KCC LE
D0268406

Tou

Knowsley Community College
Learning Centres

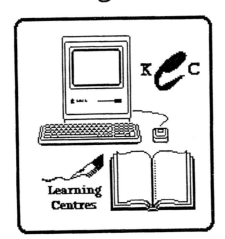

Reference Only

**This item is not available for loan.
It may not be taken out of the
Learning Centre.**

NOT TO BE
TAKEN AWAY

Knowsley Community College
Learning Centres

00034129

To the Wandering Islands

THEMES IN TOURISM

Series Editor: Professor Stephen J. Page, Centre for Tourism Research, Massey University Albany, Auckland, New Zealand.

This new book series seeks to develop a student-oriented set of texts focused on current research and thinking in tourism. By adopting a multidisciplinary perspective, the series provides an innovative and interesting range of issues for students. The purpose of each text is to introduce and systematically discuss a range of concepts and ideas related to a tourism theme, which are integral to the field of tourism studies. Each book in the series is intended to contain a core of basic principles and building blocks for the student of tourism so that the reader is taken through a series of basic concepts through to a more complex analysis of the topic under consideration. Within each book is a detailed bibliography to assist with further reading and acts as a basis for more advanced research for postgraduate students. In this respect, the series will appeal to undergraduate and postgraduate students studying tourism as a mainstream subject or as an optional subject in a wider social science context. The texts are illustrated with a range of international examples reflecting the global nature of tourism whilst paying attention to the issue of scale, where similarities and differences exist in the way tourism affects various environments, people and places. Each chapter also has suggested reading and questions to encourage readers to think critically and to review what they have just read. Each author in the series is a recognised authority in the field of tourism studies, basing their book on a depth of research experience and knowledge of tourism. Their expertise has been derived through fieldwork, experience as researchers working for the public and private sector tourism industry and above all as scholars in the field of tourism studies. The series continues an established tradition of tourism publishing at Pearson Education and adds a degree of depth and breadth to the existing range of texts already published.

Tourism Planning
Policies, Processes and Relationships

C. Michael Hall

An imprint of Pearson Education

Harlow, England · London · New York · Reading, Massachusetts · San Francisco · Toronto · Don Mills, Ontario · Sydney
Tokyo · Singapore · Hong Kong · Seoul · Taipei · Cape Town · Madrid · Mexico City · Amsterdam · Munich · Paris · Milan

00034129

063947

£23.99

338.4791

1HAL

BAT

REF

Pearson Education Limited
Edinburgh Gate
Harlow
Essex CM20 2JE
England

and Associated Companies throughout the world

Visit us on the World Wide Web at:
www.pearsoned.co.uk

© Pearson Education Limited 2000

The right of C. Michael Hall to be identified as author of this Work has been asserted by him in accordance with the Copyright, Designs and Patents Act 1988.

All rights reserved; no part of this publication may be reproduced, stored in a retrieval system, or transmitted in any form or by any means, electronic, mechanical, photocopying, recording, or otherwise without either the prior written permission of the Publishers or a licence permitting restricted copying in the United Kingdom issued by the Copyright Licensing Agency Ltd., 90 Tottenham Court Road, London W1T 4LP.

First published 2000
ISBN-10: 0-582-32028-3
ISBN-13: 978-0-582-32028-4

British Library Cataloguing-in-Publication Data
A catalogue record for this book is available from the British Library

Library of Congress Cataloging-in-Publication Data
Hall, Colin Michael, 1961–
    Tourism planning : policies, processes and relationships / C. Michael Hall.
      p.   cm.
    Includes bibliographical references.
    ISBN 0–582–32028–3
    1. Tourism—Planning.   I. Title.
G155.A1H349   1999
338.4'79104—dc21
                             99–32408
                                CIP

Typeset by 11/12pt Adobe Garamond by 35
Printed and bound by 4edge Ltd, Hockley Essex. www.4edge.co.uk

10 9 8
07 06 05

Contents

List of Figures

List of Tables

List of Plates

Preface

Writing a preface and acknowledgements is a funny thing. A part of me wants to be creative and say things that one normally couldn't write too easily in the 'normal' style of academic tourism texts, while another part is seeking to try to acknowledge, albeit usually unsuccessfully, the various influences and inspirations that cannot normally be noted just by the referencing of a publication. In the case of this book I will perhaps try and do both!

This particular book on tourism planning is hopefully a bit different from some of the other books on the subject. It doesn't provide a 'check-list' type approach to planning and then provide a series of selected cases which often don't tell you too much about what really happened. Instead, it seeks to outline a broad approach to the problem of tourism planning which attempts to encourage the reader to conceptualise the highly complex problem field within which tourism planning operates. Perhaps more significantly, it stresses that planning is difficult – it is irrational, complex, political, value-laden and, often, frustratingly incomplete. Moreover, by stressing the search for sustainability as the vision for tourism planning it becomes even more difficult!

All this being said, I make no apologies for stating it at the outset. This book is suggesting that rather than seeing the 'irrationality' of the real world as a problem, particularly in the way that tourism planning experiences often fail to match up to what the texts say should happen, we should be trying to embrace such 'irrationality' and use it creatively and positively, especially as this is how the world actually works. Therefore, this book is not a planning manual in terms of providing you with a step-by-step checklist of what you need to do, rather it tries to encourage the reader to think and reflect on the nature of the tourism planning and policy process. It emphasises the importance of conceptualising the tourism system, values, stakeholder relationships, problem definition, the issue of scale, and the means by which problems are 'solved' in terms of concerns over sustainability.

Some of these concerns are of course not new either in tourism studies or in some of my own previous work. My concern for the political found in my writing on tourism politics and policy making (e.g. Hall 1994; Hall and Jenkins 1995), including some of my early work on events, and the America's Cup in particular, led me into tourism research in the first place, having been originally more interested in environmental history and natural resource management. Tourism planning and development issues have also long been an interest and have found their way into several texts I have written or coedited on tourism in Australia, New Zealand and the Asia-Pacific region, while issues of relevance, critical analysis and counter-institutional thinking have long been a somewhat 'dirty' undercurrent in some of my work. To note these things is important for what is to come. The book notes the significance of relational approaches to tourism planning, it talks of values, one's position in the planning process, and the importance of trust as the glue which actually makes collaboration work. In short, it highlights the personal and the dialectical. This therefore makes it important, for me at least, to note some of the influences which have affected how the book has evolved and to try to convey to the reader that the book is part of a process and not an end in itself. It is imperfect, it will develop and change over time, but hopefully it is a useful means by which a staging post for dialogue and debate can be opened.

As the reader might then guess, this book has had a long gestation period, with some of the ideas within it dating back to when I was undertaking my graduate studies in geography, public policy and resource management. Therefore, several of the ideas in this book have something approaching genesis in my experiences with my graduate supervisors Michael Wood, Bruce Mitchell and Geoff McBoyle; indeed, parts of my master's thesis have found themselves in this manuscript after a number of years of lying on the back of a shelf at home unread by anyone except John Jenkins. Similarly, a number of ideas have been generated from encountering the insights of Stuart Brand, Kenneth Gergen, Peter Hall, David Harvey, Giandominico Majone and John Ralston Saul. To these people, and to my former supervisors, I find that I can only adapt the line of Wayne in *Wayne's World* to Alice Cooper, 'I am not worthy'!

Work with a number of colleagues has also provided sources for several of the ideas used in this book. Writing in the policy areas with John Jenkins (e.g. Hall and Jenkins 1995; Hall, Jenkins and Kearsley 1997; Butler, Hall and Jenkins 1998) has proved invaluable for stimulating ideas and material on the nature of the tourism policy-making process and the role of government in tourism. Similarly, work in the field of heritage management with Simon McArthur (e.g. Hall and McArthur 1993, 1996, 1998) has proven invaluable for focusing on how the planning process can be shaped and the reasons why it should be approached in certain ways. At times my own ideas cannot be separated from those of John or Simon, given that we have worked so closely together – even though they may at times wish so and despite the fact they don't get any of the royalties directly! More recently I have been fortunate to have worked with Alan Lew on geographical approaches to sustainable tourism development (Hall and Lew 1998) and Stephen Page on the geography of tourism and recreation (Hall and Page 1999a) with both of these projects strongly influencing my thoughts on sustainable tourism, issues of relevance in academic work, and the central role of values in tourism planning and policy making. In addition, work with Brock Cambourne, Gary Johnson, Niki Macionis, Richard Mitchell and Kathryn Pavlovich has been extremely valuable in studying the role of network development. I would also specifically like to thank Craig Millar for his generosity in sharing his excellent insights into the role of trust in resource management with me, and Steve Selin for his excellent work on collaboration.

The Centre for Tourism at the University of Otago has provided a conducive environment for undertaking research towards this book. I would like to thank my work colleagues James Higham, Geoff Kearsley and Alison McIntosh and the secretarial assistance of Janine Watkin for their continued support. The opportunity for discussion with colleagues at Sheffield Hallam University has been particularly valuable in terms of thinking about issues of collaboration, regional development and urban regeneration, while time spent at the University of Surrey, the University of Strathclyde, University of Victoria (Canada), Simon Fraser University, and the Scottish Agricultural College in recent years has also been helpful and stimulating. Carmen Aitken, Tim Bahaire, Bill Bramwell, Dick and Margaret Butler, Sonia Casey, Dave Crag, Ross Dowling, Martin Elliott-White, Angela Elvey, Thor Flogenfeldt, Joanna Fountain, Alison Gill, Liesl Harlen Tom Hinch, Keith Hollinshead, Sandra James, John Jenkins, Linda Kell, Alan Lew, Bernard Lane, Jim MacBeth, Simon McArthur, Alison and Brian McIntosh, Fiona McKay, Carleen and Richard Mitchell, Nigel Morpeth, Meiko Muramaya, Peter Murphy, Jenny Nicholl, Stephen Page, Kathryn Pavlovich, Rachel Piggin, Anna Dora Saethorsdottir, Brian and Delyse Springett, Megan Walker, Geoff Wall, Brian Wheeller, Alan Williams and Peter Williams have all contributed to the development of this book in various ways, although my interpretation of their thoughts is of course my own. Fiona Apple, Gavin Bryars, Bruce Cockburn, Neil and Tim Finn, JJJ, KCRW, Ed Kuepper, Lisa Loeb, Sarah McLachan, The Sundays, Bic Runga, Virtually Canadian and Chris Wilson have all assisted in providing an appropriate context within which the book was written. I would also like to gratefully thank Matthew Smith and all at Addison Wesley Longman, especially Julie Knight and Helen Hodge, for putting up with the delays in getting the manuscript to them and for being such a good team to work with. Finally, I would like to thank my friends and significant others for their love, support and understanding; hopefully this will also mean more time at the beach in coming years.

C. Michael Hall
City Rise
January 1999

Acknowledgements

The publishers wish to thank the following for permission to reproduce the following copyright material:

Dept of Resource Recreation and Tourism, College of Forestry, University of Idaho, Inter-Sectoral Unit for Tourism, Organization of American States for tables 1.1 and 4.7 from S.N. Edwards, W.J. McLaughlin and S.H. Ham, *Comparative Study of Ecotourism Policy in the Americas, Vol II, USA and Canada*, (1998).

Sage Publications for table 5.1 from Ascher, *Journal of Travel Research* (22), pp. 2–16, © 1984 by Sage Publications. Reprinted by permission of Sage Publications, Inc.

South Australian Tourism Commission for figures 4.1 and 4.2 and tables 4.1 and 4.2 from Tourism South Australia, *Making South Australia Special: South Australian Tourism Plan 1991–1993* (pp. 28–31) (1991).

The Stationery Office for figures 4.3 and 4.5 from C.M. Hall and S. McArthur, *Integrated Heritage Management* (1998). Reprinted by permission of The Stationery Office, Norwich.

University of California at Berkeley, Institute of Governmental Studies Press for table 7.2 from I. Schiffman, *Alternative Techniques for Managing Growth* (1989).

If any unknowing use has been made of copyright material, owners should contact the author via the publishers as every effort has been made to trace owners and obtain permission.

Chapter 1

Tourism planning and policy: the sustainable imperative

Tourism is now a major area of academic, government, industry and public concern. While it is now an oft-cited truism that tourism is the world's largest industry, tourism is significant not just because of its size in terms of the number of people travelling, how many people it employs, or how much money it brings into a destination. Tourism is significant also because of the enormous impact it has on people's lives and on the places in which they live, and because of the way in which tourism is itself substantially affected by the world around it.

Tourism is intimately connected with issues of sustainable development. Indeed, since the late 1980s there has been an explosion in the number of texts and articles, plus courses and consultants, which are concerned with sustainable forms of development. However, despite the plethora of discussions about sustainability in tourism we often seem no closer to finding solutions to the problems of tourism development. For every report of success it often seems that there are ten reports of failure or at least further recognition of the negative impact of tourism. Yet tourism still continues to grow. Besides, it may possibly be argued that compared with problems of global climate change, deforestation, loss of biodiversity and cultural diversity, poverty and seemingly endless economic restructuring, tourism is not an issue. It is. As noted above, given the size of the industry, tourism is both a contributing factor and a response to some of these problems. Ecotourism, for example, has been posited as a means of conserving ecological diversity through offering a higher economic value for conserving plant and animal species that might otherwise be exploited in other ways. Nevertheless, tourism has also contributed to species and habitat loss through accommodation, attraction and infrastructure development, such as in many coastal areas where a golf course, a marina and a sandy beach are regarded as having greater value than mangroves and wetlands. It is these paradoxes and problems of tourism development and the hope that they can be solved that creates the setting for tourism planning.

The sustainable tourism imperative

Sustainability is primarily an outcome of the age of ecology, although the intellectual heritage of the concept dates back at least to the early nineteenth century. Although society, and key interests within society, have long been

Plate 1.1   Waterfront development at Noosa, Queensland, Australia. Tourism development at this popular resort town has been controversial for many years. Issues include engineering works on the river mouth, replacement of cheap accommodation on the peninsula by more upmarket accommodation and resorts, proposals to build resorts in natural areas, and inappropriate siting of tourism facilities.

Plate 1.2   Canal estate development at Noosa. The canal estate development replaced existing wetlands.

Plate 1.3 Rock wall at Noosa Beach. Because the beach area and the spit is geomoropholical unstable, engineering works have been required to protect the valuable real estate on the spit.

Plate 1.4 Severe gully erosion, Noosa, Queensland. Inadequate consideration of drainage needs following estate development led to severe erosion.

Plate 1.5 Replacement of wetlands and coastal heath with a golf course. Hyatt Coolum, Queensland.

concerned with how best to utilise and conserve natural resources, it has been in the twentieth century and in the globalised world of the new millennium that we have come to realise the way that everything is tied together. Environment, economy and society are inextricably linked.

Sustainability is everyone's concern. The famous Brundtland definition, that 'sustainable development is development that meets the needs of the present without compromising the ability of future generations to meet their own needs' (WCED 1987 : 49), has come to feature in many a textbook and student essay. However, sustainable development and sustainability are important concepts, the interpretation and operationalisation of which have been hard fought over in policy and planning decisions throughout the world. They are not just abstract academic ideas, they are concepts which trickle down and affect the day-to-day lives of everyone on the planet, even if people never realise it. As the then Prime Minister of the United Kingdom, John Major, noted in his Foreword to *Sustainable Development: The UK Strategy* : 'Sustainable development is difficult to define. But the goal of sustainable development can guide future strategy' (HMSO 1994 : 3).

The report of the World Commission on Environment and Development (WCED 1987), commonly known as the Brundtland Report, provided substantial impetus to the concept and practice of sustainable development. Five basic principles of sustainability were identified in the report. First, the idea of holistic planning and strategy-making. Second, the importance of preserving essential ecological processes. Third, the need to protect both human heritage and biodiversity. Fourth, the need to develop in such a way that productivity can be sustained over the long term for future generations (the concept of intergenerational equity). Fifth, the goal of achieving a better balance of fairness and opportunity between nations (Bramwell and Lane 1993 : 2).

The scope of the challenge which needs to be met in order for economic activity to be environmentally sustainable has been outlined by Ekins (1993), who argues that certain conditions need to be rigorously adhered to with respect to resource use, pollution and environmental impacts:

- destabilisation of global environmental features such as climate patterns and the ozone layer must be prevented
- important ecosystems and ecological features must receive absolute protection in order to maintain biological diversity
- renewable resources must be maintained with sustainable harvesting measures rigorously enforced
- non-renewable resources must be used as intensively as possible
- depletion of non-renewable resources should proceed on the basis of maintaining minimum life expectancies of such resources, at which level consumption should be matched by new discoveries of these resources and technological innovation
- emissions into the biosphere should not exceed the biosphere's capacity to absorb such emissions
- risks of life-damaging events from human activity, i.e. nuclear power generation, must be kept at a very low level.

Clearly, meeting such conditions for sustainability is a major political, economic and environmental issue as it requires new ways of thinking about the nature and purpose of development and growth, and the role of individuals, government and the private sector in developing sustainable futures, a concern which is increasingly at the forefront of the analysis of tourism.

The idea of sustainable development requires a broader view of development and the natural environment than has hitherto been the case in much of Western society, particularly in recent years when monetarist economics and the denial of a public interest has featured in so much government policy. 'The term "sustainable development" suggests that the lessons of ecology can, and should, be applied to economic processes' (Redclift 1987 : 33). Therefore, sustainable development stresses that economic development is dependent upon the continued well-being of the physical and social environment on which it is based (Barbier 1987; Brookfield 1988; Butler 1991). A purely economic approach to development does not give any appreciation of the environmental and social implications on development or an empirical measure of the quality of life and 'any development indicator based on monetary value of production is subject to both technical and conceptual shortcomings' (Smith 1977 : 203). Similarly, economic data alone does not give any appreciation of the productive utilisation of resources – for example, whether or not the resources are renewable. A solely economic approach does not record the environmental and social costs that may have been associated with economic production (Pearce 1989). 'By valuing the environment predominantly in monetary terms, we may be *de*valuing its importance. We may end up, as Oscar Wilde put it, "knowing the price of everything and the value of nothing"' (Redclift and Sage 1994a : 1–2). As Redclift (1987 : 16) argued:

From an environmental standpoint . . . GNP is a particularly inadequate guide to development since it treats sustainable and unsustainable production alike and compounds the error by including the costs of unsustainable economic activity on the credit side, while largely ignoring processes of recycling and energy conversion which do not lead to the production of goods and marketable services.

An increasingly important conception of sustainability is that of maintaining 'environmental capital' (Pearce and Turner 1990; Jacobs 1991) and, in terms of the ideas of equity which are a component of sustainability, the notion of social capital (Healey 1997). For example, Redclift and Sage (1994b : 1) notes that 'development is about the creation of economic (often market) "value" as natural resources are transformed into "goods", into commodities. The process of economic development involves the substitution of resources by human-made "capital" . . . we need to enlarge our view of capital to include nature, if we are to preserve lifeforms on the planet.' Such notions draw on economic metaphors and analysis and are based on two main principles:

- Intergenerational equity requires 'bequeathing to the next generation a stock of 'capital', with its assumed capacity to produce well-being at least equivalent to that enjoyed by the present' (Cowell and Owens 1997 : 16–17); and
- Biophysical capacities are not infinitely elastic. In other words, all forms of capital are not substitutable – 'Some functions of the environment are vital and irreplaceable . . . [therefore], social and economic activity should be managed at least to conserve such 'critical environmental capital', which not only protects what is critical but maintains at least the present value of the environmental capital stock' (Cowell and Owens 1997 : 17).

Such an interpretation is significant, because, when understood in terms of the maintenance of environmental capital, sustainability shows its relation to the older idea of 'limits to growth' and 'capacity'. 'This does not mean that growth is necessarily limited but it does imply that, in order to be sustainable in the long term, the nature of growth must be such that it respects constraints set by the need to maintain critical environmental capital (and in some interpretations the total value of the environmental capital stock) intact' (Cowell and Owens 1997 : 17).

As history has demonstrated, maintaining environmental capital is extremely difficult in a political-economic system within which maintaining or increasing levels of economic growth has been a virtually unassailable policy goal. Sustainability is a qualitatively different policy goal – it is not specific, it is not easily understandable, it is not easily quantifiable, and it deals in time horizons which are not usually adopted. However, despite these characteristics it is still probably the most important planning and policy issue of our time. It is also the major imperative behind a thorough assessment of the manner in which tourism planning may be able to contribute to more sustainable forms of development.

Policy and planning

The terms planning and policy are intimately related. Planning is an extremely ambiguous and difficult word to define. 'The trouble arises because, although people realize that planning has a more general meaning, they tend to remember the idea of the plan as a physical representation or design. Thus they imagine that planning must include the preparation of such a design' (Hall 1992 : 1). Veal (1992 : 3) states that 'planning can be seen as the process of deciding'. Similarly, Dror (1973 : 330) argues that 'Planning is the process of preparing a set of decisions for action in the future, directed at achieving goals by preferable means.' However, the tourism planning process is not just about *deciding* what is to be provided in the future for a given area of land or a community. It is far much more complex than that. Chadwick's (1971) response to 'what is planning?' is extremely relevant. Chadwick states 'that planning is a process, a process of human thought and action based upon that thought – in point of fact, forethought, thought for the future – nothing more or less than this is planning, which is a very general human activity' (1971 : 24).

Planning is a kind of decision-making and policy-making; however, it deals with a set of interdependent and systematically related decisions rather than individual decisions. Therefore, planning is only one part of an overall 'planning-decision-action' process. Furthermore, various activities in that process may be difficult to isolate as the planning process and other activities involve such things as bargaining and negotiation, compromise, coercion, values, choice and politics. Planning as a process must therefore be distinguished from a 'plan', which is 'a set of decisions for action in the future' (Dror 1973) and, in the case of much tourism planning, is related to land use planning in particular (e.g. Gunn 1988, 1994). As P. Hall (1992 : 2) noted, there are many types of planning, 'though they will almost certainly require the production of many symbols on pieces of paper, in the form of words or diagrams, may never involve the production of a single exact physical representation of the entity which is being produced'.

There are several ways in which some of the different types of planning may be identified. For example, Friedmann (1973) conceived of two different types of planning which lay at opposite ends of an autonomy-dependency continuum depending on where the planner or the planning agency lay within the planning system:

- *developmental planning*, which has a high degree of autonomy with respect to the setting of ends and the choice of means, and which tends to merge into what is usually described as policy making, and
- *adaptive planning*, in which most decisions are heavily contingent on the actions of others external to the planning system and which tends to merge into programming.

Healey (1997) also recognised several strands of planning:

- economic planning which aims to manage the productive forces of a country or region
- the management of the physical development of towns and regions and
- the management of public administration and policy analysis which aims to manage the efficiency and effectiveness of public agencies.

Indeed, Healey noted that most who criticise 'planning' often have the state socialist 'command and control' model of centralised economic planning in mind, rather than other forms of planning which are, in fact, in common usage in western democratic societies.

The most important characteristic of planning is that it is directed toward the future. Friedmann (1959 : 334) provides an interesting list of planning characteristics that arise out of the future orientation of planning:

- it places a limit upon the time period over which projections into the future can be made without loss of practical significance for present decisions
- it establishes the necessity for continuing planning analysis and assessment throughout the planning period and the constant reevaluation and adjustment of means to ends
- it suggests the use of expectational calculus in connection with statements about the future
- it argues for the adoption of a system of framework or structural planning
- it forces the careful consideration of flexibility in planning where the degree of flexibility introduced into a solution must be proportionate to the degree of uncertainty over future events. It is an approach such as this that reason can come to terms with uncertainty.

As already noted, planning and policy are terms which are intimately related. According to Cullingsworth (1997 : 5), 'Planning is the purposive process in which goals are set and policies elaborated to implement them.' In contrast, policy analysis is 'concerned with understanding and explaining the substance of policy content and policy decisions and the way in which policy decisions are made' (Barrett and Fudge 1981 : 6), where public policy is 'the structure or confluence of values and behaviour involving a governmental prescription' (Kroll 1969 : 9). Public policy is therefore the focal point of government activity. Public policy-making is first and foremost a political activity. Public policy is influenced by the economic, social, and cultural characteristics of society, as well as by the formal structures of government and other features of the political system. Policy should therefore be seen as a consequence of the political environment, values and ideologies, the distribution of power, institutional frameworks, and of decision-making processes (Simeon 1976; Hall and Jenkins 1995; Elliot 1997).

Public policy 'is whatever governments choose to do or not to do' (Dye 1992 : 2). This definition covers government action, inaction, decisions and non-decisions as it implies a deliberate choice between alternatives. For a policy to be regarded as public policy, at the very least it must have been processed, even if only authorised or ratified, by public agencies (Hall and Jenkins 1995). This is an important caveat because it means that the 'policy may not have been significantly developed within the framework of government' (Hogwood and Gunn 1984 : 23). Pressure groups (e.g. tourism industry associations, conservation groups, community groups), significant individuals (e.g. local government councillors, business leaders), members of the bureaucracy (e.g. employees within tourism organisations or development agencies) and others (e.g. academics and consultants), all influence and perceive public policies in significant and often markedly different ways.

Tourism has become an integral part of the machinery of many governments. Tourism public policy is whatever governments choose to do or not to do with respect to tourism (Jenkins 1993; Hall 1994; Hall and Jenkins 1995). However, there is increasing scepticism about the effectiveness of government, particularly central government, and the intended consequences and impacts of much government policy, including with respect to tourism (Jenkins 1997; Jenkins et al. 1998). For example, as Richter (1989 : 21) observed, 'critics of current tourism policies are becoming aware and are more than a little cynical about the excesses and "mistakes" occasioned by national tourism development schemes'. Nevertheless, even given demands for 'smaller government' in much of the Western world, market failure still provides a number of rationales for state economic intervention including:

- improving economic competitiveness
- amending property rights
- enabling state decision makers to take account of externalities
- providing widely available public benefits
- reducing risk and uncertainty
- supporting projects with high capital costs and involving new technologies
- educating and providing information (Haughton and Hunter 1994 : 263).

Policy should therefore be an important area of concern to the student of tourism. One of the most interesting studies of policy in the context of tourism was a survey of the range of tourism policy roles of agencies in Canada and the United States with respect to ecotourism (Edwards et al. 1998). Respondents comments as to the nature of their roles indicate that there are tremendous variations in government tourism agency involvement in tourism policy (Table 1.1), ranging from a more reactive, passive role in which agencies provide input and react to policies established by other agencies, to a proactive role in which government tourism agencies are researching, writing, lobbying for and implementing tourism policy. One of the most detailed explanations as to why greater attention should be devoted to the study of public policy was presented by Dye (1992) who argued that public policy can be studied for three primary reasons:

- Public policy can be studied so as to gain an understanding of the causes and consequences of policy decisions, and to improve our knowledge about society. In this instance, public policy can be viewed as either a dependent variable *or* as an independent variable. If policy is viewed as a dependent variable, the critical question becomes 'what socioeconomic [or environmental forces] and political system characteristics operate to shape the content of policy' (Dye 1992 : 4). If tourism public policy is viewed as an independent variable, then the central question becomes *what impact does public policy (including tourism) have on society [the environment] and on the political system?*
- Public policy can also be studied for professional reasons in order to understand the causes and consequences of policy. Thus, *we might seek solutions of practical problems with respect to tourism, and feed that knowledge into the political process.*

Table 1.1   Range of tourism policy roles in Canadian and American agencies

actively involved	adapt/change agency structure
administer	advise/consult
advocate policies	answer to a commission
assist in writing	collaborate with other agencies
coordinate with others	depends on issue
develop legislation	facilitate
find solutions to tourism issues	follow governor's policy
write/formulate policy	involved in land use planning
fund policy	get people involved
implement policy	official agency for tourism policy
initiate tourism policy	serve as mediator
serve on committees	strategic/tourism planning
monitor policy	no role/not involved
lobby	persuade
participate in policy process	partner with others
play lead/key role	propose policy
provide input on policy	react to policy
recommend/suggest policy	represent tourism in policy issues
research policy	involved in licensing
form/attend councils/taskforce	follow policies set by other agencies
work with others (private sector,	information/technical assistance provider
Governor's Office, industry,	primarily involved in promotions and marketing
legislature, Tourism Commission,	writing
Regional Councils, etc.)	

Source: Edwards et al. (1998 : 25).

- Public policy can be studied for political purposes so as to ensure that the 'right' policies are adopted 'to achieve the "right" goals' (Dye 1992 : 5). This latter focus raises the critical issues of defining *what is 'right', and identifying by whom 'right' is determined*. These issues reflect the play of interests and values in the influence and determination of the tourism planning and policy processes (Hall and Jenkins 1995).

Planning for tourism

Demands for tourism planning and government intervention in the development process are typically a response to the unwanted effects of tourism development, particularly at the local level. The rapid pace of tourism growth and development, the nature of tourism itself and the corresponding absence of single agency responsibility for tourism-related development has often meant that public sector responses to the impacts of tourism on destinations have been *ad hoc*, rather than predetermined strategies oriented toward development objectives. Such an approach is the antithesis of planning.

Although planning is not a cure-all, in its fullest process-oriented sense planning may be able to minimise potential negative impacts, maximise economic returns to the destination, and hence encourage a more positive response from the host community towards tourism in the longer term. As Murphy (1985 : 156) argued, 'Planning is concerned with anticipating and regulating change in a system, to promote orderly development so as to increase the social, economic, and environmental benefits of the development process.' Therefore, planning must be regarded as a critical element in ensuring the long-term sustainable development of tourist destinations. Nevertheless, as Gunn (1979 : 1) observed, 'on the surface, the planning of tourism is a contradiction . . . tourism implies non-directed, voluntary and personal goal-oriented travel and its corollary of free-enterprise development'. Gunn (1988) identified a number of assumptions regarding the value of, and approaches to, tourism planning:

1 Only planning can avert negative impacts, although for planning to be effective, all 'actors' must be involved – not just professional planners.
2 Tourism is symbiotic with conservation and recreation, not a conflicting use with irreconcilably incompatible objectives or effects.
3 Planning today should be pluralistic, involving social, economic and physical dimensions.
4 Planning is political, and as such there is a vital need to take into account societal objectives and balance these in the contact of other (often conflicting) aspirations.
5 Tourism planning must be strategic and integrative.
6 Tourism planning must have a regional planning perspective – because many problems arise at the interface of smaller areas, a broader planning horizon is essential.

The assumptions identified by Gunn (1988) provide a useful basis for realising the benefits of tourism planning, although they cannot provide the only means of minimising the costs of tourism. However, the implications of some of the assumptions, particularly regarding its political nature, have been little discussed, even by Gunn! Moreover, Gunn tended to concentrate on the land use dimensions of planning, rather than the fuller dimensions of the concept. Nevertheless, completely unregulated or unplanned tourism development would almost certainly lead to the degradation of the physical and social resource base upon which tourism depends.

As a general field of research, tourism planning has mirrored broader trends within the urban and regional planning traditions (e.g. Getz 1986, 1987; Inskeep 1991), primarily because it has tended to be focused on destination planning rather than individual tourism business planning (e.g. Gunn 1977, 1988, 1994; Inskeep 1991). In recent years, as ecotourism and sustainability have become major issues in tourism, it has also been substantially influenced by developments in the field of environmental planning (e.g. Inskeep 1987; Dowling 1993a, 1993b, 1997; Hunter and Green 1995), while increasing attention is also being given to the relationship to policy (e.g. Hall and Jenkins 1995; Davidson and Maitland 1997; Hall et al. 1997). These recent developments are extremely important for our understanding of tourism planning as no longer can tourism planning be simply seen as an exercise in land-use planning at either the regional or, more typically, the local or site level. Undoubtedly, local or site level land use planning is extremely important for destination regions. However, such activities need to be conceived as occurring at one end of a continuum of planning-related activities which range from the local to the global and which similarly range from being land-use oriented at the site and local level to being policy oriented at the global level. Planning for tourism therefore occurs in a number of forms (e.g. development, infrastructure, land and resource use, organisation, human resource, promotion and marketing); structures (e.g. different government, quasi-government and non-government organisations); scales (international, transnational, national, regional, local, site and sectoral) and over different time scales (for development, implementation, evaluation and satisfactory fulfilment of planning objectives) (Hall 1998b). Furthermore, planning is rarely exclusively devoted to tourism *per se*. Instead, planning for tourism tends to be 'an amalgam of economic, social and environmental considerations' which reflect the diversity of the factors which influence tourism development (Heely 1981 : 61).

Undoubtedly, the emergence of public and interest group concern over the perceived negative effects of tourism has led to demands for improved planning for tourism in the belief that this will help ameliorate such impacts. Furthermore, in recent years demand for public tourism planning has also been driven by perceived changes in the tourist marketplace and by government responses to the problems of economic restructuring in both urban and rural areas. As greater competition has begun to develop in the tourism marketplace so destinations have sought to improve various aspects of attractions, facilities and infrastructure in order that they may continue to be attractive to visitors or at least extend their product life cycle. Many areas which have recently undergone substantial economic restructuring also now want to develop tourism in order to attract investment, promote economic growth and generate employment. Such demands on tourism – and on the means by which we understand tourism-related development – are enormous, while the capacity of tourism and tourism studies as an area of academic concern to meet such challenges is mixed.

This book is concerned with the tourism planning process. It aims to place concerns over values, the significance of politics, and issues of scale, approach and sustainability at the centre of tourism planning. It is also primarily concerned with public tourism planning, although there is substantial discussion of private sector-related planning, particularly at the destination level. It is not a technical guide to tourism planning legislation or certain related planning tools, such as environmental impact statements, although the importance of such tools and aspects of institutional arrangements are noted. Being international in scope it is clearly infeasible for this book to list and discuss all relevant tourism planning legislation although various examples will be provided. Instead, it is expected that readers will be able to follow up such legislation in their own time or as part of class exercises. Rather, the reader is being asked to see relevant legislation or land use regulations within the wider context of the tourism planning process and the tourism planning system.

Outline of the book

This book is divided into nine chapters. This chapter sets some of the context within which tourism and tourism planning occurs. Most significantly, it has identified the sustainable tourism imperative as being one of the major driving forces behind the desire for tourism planning. It has also outlined some of the characteristics of planning and policy which will be discussed in more detail as the book goes on.

Chapter 2 provides a brief overview of some of the major traditions or approaches to tourism planning. It discusses the traditions of boosterism, economic approaches, the physical/spatial approach which is increasingly becoming described under the heading of environmental planning, community-based planning and some of the emerging dimensions of sustainable tourism planning from which some of the concepts utilised in this book are based.

Chapter 3 examines the nature of a systems approach to planning and how that affects our understanding of the tourism planning process. It discusses the idea of planning as theory, the nature of systems and systems thinking and how such concepts have been applied in fields such as ecology, geography, planning, management and, more recently, tourism. The chapter emphasises that process, flux and change are fundamental to a systems view of the world and need to be incorporated into our understanding of tourism. Several approaches to tourism systems are noted including the significance of the partial industrialisation of tourism. However, as part of our understanding of systems the chapter also argues that it is important to understand issues of scale, the standpoint of the participant, the role of values, the significance of relationships and the role of argument and persuasion in the planning process.

Chapter 4 examines the development of integrated approaches towards planning in complex systems. It provides an idealised model of the policy, planning and decision-making process which is then used to discuss issues in the operationalisation of planning theory particularly with respect to identifying stakeholders, goal and objective setting, negotiation and cooperation, and our understanding of implementation. It argues for the concept of integration to be conceived of in terms of the centrality of interrelationships, which means that problem definition becomes vital to planning as does the actual shape of planning solutions. The chapter concludes with a discussion of the importance of dialectical analysis to a systems view of planning and the importance of argument and persuasion in a craft approach to tourism planning.

Chapters 5 to 8 look at the operation of tourism policy and planning at different scales. Chapter 5 examines policy and planning at the international and transnational levels and it discusses the influence of various international institutions such as the World Tourism Organisation and the role of institutional arrangements through hard and soft international law on tourism development.

Chapter 6 examines tourism planning and policies at the national and subnational level. It discusses the role of government and the private sector in

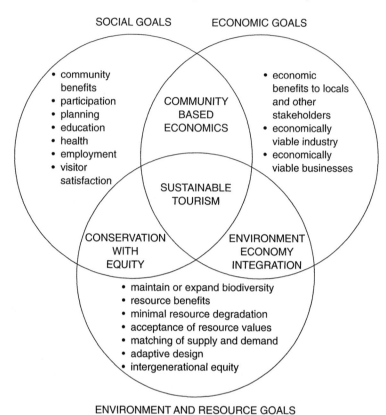

SOCIAL GOALS   ECONOMIC GOALS

- community benefits
- participation
- planning
- education
- health
- employment
- visitor satisfaction

COMMUNITY BASED ECONOMICS

- economic benefits to locals and other stakeholders
- economically viable industry
- economically viable businesses

SUSTAINABLE TOURISM

CONSERVATION WITH EQUITY

ENVIRONMENT ECONOMY INTEGRATION

- maintain or expand biodiversity
- resource benefits
- minimal resource degradation
- acceptance of resource values
- matching of supply and demand
- adaptive design
- intergenerational equity

ENVIRONMENT AND RESOURCE GOALS

Figure 1.1   Sustainable tourism values and principles (after Hall 1998b)

tourism planning and development and the key concepts of coordination, cooperation and competition in tourism. It also notes the importance of interest groups in the tourism policy and planning process and their influence on the planning process.

Chapter 7 examines tourism planning at the destination level in an increasingly globalised competitive environment. It argues that the structure of destinations needs to be reconsidered in the tourism planning process with greater emphasis being placed on the need to create cooperative structures rather than simply providing greater amounts of money for destination promotion or development organisations.

Chapter 8 examines the linkage between policies and operations in terms of design principles and site development. It discusses sustainable development in terms of principles of adaptivity and rates of change and their potential application to tourism.

Chapter 9 concludes by reflecting on issues of cooperation, integration and relationships within complex tourism planning environments. It argues that there needs to be greater reflection on the assumptions and bases of tourism planning with the intention being that tourism planning needs to be able to reflect how the real world actually operates. In short, it argues that planning is political. This, then, has certain implications for the skill development of tourism planners. It argues that tourism planners need to have greater understanding of the role of communication and mediation as well as the idea of planning as argument and negotiation in addition to the more traditional technical knowledge of legislation, regulation and planning techniques.

Conclusion

Tourism planning does not just refer specifically to tourism development and promotion, although these are certainly important. Tourism must be integrated within the wider planning processes in order to promote certain goals of economic, social and environmental enhancement or maximisation that may be achieved through appropriate tourism development (Figure 1.1). Therefore, tourism planning must be, as Getz (1987 : 3) emphasised, 'a process, based on research and evaluation, which seeks to optimize the potential contribution of tourism to human welfare and environmental quality'.

Such a statement reflects the value basis of this book as well. This book argues that values lie at the core of tourism planning. Planning assists in determining who wins and who loses in the tourism development process. It also assists in contributing to more sustainable forms of tourism in which economic, environmental and social goals are seen to be in balance and in which there is greater equity of outcomes for stakeholders in tourism, which means not just the developers, tourism industry and the tourist but also the wider community whose destination is being consumed. Most fundamentally, tourism planning should be about the creation of sustainable places. It is hoped that this book makes at least some small contribution to such a goal.

Questions and further reading

What are the limitations of a purely economic approach to development?
Why does the idea of 'sustainability' challenge conventional ways of thinking about development?
To what extent can we describe the differences between planning and policy as one of degree?

The WCED (1987) 'Brundtland' report and Redclift (1987) provides a valuable introduction to the concept of sustainable development. There has been an explosion of literature on the relationship between tourism and sustainable development in recent years. See Butler (1991), Bramwell and Lane (1993), and Hall and Lew (1998) for an introduction to the main threads of the debate on sustainable tourism which have been in place for the past decade. Excellent introductions to public planning are Peter Hall (1992) and Healey (1997), while Hogwood and Gunn introduces the field of public policy. The most comprehensive introductions to tourism policy are Hall and Jenkins (1995) and Elliot (1997).

Chapter 2

Changing dimensions of tourism planning

The focus and methods of tourism planning have not remained constant and have evolved to meet the new demands which have been placed on the tourism industry. International tourism policies among the developed nations can be divided into four distinct phases (Table 2.1). Of particular importance has been the increased direct involvement of government in regional development, environmental regulation and the marketing of tourism, although more recently there has been reduced direct government involvement in the supply of tourism infrastructure, and greater emphasis on the development of public–private partnerships and industry self-regulation (Hall 1994). Similarly, Airey (1983) identified the principal issues in the tourism policies of Belgium, France, the Federal Republic of Germany, Italy, the Netherlands and the United Kingdom, between 1972–82 (regional development, seasonality, consumer protection, balance of payments, social tourism, rural/green tourism, and environmental protection). The issues identified by Airey (1983) are generally reflected in the wider concerns of Western governments (Williams and Shaw 1988a, 1988b; Hall 1994). In particular, the attention of government on the potential benefits of economic and regional development has provided the main driving force for tourism planning, but the result has often been 'top-down planning

Table 2.1   International tourism policies from 1945 to the present

Phase	Characteristics
1945–1955	The dismantling and streamlining of the police, customs, currency, and health regulations that had been put into place following the second world war.
1955–1970	Greater government involvement in tourism marketing in order to increase tourism earning potential.
1970–1985	Government involvement in the supply of tourism infrastructure and in the use of tourism as a tool of regional development.
1985–present	Continued use of tourism as a tool for regional development, increased focus on environmental issues, reduced direct government involvement in the supply of tourism infrastructure, greater emphasis on the development of public–private partnerships and industry self-regulation.

Source: After OECD (1974); Hall (1994); Hall and Jenkins (1995).

Plate 2.1   Bristol City Treasury, England. I could not resist taking this slide of the road sign outside the Treasury in the last years of Thatcher's reign. It summed up the changed priorities for government under the Conservative Party very nicely and the continuing challenges which local government face.

and promotion that leaves destination communities with little input or control over their own destinies' (Murphy 1985 : 153).

Within Western society, considerable debate has emerged in the past two decades over the appropriate role of the state in society. Such a debate has considerable impact on both the form of, and the organisations which, undertake tourism planning. Throughout most of the 1980s and the early 1990s, 'Thatcherism' (named after Conservative Prime Minister Margaret Thatcher) in the United Kingdom and 'Reaganism' (named after Republican President Ronald Reagan) in the United States, saw a period of supposed retreat by central government from active intervention. At the national level, policies of deregulation, corporatisation, privatisation, free-trade, the elimination of tax incentives, and a move away from discretionary forms of macro-economic intervention, were and have been the hallmarks of a push towards 'smaller' government and lower levels of central government intervention in various countries around the world.

Tourism is clearly not immune from changes in political philosophy in its wider policy environment. The dominant ideological trend in Western societies in the 1980s and for much of the 1990s to deregulate the market and reduce the extent of government involvement has led to government often becoming entrepreneurial in its involvement with tourism in order to increase the financial contribution of tourism to government income. Therefore, government has increasingly been involved in the promotion and marketing of destinations, and the joint development of tourist attractions or facilities with the private sector (Pearce 1989; also see Burns 1999 for an excellent discussion on the changing role of tourism planning in developing countries).

Tourism is subject to direct and indirect government intervention often because of its employment and income producing possibilities and therefore its potential to diversify and contribute to national and regional economies. Given calls from some interests for reduced government in Western society in recent years, there have been increasing demands from conservative national governments and economic rationalists in the public and private sectors for greater industry self-sufficiency in tourism marketing and promotion, often through the privatisation or corporatisation of tourism agencies or boards (Jeffries 1989). The implications of such an approach for the tourism industry are substantial. As Hughes (1984 : 14) noted with respect to tourism in the United Kingdom, 'The advocates of a free enterprise economy would look to consumer freedom of choice and not to governments to promote firms; the consumer ought to be sovereign in decisions relating to the allocation of the nation's resources.' Such sentiments are far away from ideas of the role of the state in tourism espoused by the International Union of Travel Organizations (IUOTO), the forerunner to the World Tourism Organization (WTO), which, in the 1970s, argued that tourism was such an important sector that in order to foster and develop tourism

> on a scale proportionate to its national importance and to mobilize all resources to that end, it is necessary to centralize the policy-making powers in the hands of the state so that it can take appropriate measures for creating a suitable framework for the promotion and development of tourism by the various sectors concerned (IUOTO 1974 : 71).

Over 25 years later, the comments of IUOTO are far removed from contemporary debates concerning the role of the state and government in tourism (see Chapter 5 for a more recent perspective on WTO's approach to tourism development).

Much intervention in tourism and other public policy arenas (e.g. education, health and welfare) is related to market failure, market imperfection and social need. The market method of deciding who gets what and how is not always adequate, and therefore government often changes the distribution of income and wealth by measures that work within the price system. Across the globe almost every industry has been supported at various times by subsidies, the imposition of tariff regulations, taxation concessions, direct grants and other forms of government intervention, all of which serve to affect the price of goods and services and therefore influence the distribution of income, production and wealth. The size or economic importance of the tourism industry, so commonly emphasised by the public and private sector sectors (e.g. World Tourism Organization 1996), is no justification in itself for government intervention; within market-driven economies justification must lie in some aspect of: (1) market failure; (2) market imperfection, or (3) public/social concerns about market outcomes. In other words, 'implicit in each justification for political action is the view that government offers a corrective alternative to the market' (Hula 1988 : 6).

Market failure takes many forms. For instance, the market often fails to protect adequately the environment on which much of the tourist industry depends for its survival. One would expect that a business or industry that receives income from environmental quality would largely maintain that quality. However, there is a real risk that, where several businesses rely on the same environmental space or where others are competing for resources, the 'tragedy of the commons' (Hardin 1968) – the inability of individuals or the private sector on many occasions to come together to coordinate a strategy to protect (or enhance) the environment because they regard it as a 'free' resource to which their own individual activities do little harm – will emerge. This arises for such reasons as the inclination of businesses to freeload on the activities of others, and the difficulty in getting private interests to pool their resources. In addition, business is rarely interested in long-term social and environmental need as opposed to short-term revenue and profits, and yet tourism development may impact adversely on some sections of the community to the extent that government has to step in to rectify the problem (Hall and Jenkins 1998).

Infrastructure supply is another avenue for market failure, market imperfection or social need. This is illustrated in the manner in which governments in many parts of the world usually find themselves as the main providers and managers of roads, airports, railways, power supply, sewage and water supply, although increasingly infrastructure is being provided by way of public–private sector partnerships or statutory or corporate authorities in which government is a major shareholder or partner.

Market imperfections can be found in areas where the market does not cater to the needs of individual citizens. In many countries, government, in consultation with industry, unions and other interests, has established equal employment opportunity legislation, anti-discrimination legislation, occupational health and safety practices, minimum wage structures, the provision of facilities for disabled people, and other workplace and social/cultural arrangements. Public consensus may also deem that a particular market outcome is unacceptable. A prime example is social welfare policy because there is usually a political consensus that aid ought to be targeted to those who are unable to compete in the market (Hall and Jenkins 1998).

Tourism, like any other industry, has problems which stem from market failures and imperfections and from subsequent government responses. However, as an industry, tourism is poorly understood, as are its various impacts. Hard to define because of its particular service and structural characteristics, tourism is consequently beset by problems of analysis, monitoring, coordination and policy-making. Moreover, until recently, tourism research, and notably analysis of tourism public policy and planning (Hall and Jenkins 1995), has been a low priority, with the tourism industry and governments at all levels more often concerned with promotion and short-term returns than strategic investment and sustainability. The major proportion of tourism industry and even government tourism agency research has therefore been focused on understanding the market and the means by which potential consumers can be persuaded to buy tourism products. According to Hall and Jenkins (1998) understanding of

- the dynamics of the tourism destination system in terms of the most appropriate set of supply-side linkages to maximise the returns from visitor expenditure
- the long-term effects of tourism on the socio-cultural and physical environment, and
- the relationship of tourism to other industries

is minimal. To this we can perhaps add our understanding of the dynamic nature of tourism planning as a whole. While the desirability for tourism planning is generally accepted, the most effective form and method of planning remains a contested concept. The consequences of tourism development are wide ranging and often unpredictable. As a result, planning can often only articulate concerns or uncertainties, society must guide planners in assessing their acceptability. Furthermore, as the discussion below illustrates, planning occurs at different levels and within a number of planning traditions.

While we have substantial numbers of local case studies of tourism planning and development on the one hand, and a desire for more sustainable tourism on the other, often being driven by international agreements regarding sustainability and the environment, the development of more appropriate forms of tourism on anything in the space in between has not been terribly successful.

Planning for tourism has traditionally been associated with land-use zoning or development planning at the local or regional government level. Concerns have typically been focused on site development, accommodation and building regulations, the density of tourist development, the presentation of cultural, historical and natural tourist features, and the provision of infrastructure including roads and sewage. However, as noted above, tourism planning at all levels of government has increasingly had to adapt its tourism planning programme in recent years to include concerns over the environmental and social impacts of tourism and, given the changing context within which government occurs, demands for 'smaller government', particularly from some business interests which argue that self-regulation is more economically efficient than government regulation. As the following pages will indicate, economic motivations have been foremost in tourism planning. However, attention is gradually becoming focused on the social and environmental aspects of tourism development, and the creation of more sustainable forms of tourism overall.

Approaches to tourism planning

One of the most useful outlines of the field of tourism planning was provided by Getz (1987) who identified four broad traditions of tourism planning:

- 'boosterism'
- an economic, industry-oriented approach
- a physical/spatial approach
- a community-oriented approach which emphasises the role that the host plays in the tourism experience.

As Getz (1987 : 5) noted, 'the four traditions are not mutually exclusive, nor are they necessarily sequential. Nevertheless, this categorisation is a convenient way to examine the different and sometimes overlapping ways in which tourism is planned, and the research and planning methods, problems and models associated with each.' The following sections will review each of these traditions and conclude with a discussion of the development of a sustainable model of tourism planning. The various approaches to tourism planning are outlined in Table 2.2.

Boosterism

Boosterism has long been the dominant tradition towards tourism development and planning since mass tourism began. Indeed, in many ways it is debatable whether one can describe boosterism as form of planning at all. Boosterism is a simplistic attitude that tourism development is inherently good and of automatic benefit to the hosts. Under this approach little consideration is given to the potential negative economic, social and environmental impacts of tourism and instead cultural and natural resources are regarded as objects to be exploited for the sake of tourism development. Therefore, in many ways boosterism may be more aptly described as a form of non-planning. However, boosterism has had a marked impression on the economic and physical landscape.

Elements of the idea of boosterism have their origins not only in nineteenth-century European laissez-faire economic utilitarianism and North American frontier capitalism but also in the relatively small size of organized tourism for much of the past 150 years. When tourist numbers were so small and natural resources so overwhelming in some areas, such as the frontier United States where the first national parks were created, then the effects of tourism were relatively small. However, although tourism grew, the perception of tourism as a benign, 'smokeless' industry did not change until relatively recently.

Under the boosterism tradition, residents of tourist destinations are not involved in the decision-making and planning processes surrounding tourism development and those who oppose such development may be regarded as unpatriotic or excessively negative. In recent years boosterism is probably best noted in the hosting of mega-events, such as the Olympic Games, in which such large events are held to be automatically good for the host city and region (Olds 1998). Research in this tradition focuses on the forecasting of tourism demand solely for the purposes of promotion and development rather than to ensure that levels of demand are appropriate to the resources and social carrying capacity of a region. According to Getz (1987 : 10):

> Boosterism is still practiced, and always will be, by two groups of people: politicians who philosophically or pragmatically believe that economic growth is always to be promoted, and by others who will gain financially by tourism. They will go on promoting it until the evidence mounts that they have run out of resources to

Table 2.2   Tourism planning approaches: assumptions, problem definition, methods, models and literature

Planning tradition	Underlying assumptions and related attitudes	Definition of the tourism planning problem	Some examples of related methods	Some examples of related models	Some examples of related literature
Boosterism	• tourism is inherently good • tourism should be developed • cultural and natural resources should be exploited • industry as expert • development defined in business/corporate terms	• how many tourists can be attracted and accommodated? • how can obstacles be overcome? • convincing hosts to be good to tourists	• promotion • public relations • advertising • growth targets	• demand forecasting models	Usually associated with tourism policy statements
Economic	• tourism equal to other industries • use tourism to: create employment, earn foreign revenue and improve terms of trade, encourage regional development, overcome regional economic disparities • planner as expert • development defined in economic terms	• can tourism be used as a growth pole? • maximisation of income and employment multipliers • influencing consumer choice • providing economic values for externalities • providing economic values for conservation purposes	• supply–demand analysis • benefit–cost analysis • product-market matching • development incentives • market segmentation	• management processes • tourism master plans • motivation • economic impact • economic multipliers • hedonistic pricing	Economic impact statements and feasibility studies. Examples would be analyses of the potential benefits of hosting an Olympics

Physical/spatial	• tourism as a resource user • ecological basis to development • tourism as a spatial and regional phenomenon • environmental conservation • development defined in environmental terms • preservation of genetic diversity	• physical carrying capacity • manipulating travel patterns and visitor flows • visitor management • concentration or dispersal of visitors • perceptions of natural environment • wilderness and national park management • designation of environmentally sensitive areas	• ecological studies • environmental impact assessment • regional planning • perceptual studies	• spatial patterns and processes • physical impacts • resort morphology • LAC (limits of acceptable change) • ROS (recreational opportunity spectrum) • TOS (tourism opportunity spectrum) • destination lifecycles	Gunn 1994; Inskeep 1991; Dowling 1997
Community	• need for local control • search for balanced development • search for alternatives to 'mass' tourism development • planner as facilitator rather than expert • development defined in socio-cultural terms	• how to foster community control? • understanding community attitudes towards tourism • understanding the impacts of tourism on a community • social impact	• community development • awareness and education • attitudinal surveys • social impact assessment	• ecological view of community • social/perceptual carrying capacity • attitudinal change • social multiplier	Murphy 1985; Blank 1989; Macbeth 1997

Table 2.2 (cont'd)

Planning tradition	Underlying assumptions and related attitudes	Definition of the tourism planning problem	Some examples of related methods	Some examples of related models	Some examples of related literature
Sustainable	• integration of economic, environmental and socio-cultural values • tourism planning integrated with other planning processes • holistic planning • preservation of essential ecological processes • protection of human heritage and biodiversity • inter- and intra-generational equity • achievement of a better balance of fairness and opportunity between nations • planning and policy as argument • planning as process • planning and implementation as two sides of the same coin • recognition of political dimension of tourism	• understanding the tourism system • setting goals, objectives and priorities • achieving policy and administrative coordination in and between the public and private sectors • cooperative and integrated control systems • understanding the political dimensions of tourism • planning for tourism that meets local needs and trades successfully in a competitive marketplace	• strategic planning to supersede conventional approaches • raising producer awareness • raising consumer awareness • raising community awareness • stakeholder input • policy analysis • evaluative research • political economy • aspirations analysis • stakeholder audit • environmental analysis and audit • interpretation	• systems models • integrated models focused on places and links and relationships between such places • resources as culturally constituted • environmental perception • business ecology • learning organisations	Krippendorf 1987; Hall & McArthur 1996, 1998; Mathieson & Wall 1982; McKercher 1997; Lindberg & McKercher 1997

Source: After Getz (1987), Hall et al. (1997).

exploit, that the real or opportunity costs are too high, or that political opposition to growth can no longer be countered. By then the real damage has usually been done.

The economic tradition: tourism as an industry

Under the economic tradition, tourism is seen as an industry which can be used as a tool by governments to achieve certain goals of economic growth and restructuring, employment generation, and regional development through the provision of financial incentives, research, marketing and promotional assistance. Although the economic model does not claim tourism to be the panacea for all economic ills, the approach does emphasise the potential value of tourism as an export industry, sometimes nebulously defined, which can positively contribute to national and regional imbalances in such things as terms of trade, balance of payments or levels of foreign exchange. For example, in promoting tourism as a response to the substantial economic restructuring of agriculture in rural Australia, the Department of Tourism (1993a : 24) noted

> Diversification of traditional rural enterprises into tourism would provide considerable benefits to local rural economies including:
> - wider employment opportunities;
> - diversifying the income base of farmers and rural towns;
> - additional justification for the development of infrastructure;
> - a broader base for the establishment, maintenance and/or expansion of local services;
> - scope for the integration of regional development strategies; and
> - an enhanced quality of life through extended leisure and cultural opportunities.

without also acknowledging some of the downsides of rural tourism or the difficulties for some marginal farming operations to get into the tourism business.

Within the economic tradition, government utilises tourism as a means to promote growth and development in specific areas. Therefore, the planning emphasis is on the economic impacts of tourism and its most efficient use to create income and employment benefits for regions or communities. Attention is given to the means by which tourism can be defined as an industry in order that its economic contribution and production can be measured, and so the role of government regulation and support can be adequately appraised.

One of the main characteristics of the economic approach is the use of marketing and promotion to attract the type of visitor who will provide the greatest economic benefit to the destination given the destination's specific tourist resources. Both government and industry emphasise market segmentation studies and matching product and markets. Economic goals are given priority over social and ecological questions; however, issues of opportunity costs, the assessment of visitor satisfaction and the economic necessity of generating a positive attitude towards tourists in host communities does mean that limited attention is paid to the negative impacts of tourism. Under the economic approach the issue of who benefits and who loses from tourism development does not usually arise.

The land use/physical/spatial approach

The physical/spatial approach has its origins in the work of geographers, urban and regional land-use planners and conservationists who advocate a rational approach to the planning of natural resources. Land use planning is one of the oldest forms of environmental protection. For many readers the land use/ spatial approach is the dominant form of public tourism planning through its close relationship with regional and destination planning, for example, the early work of Gunn (1979, 1988) before he incorporated the concept of sustainability in his later work (Gunn 1994).

Physical or spatial planning refers to 'planning with a spatial, or geographical, component, in which the general objective is to provide for a spatial structure of activities (or of land uses) which in some way is better than the pattern existing without planning' (P. Hall 1992 : 4). Typically, spatial planning is multi-dimensional and multi-objective. Within this approach, tourism is often regarded as having an ecological base with a resultant need for development to be based upon certain spatial patterns that would minimise the negative impacts of tourism on the physical environment. Comprising one of the main focuses within this framework are the related issues of physical and social carrying capacity (e.g. Mathieson and Wall 1982), environmental

Plate 2.2 Canterbury, England. The large numbers of visitors to the city has created substantial congestion problems which tourism planning strategies have sought to overcome.

Plate 2.3 Canterbury Cathedral, England. Large numbers of tourists has placed enormous stress on the physical and spiritual fabric of the Cathedral. A Visitor Centre has been built to help manage crowds alongside a visitor management strategy.

thresholds (e.g. Hill and Rosier 1989), and limits to or acceptable/desirable rates of change (e.g. McCool 1994; Wight 1998).

In order to minimise the impact of tourists on the physical environment, many visitor managers seek to manipulate travel patterns by concentrating or dispersing tourists in sensitive areas. For example, many national parks and marine parks have management plans which zone sections of the park in relation to certain levels of visitation, the provision of certain desired experiences and the nature of the resource itself. However, visitor management strategies at heritage attractions are increasingly being revised as past strategies appear not to be able to cope with either the increased numbers or the increased demands for positive experiences being placed on such sites (Hall and McArthur 1998). As Lindberg and McKercher (1997 : 72) noted 'As soon as an area starts to show signs of damage through overuse, the walking paths, roads, boating and other activities can be shifted to a different location . . . the common strategy of dispersion may be misguided . . . From the perspective of minimizing overall environmental change due to ecotourism, shifting locations may be the wrong strategy, because the new location may be damaged before the old location recovers.'

Within the spatial tradition, geographers have emphasised the tendency for destinations to evolve and decline in relation to the market (an economic approach) and the resources of a region (the physical approach) (e.g. Butler 1980; Pearce 1992). It is therefore not surprising that the spatial tradition emphasises the production of tourism development plans that are based on the natural resources of a region and on the capacity or limitations of sites to withstand tourism infrastructure. However, while such plans provide valuable insights into the potential natural resource capacities and travel patterns that occur within a region, they often fail to give attention to the social and cultural attributes of a destination. Therefore, another significant strand within the land use and physical planning aspects of the spatial tradition is the attention given to environmental impact and social impact assessments and statements. Such statements have increasingly become required under planning law for the development of major infrastructure projects (e.g. airports and roads), resort developments and facilities (e.g. visitor centres in wilderness areas). Although often thought of as primarily being related to developments in non-urban areas, the impacts of tourism-related development in urban areas, particularly large waterfront developments, are also often subject to an environmental impact statement (EIS), which will often include a number of social factors. For example, some of the urban impacts considered appropriate for inclusion in an EIS by Haughton and Hunter (1994 : 256) are:

- employment
- accessibility
- safety
- air and water quality, pollution
- urban sprawl
- displacement
- community facilities and services
- tax base

As the land use/spatial approach has evolved it has increasingly taken on aspects of wider developments in the land use and physical planning field. Indeed, land use planning has increasingly sought to integrate social and cultural planning concerns within an ecological approach as environmental problems have come to be defined in terms of human–environment relationships, particularly as land use planners have sought to respond to the challenge of sustainable development. This new development in the physical planning field is broadly described under the heading of environmental planning.

According to Evans (1997 : 5), contemporary environmental planning 'is conceived as an integrated and holistic approach to the environment that transcends traditional departmental and professional boundaries, and is directed towards securing the long-term goal of environmental sustainability'.

According to Cowell and Owens (1997), an environment-led system of planning will have certain implications, including

- the construction of defensible arguments for protecting any particular function of the environment as 'environmental capital'
- defining what is sustainable in the first place will create conflict as it preempts future decisions
- issues will be intensely political because of the constraints they will place on economic activity
- there will be debate over the various technical discourses of impact management and compensation
- issues of linkages will arise – with other policy instruments and between localities and scales.

The issues noted by Cowell and Owens bear great similarity to a number of the issues identified in the first chapter and, as we shall see, are points which the following chapters will frequently return to. Nevertheless, as Cowell and Owens (1997 : 21) emphasise, 'These issues must be confronted if we are to make sense of sustainability in real policy contexts.' Similarly, as Evans (1997 : 8) argues, 'if environmental planning for sustainability . . . is to be anywhere near effective, the political processes of public debate and controversy, both formal and informal, will need to play a much more significant role than has hitherto been the case'.

Community oriented tourism planning

Since the late 1970s increasing attention has come to be given to the negative environmental and social impacts of tourism. Although the negative effects of tourism was initially associated with the less developed nations (e.g. de Kadt 1979; Smith, V. 1989a; Harrison 1992), it was gradually recognised that as tourism grew undesirable impacts were also occurring in the developed nations and in parts of Europe and North America in particular. Indeed, Craik (1988 : 26) argued that despite difficulties in quantifying the social impacts of tourism 'in the same way as carrying capacities, bed requirements and even environmental impacts . . . it is perhaps the most important aspect of tourism development'. Therefore, an examination of the social impacts of tourism became to be regarded as essential not only from an ethical perspective of the need for community involvement in decision-making processes but also because without it, tourism growth and development may become increasingly difficult. As Ross (1991 : 157) observed:

> If pleasant and satisfying experiences involving local residents are important in the destination images of tourists, and in their decision-making processes, then a consideration of the well-being of local residents in the context of tourist development would seem critical. Should residents of tourist communities come to believe that

continual tourist development is destroying their physical and social environment, and that tourists are the symbols of this process, then a degree of unpleasantness may eventually characterize many resident–visitor interactions, which would ultimately damage the image of friendliness in the locals, so prized by overseas tourists at present.

In response to the perceived negative effects of tourism development, alternative strategies of tourism development were espoused, including what we now describe as ecotourism, which highlighted the social and physical context within which tourism occurred (e.g. Smith and Eadington 1992). For example, although Gunn (1979) emphasised a laissez-faire perspective in the first two of his three goals of tourism planning in the form of satisfactions to users and rewards to owners, the third goal, that of the protected utilisation of environmental resources did signify a new appreciation of the renewable nature of tourism resources – although it was clearly different from what we would now conceive of as sustainable tourism. Similarly, McIntosh and Goeldner (1986 : 308, 310) highlighted the need for wider community involvement in tourism in their five goals of tourism development, in which they argued that tourism development should aim to:

1 provide a framework for raising the living standard of local people through the economic benefits of tourism;
2 develop an infrastructure and provide recreation facilities for both residents and visitors;
3 ensure that the types of development within visitor centres and resorts are appropriate to the purposes of these areas;
4 establish a development programme that is consistent with the cultural, social and economic philosophy of the government and the people of the host area; and
5 optimise visitor satisfaction.

One of the clearest and most influential statements of the community approach to tourism development is to be found in Murphy's seminal book *Tourism: A Community Approach* (1985). Murphy advocated the use of an ecological approach to tourism planning which emphasised the need for local control over the development process. One of the key components of the approach is the notion that in satisfying local needs it may also be possible to satisfy the needs of the tourist, a 'win-win' philosophy that is immensely attractive. Nevertheless, despite the undoubted conceptual attraction to many destinations of the establishment of a community approach to tourism planning, substantial problems remain in the way such a process may operate and how it may be implemented (Haywood 1988; Murphy 1988).

Community tourism planning is a response to the need to develop more socially acceptable guidelines for tourism expansion. Cooke's (1982) study of social sensitivity to tourism in British Columbia provides some important insights into the manner in which the social impacts of tourism on a community can be ameliorated through appropriate planning measures. Cooke (1982 : 26) identified several sets of conditions that are appropriate and inappropriate to local tourism development:

Conditions associated with locally appropriate tourism development:
- Tourists respect local or ethnic traditions and values.
- Opportunities for extensive local involvement in the tourism industry at three levels:
  - through decisions made by local government;
  - through community-wide support for volunteer support programs for tourism; and
  - active participation in the direction of tourist development.
- Tourism is an economic mainstay or is viewed as a desirable alternative to other industries.
- Themes and events that attract tourists are supported and developed by the local community.

Conditions associated with locally inappropriate tourism development:
- Tourists do not respect local or ethnic traditions and values.
- There are uncertainties about the future direction of tourism development with local people feeling that they have little control.
- Residents feel that visitors are catered to ahead of locals, and that infrastructure and facilities have been designed for the benefit of tourists rather than the local community.
- Growth in the host community is proceeding faster than what the residents feel appropriate.
- There are perceived conflicts over natural resource use.

Cooke's study recommended that all tourism planning be based on the goals and priorities of residents. Indeed, she even went further and recommended that local attractions be promoted only when endorsed by residents. While many readers may have a sympathy with this approach and while this idea underlies much of the community development literature, its practical exercise will have substantial implications for tourism development which could even mean stopping certain types of development which may be favoured by certain stakeholders in the planning process. For example, opposition has often emerged towards the development of casinos by various interests in a destination because of the perceived impact of casinos on host communities, particularly in relation to a perceived increase in crime and prostitution and the effectiveness of governments at regulating casino gambling.

A community approach to tourism planning is therefore a 'bottom up' form of planning, which emphasises development *in* the community rather than development *of* the community. As Blank (1989 : 4) recognised, '*Communities* are the destination of most travellers. Therefore *it is in communities that tourism happens*. Because of this, *tourism industry development and management must be brought effectively to bear in communities*'. Under this approach, residents are regarded as the focal point of the tourism planning exercise, not the tourists, and the community, which is often equated with a region of local government, is regarded as the basic planning unit. Nevertheless, substantial difficulties will arise in attempting to implement the concept of community planning in tourist destinations. As Dowling (1993a : 53) noted, 'research into community attitudes towards tourism is reasonably well developed, although incorporation of such views into the planning process is far less common'.

One of the major difficulties in implementing a community approach to tourism planning is the political nature of the planning process. Community planning implies a high degree of public participation in the planning process (Haywood 1988). As Arnstein (1969) argued, public participation implies that the local community will have a degree of control over the planning and decision-making process. Therefore, a community approach to tourism planning implies that there will be a need for partnership in, or community control of, the tourism development process. However, such a community approach has generally not been adopted by government authorities, often because of complaints from business interests of the economic impact of decision-making delays which arise out of any statutory requirement for participation. Moreover, for many government officials, whether elected or otherwise, community control can also be interpreted as a loss of their power and their control over the planning process. Indeed, the level of public involvement in tourism planning throughout most of the world can be more accurately described as a form of tokenism in which decisions or, just as importantly, the direction of decisions has already been prescribed by government. Communities rarely have the opportunity to say no (Hall 1998b).

Substantial problems also exist in implementing public participation programmes at the community level (Sewell and Phillips 1979; Timothy 1999). For example, formal legalistic processes of consultation usually require the hosting of public meetings. However, public meetings can be exploited by those individuals and organisations who best know how to utilise meeting procedures and dynamics in their favour. Indeed, the more formal the participation process the more legalistic it tends to become thereby disadvantaging poorer resourced stakeholders. In discussing tourism policy in rural New South Wales, Australia, Jenkins (1993) identified seven impediments to public participation in tourism planning:

- the public generally has difficulty in comprehending complex and technical planning issues
- the public is not always aware of or understands the decision-making process
- the difficulty in attaining and maintaining representativeness in the decision-making process
- the apathy of citizens
- the increased costs in terms of staff and money
- the prolonging of the decision-making process
- adverse effects on the efficiency of decision-making.

A further problem in utilising a community approach to tourism planning is the structure of government. The nature of systems of governance leads to difficulties in ensuring that tourism policies at different levels of government are adequately coordinated and that decisions and policies at one level are not at odds with decisions at another. For example, a locally based community decision not to allow tourism development at a particular site may well be at odds with a regional or national tourism plan which has been drawn up by a superior level of government. Alternatively, a local government decision to proceed with a tourism related development may be opposed at another level if it impinges on legislative requirements or policy settings. However, if tourism resource conflicts are to be resolved at the community level then the institutional arrangements for decision-making processes related to management also need to be based at the local level (Millar and Aitken 1995). One major concern with such measures is the role that local elites may have in skewing decisions towards their own interests rather than wider community needs. However, the holding of reserve powers at higher levels of government can often act as a restraint on the roles of local elites (Ostrom 1990).

Despite the difficulties in implementing a community approach to tourism development, elements of the approach have proven to be attractive in the tourism planning literature (e.g. Getz 1994; Ryan and Montgomery 1994; Simmons 1994). Many readers would likely agree with Murphy that, 'If tourism is to become the successful and self-perpetuating industry many have advocated, it needs to be planned and managed as a renewable resource industry, based on local capacities and community decision making' (Murphy 1985 : 153).

As noted above, tourism planning is not static. Planning approaches evolve in relation to the demands made upon them by various stakeholders and interests, the changing values of a community and a society, and the broader socio-economic-environmental context within which planning occurs. Nevertheless, elements of a community approach to planning would appear to provide a basis for the formulation of tourism policies which would assist both residents and visitors in the longer term, satisfying local desires to control the rate of change, if any, and meeting visitor interest in the maintenance of unique attributes of a destination. However, a community approach is only a starting point. Tourism planning must also be able to accommodate the physical and economic dimensions of tourism, not only in order to ensure the long-term viability of the tourism industry but also to assist in the creation of sustainable places. The next section will examine some of the aspects of the emerging sustainable approach to tourism planning.

A sustainable approach to tourism planning: towards integrated tourism planning and development?

As noted in the first chapter, sustainable development has a primary objective of providing lasting and secure livelihoods which minimise resource depletion, environmental degradation, cultural disruption and social instability. The WCED (Bruntland Commission) (1987) report extended this basic objective to include concerns of equity; the needs of economically marginal populations; and the idea of technological and social limitations on the ability of the environment to meet present and future needs.

While tourism ostensibly seeks to meet the primary objective of sustainable development (i.e. 'not to foul its own nest' and in so doing to continue over time to return benefits to society), there are many contradictions within both the concept of sustainable development and the nature of tourism which will mean that complete satisfaction of the concept will be extremely difficult (e.g. see Dutton and Hall 1989; Bramwell and Lane 1993; Hall and Butler 1995; Hall and Lew 1998). For example, Pearce, Barbier and Markandya (1988) noted that sustainability implies an infinite time horizon, whereas practical decision-making requires the adoption of finite horizons. Although these factors complicate the attainment of sustainable development planning objectives, they are not 'hard barriers'. Rather, they serve to emphasise the pre-conditions for tourism to become a sustainable land use. Paramount among these is an effective coordination and control mechanism – a system which is able to give practical and ongoing effect to the policy and planning intent of sustainable development.

The complex nature of the tourism industry and the often poorly defined linkages between its components are major barriers to the integrative strategic planning which is a prerequisite for sustainable development. Tourism development is often fragmented and poorly coordinated (Hall and Jenkins 1995). The poor record of synchronisation of policy and practice therefore appears to be one of the major impediments to attainment of sustainable development objectives. The existence of tourist infrastructure and 'ready-made' attractions alone are not sufficient by themselves to ensure the long-term future of a tourist destination. Furthermore, an imbalance between the supply and demand components of tourism, together with inadequate attention to factors determining economic, social and environmental sustainability, have the potential to lead to undesirable and unforeseen consequences (Butler 1990, 1991).

As tourism developed around the world in the immediate post Second World War era, there was little evidence to suggest that the nature and scale of tourism activities was not sustainable. The number of people travelling was minimal by today's standards. It is only since the rapid growth of international tourism began in the early 1970s with the advent of the jumbo jet that questions about factors affecting sustainability, such as environmental and social constraints to development, have become prominent. Therefore, it should not be surprising that the need for incorporation of sustainable development principles into tourism development has only recently emerged as one of the key management issues in tourism.

Community planning provides a basis for the development of a longer-term approach to tourism, but the tenets of community-based planning need to be extended to incorporate the coordinative, iterative, integrative and strategic aspects of planning before a sustainable approach can be realised. One of the means to developing more sustainable forms of tourism lies in convincing government and the tourism industry of the importance of incorporating sustainable development principles into planning and operations. Dutton and Hall (1989) identified five mechanisms by which this goal can be achieved:

- cooperative and integrated control systems
- development of industry coordination mechanisms

- raising consumer awareness
- raising producer awareness
- strategic planning to supersede conventional approaches.

Cooperative and integrated control systems
Unfortunately, in a typical public planning process, stakeholders are often consulted minimally, near the end of the process, and often via formal public meetings. 'The plan that results under these conditions tends to be a prescriptive statement by the professionals rather than an agreement among the various parties'; by contrast, an interactive style 'assumes that better decisions result from open, participative processes' (Lang 1988, quoted in Wight 1998). An integrative planning approach to tourism planning and management at all levels (from the regional plan to individual resort projects) would assist in the distribution of the benefits and costs of tourism development more equitably, while focusing on improving relationships and understanding between stakeholders may also assist in agreement on planning directions and goals. However, cooperation alone will not foster commitment to sustainable development without the incentive of increased mutual benefits.

Development of industry coordination mechanisms
While a range of formal and informal industry bodies exist, few of these address such complex issues as sustainable development. The support by industry groups of voluntary development codes, environmental codes, or codes of conduct is perhaps indicative of possible directions if common needs can be agreed upon. However, for such guidelines to be effective, it must be ensured that they do not constitute a 'lowest common denominator' approach to development and implementation. Therefore, it becomes imperative that government, at all levels, uses its influence to encourage greater industry coordination on planning issues by creating structures and processes which enable stakeholders to talk to each other and create effective relationships and partnerships.

Raising consumer awareness
In many cases, the difference between a sustainable and non-sustainable tourism operation can be difficult for consumers to detect, particularly in the short term. Even in the long term the various market segments will react differently to different levels of impact. For example, some users of national parks continue to use areas even when they become crowded, while others divert to other areas. Nevertheless, if consumers are to enjoy the benefits of better quality experiences, while minimising the costs of that experience to their own or external communities, then they will be more likely to make informed judgements about the types of tourism products and services (Botterill 1991; Wood and House 1991; Elkington and Hailes 1992; Hall and McArthur 1998). For example, the shift in adventure travellers from consumptive to experiential services (from hunting to wildlife photography) is illustrative of the capacity of markets to readjust and make value judgements compatible

with the values inherent in the philosophy of sustainable development (Barbier 1987).

On the demand side, tourist codes of behaviour have been developed in order to minimise the negative impacts of tourists on the social and physical environment (e.g. Ecotourism Association of Australia 1993; Mason and Mowforth 1996). For example, the Audubon Society, one of the largest conservation groups in the United States, has developed the Audubon Travel Ethic which draws attention to the appropriate behaviours and ethics to which individuals travelling with the Society should subscribe (cited in Valentine 1992):

1 The biota shall not be disturbed.
2 Audubon tours to natural areas will be sustainable.
3 The sensibilities of other cultures will be respected.
4 Waste disposal shall have neither environmental nor aesthetic impacts.
5 The experience a tourist gains in travelling with Audubon shall enrich his or her appreciation of nature, conservation, and the environment.
6 The effect of an Audubon tour shall be to strengthen the conservation effort and enhance the natural integrity of places visited.
7 Traffic in products that threaten wildlife and plant populations shall not occur.

However, while alterations to the demand side of the tourism equation may well be possible through the modification of tourist behaviour via the development of codes of behaviour, it may be argued that the tourists who read and take note of such material are those who represent the least worry in terms of negative impacts on the physical and social environment (Mason and Mowforth 1996). Therefore, if sustainable forms of tourism are to be developed, then it clearly becomes essential to develop more sustainable forms of tourist product that are supplied to the consumer.

Raising producer awareness

Greater attention has been given to meeting the demands of different consumer segments than to the needs of the supplier of the tourist product. Such an approach is extremely short-sighted as there is clearly a need to balance the supply and demand of the tourist experience. In the environmental sphere, producer awareness may be raised through the production of environmental codes of conduct or practice (e.g. Mason and Mowforth 1996; Hall and McArthur 1998). However, such documents, while influencing the perceptions of some tourism developers, may need to be backed up by government regulation and environmental planning legislation if they are to have any overall affect on development practices. Indeed, the more cynical commentator may note that such developments have only occurred in order to reduce the likelihood of greater government intervention in the environmental dimensions of the tourism industry.

Strategic tourism planning to supersede conventional approaches

Strategic tourism planning at the destination level is facilitated by greater involvement of host communities in the decision-making process (Gunn 1988;

Dowling 1993a, 1993b). Such an approach requires a willingness on the part of decision-making agencies to actively solicit and take account of host community attitudes if genuine public involvement in planning is to be achieved. Moreover, strategic tourism planning at the destination level needs to be conceived of in terms of strategic planning for the destination rather than strategic planning for destination organisations, which are related but significantly different things.

Strategic tourism planning in its fullest sense is proactive, responsive to community needs, perceiving planning and implementation as part of a single process, and ongoing (Lang 1986). Similarly, Dredge and Moore (1992 : 15) highlighted the need to integrate tourism in town planning and emphasised that strategic plans need 'to be backed up by statements of implementation that guide the pattern of tourism development'.

Strategy is a means of achieving a desired end, e.g. the objectives identified for the management of tourism resources (Chaffee 1985). In the case of sustainable tourism planning and development, 'the strategy' is the use of appropriate visitor management, marketing, management and planning practices to achieve three basic strategic objectives:

- ensuring the conservation of tourism resource values
- enhancing the experiences of the visitors who interact with tourism resources
- maximising the economic, social and environmental returns to stakeholders in the host community (McArthur and Hall 1993; Hall and McArthur 1998).

Strategic analysis combines three different types of analysis:

- *Environmental analysis* which assists planners and managers in anticipating short- and long-term changes in the operational environment.
- *Resource analysis* which helps the tourism planner to understand the significance of the site's physical and human resource base to successful ongoing environmental adaptation.
- *Aspirations analysis* which identifies the aspirations and interests of the major stakeholders in the destination or tourism development and assists management to formulate their own strategic objectives in light of the desires and interests of others.

As Richardson and Richardson (1989 : 58) observed: 'If performed effectively, strategic analysis can generate tremendous insight (particularly for first time users) into the factors which underpin present success/failure levels and into the organisational changes which make greatest sense in the context of the anticipated future.' Indeed, strategic analysis is part of the process by which tourism agencies and operators can be turned into 'learning organisations' that can constantly adapt to the demands of their stakeholders (Garratt 1987). Therefore, measures which private and public sector tourism organisations can take to evaluate the strategic basis for tourism planning and development might include (Hall and McArthur 1998):

- an aspirations analysis to determine who the important stakeholders are/will be and to ascertain their power positions, aspirations and propensities for or against alternative potential developments

- an environmental analysis for the insight this might stimulate on questions of organisational restructuring as well as potential product/market competitive developments
- pertinent market segmentation exercises
- analysis of the present and potential competitive market structure to identify the inherent attractiveness of the markets, and the openings which might exist for managers to exploit
- analysis of the wider and more futuristic environment in order to anticipate futures which the event might seek to exploit, change or avoid as necessary.

At a local level, elements of the strategic planning process can be employed to achieve a manageable, timely and cost-efficient plan. Open community workshops and consultative processes may be especially useful to identify a range of issues which arise in tourism development, including

- *primary values* – what is it that residents and visitors value about the area?
- *aspirations* – what role do residents wish tourism to play in the economic and social development of the community?
- *fears* – what concerns do residents have about the impact of tourism on the community?
- *possibilities* – what are the special characteristics of the area that locals wish to share with visitors?
- *warts* – what are the things that detract from the area being a pleasant place to visit?

(Tourism South Australia 1991)

By going through a local tourism planning process and determining community response to some of the issues raised above, Tourism South Australia (1991) argued that destinations, townships and local councils can be in a far better position to determine their positioning in the tourism market, product development, infrastructure development, development constraints, preferred futures, local needs and the indicators by which success will be measured.

This last point is particularly important as the role of an indicator is to make complex systems understandable. An effective indicator or set of indicators helps a destination, community or organisation determine where it is, where it is going, and how far it is from chosen goals. Sustainability indicators provide a measure of the long-term viability of a destination or community based on the degree to which its economic, environmental, and social systems are efficient and integrated (Gill and Williams 1994). However, indicators are only useful in the context of appropriately framed questions (Hall and McArthur 1998). In choosing indicators, one must have a clear understanding of planning and policy goals. For example, a typology of indicators might include:

- economic, environmental and social indicators (measuring changes in the state of the economy, environment and society)
- sustainability indicators (measuring distance between that change and a sustainable state of the environment)
- sustainable development indicators (measuring progress to the broader goal of sustainable development in a national context).

Unfortunately, there has been a tendency to pick indicators that are easiest to measure and reflect most visible change, thus important issues, such as the social and cultural impacts of tourism, may be dropped (e.g. Craik 1988). In addition, appropriate indicators may not be selected because organisations may not want to be held accountable for the results of evaluations (Hall and McArthur 1998). Nevertheless, substantial progress has been made with the selection of various sustainable tourism indicators (e.g. NcCol 1994; Wight 1998).

The five mechanisms identified by Dutton and Hall (1989) for sustainable tourism practice still appear to be applicable planning strategies at a destination or operational level but do not deal with the contextual issues that emerge in attempting to implement such tourism strategies. More recently, Lew and Hall (1998), in a review of recent research on sustainable tourism development, identified a number of 'lessons' regarding sustainable tourism, that do provide something of the context which planners need to understand in order to be able to make principles of sustainability work:

- Sustainable tourism represents a value orientation in which the management of tourism impacts takes precedence over market economics – although tension between the two are ever present.
- Implementing sustainable tourism development requires measures that are both scale and context specific.
- Sustainable tourism issues are shaped by global economic restructuring and are fundamentally different in developing and developed economies.
- At the community scale, sustainable tourism requires local control of resources.
- Sustainable tourism development requires patience, diligence, and a long-term commitment.

It is the implications of these lessons for the successful application of sustainable tourism strategies that the following chapters will address. However, before moving on to the next chapter which describes the significance of a systems approach to tourism planning, we will briefly discuss prescriptive versus descriptive approaches to tourism planning.

Prescriptive and descriptive approaches to tourism planning and policy

Tourism planning and policy research, and, indeed, research throughout the social sciences, can be built up on two main types of theory: that which adopts prescriptive models and that which adopts descriptive models (Mitchell 1989; Hall and Jenkins 1995). 'Prescriptive or normative models seek to demonstrate how [planning and] policy making should occur relative to pre-established standards,' whereas 'descriptive models document the way in which the policy process actually occurs' (Mitchell 1989 : 264). Prescriptive (normative) models serve as a guide to an ideal situation. The majority of tourism planning texts have adopted prescriptive models of the planning process (e.g. Inskeep 1991; Gunn 1994). However, while these may be useful rational models against which to compare reality, they do not provide detailed insights into the real world of planning and policy and its associated set of values, power and interests (Hall and Jenkins 1995). Instead, approaches, methods and techniques need to be evaluated within the context of the goals, objectives and outcomes of tourism planning and development (Hall and McArthur 1998).

Descriptive approaches give rise to explanations about what happened during the decision-making, planning and policy-making processes. Indeed, one of the great problems with prescriptive tourism planning approaches is that their value has often failed to be evaluated in terms of their economic, cultural, environmental and political context. Many tourism plans are never or only partially implemented (Pearce 1989). Perhaps one of the main reasons for this is that they represent 'rational' planning approaches which fail to consider the world in which the plans will operate. In other words, although prescriptive tourism planning models are deductive, one cannot deduce in the absence of prior knowledge. This book uses a combination of both descriptive and prescriptive approaches. While several of the chapters outline what is happening with respect to tourism planning and policy they also outline ways in which it might be improved. Although the model of the policy and planning process used in this book is essentially descriptive in that it focuses on power, institutional arrangements and values as elements of planning and decision-making processes, the articulation of values of sustainability, the proposed establishment of certain forms of institutional arrangements, and arguments for certain approaches towards sustainable tourism are prescriptive. It is hoped that by placing arguments and values at the forefront of tourism planning that the planning and policy process will be seen in terms of the contested, political, terrain that it really is. However, rather than be regarded as a weakness, a public sphere of debate should be seen as a strength, as it is only through open debate, communication and exchange of ideas that the public interest which tourism planning seeks to represent can actually be gained.

Conclusion

As with all forms of resource development, tourism requires appropriate management regimes. The free market is not an adequate mechanism by itself to protect the interests of all parties and stakeholders in the tourism development process. Management regimes evolve as a solution to the challenge of collective action (Ostrom 1990). In the case of tourism planning we are looking at a way in which such collective action can be understood and furthered within the context of tourism development. As this chapter has highlighted, a number of approaches to tourism planning have developed, ranging from unrestrained boosterism through to economic emphasis and, more recently, there have been approaches which emphasise the environmental and community dimensions of tourism. Since the mid-1980s several strands of these approaches have become integrated to various degrees in an attempt to formulate more sustainable approaches towards tourism development.

The increasing recognition by government and industry of the nexus between tourism and sustainable development augurs well for a more socially responsive and environmentally sensitive tourism industry. However, the design, planning and management of tourism environments requires more than the simplistic adoption of codes and guidelines or industry self-regulation, valid though these strategies may be. Instead, a sustainable tourism industry requires a commitment by all parties involved in the planning process to sustainable development principles. Only through such widespread commitment can the long-term integration of social, environmental and economic goals be attained, issues that we will return to as we progress through the various dimensions and scales of tourism planning and policy.

Questions and further reading

How does market failure provide a justification for government intervention in tourism?
Why are community-based approaches to tourism planning difficult to implement?
To what extent are Dutton and Hall's (1989) five mechanisms to achieve sustainable tourism development still relevant in the Twenty-First Century?

Key texts in traditional approaches to tourism planning are Gunn (1994) and Inskeep (1991). Compare Gunn (1994) with Gunn (1988) to see the influence that ideas of sustainability can have on tourism planning. Murphy (1985) still provides the best introduction to a community approach to tourism planning and development. Blowers (1997) and Evans (1997) detail the contribution of contemporary environmental planning approaches to sustainable development, while various contributors to Hall and Lew (1998) outline a broad range of geographical perspectives on sustainable development. Discussion of a strategic approach to community and visitor management are to be found in Hall and McArthur (1998) as well as details of techniques to incorporate stakeholder values in the planning process.

Chapter 3

Tourism planning systems: theory, thinking and exorcism

Theory allows for both professional and intellectual self-reflection. It tries to make sense of the seemingly unrelated, contradictory aspects of urban development and create a rational system with which to compare and evaluate the merits of different planning ideas and strategies. It also allows planners to translate their specific issues into the language of more general social theory so that planning may interchange ideas with other disciplines (Campbell and Fainstein 1996 : 3).

The concept of a system is a very powerful analytical tool. At its simplest level a system is an integrated whole whose essential properties arise from the relationships between its constituent parts. Systems thinking is therefore the understanding of a phenomenon within the context of a larger whole (Capra 1997). Systems and systems thinking has greatly influenced fields of study such as biology, ecology and physics, from which some of the first ideas regarding systems were developed early in the twentieth century, through to engineering, building construction, sociology, geography, planning and, of course, tourism studies.

This chapter aims to provide an overview of the nature of systems and systems thinking. It examines how some of the ideas of systems have been applied to tourism, and aims to understand the complex environment within which tourism occurs and which it influences. Finally, the chapter outlines the shape of the tourism planning system adopted in this book and some of the various elements within such a system. Key issues to be addressed include such concepts as scale, standpoint and relationships.

Planning and policy as theory

Planning and public policy are troublesome as a research focus because of their inherent complexity, 'specifically because of the temporal nature of the process, the multiplicity of participants and of policy provisions, and the contingent nature of theoretical effects' (Greenberg et al. 1977 : 1532). As Lyden et al. (1969 : 156–157) wrote:

Altogether the realistic working assumption is that a public decision is an amalgam of a variety of contributions – public attitudes amongst them – fed into a network of social interactions. The interaction path rarely shows a constant, unchanging structure; instead it develops, evolves, and changes shape and form over time. One of the primary reasons why the public policy process has always appeared to be such a mystery to many people is this fluidity, this refusal to remain within the confines of institutional structures designed to deal with public issues.

This highly complex and volatile situation has given rise to a wide and diverse body of theoretical approaches to the study of planning and policy although many of these approaches have not been fully articulated within the context of tourism (Hall and Jenkins 1995). The study of policy and planning has become an interdisciplinary field; however, 'popularisation of the field has not led to a great deal of theoretical cohesion . . . interpretations . . . may differ sharply depending on the pedigree of the analyst' (Jenkins 1978 : ix). Similarly, Campbell and Fainstein (1996 : 2) note that 'the amorphous quality of planning theory means that practitioners largely disregard it'.

Different models exist to interpret the same events, leading in many cases to different conclusions (e.g. Rakoff and Schaefer 1970; Allison 1971; Fagence 1979). Yet this situation, while frustrating to many students of planning and tourism who wish to see 'solutions' in black and white, reflects the importance of understanding the various standpoints from which planning problems may be perceived. Different values and interests of individuals involved in the planning process will give rise to different interpretations of the planning problem and, therefore, of planning solutions. Moreover, such a situation reflects the interrelationship between planning and policy and theory.

One of the basic tenets of this book is that plans and policies imply theories. Planning and policy making reflect assumptions about the manner in which people, organisations and, in some cases, the environment, will act given an authoritative decision or set of decisions. As Pressman and Wildavsky (1973 : xv) have stated:

> Whether stated explicitly or not, policies point to a chain of causation between initial conditions and future consequences. If X, then Y. Policies become programs when, by authoritative action, the initial conditions are created, X now exists. Programs make the theories operational by forging the first link in the causal chain connecting actions to objectives. Given X, we act to obtain Y.

Similarly, Majone (1980a : 178) has argued that 'policies may be viewed as theories from two different but related perspectives'. First, 'they can be seen as an analyst's rational reconstruction of a complex sequence of events'. Second, 'they can be seen from the point of view of actions, giving them stability and internal coherence' (Majone 1980a : 178). More recently, Campbell and Fainstein (1996 : 2) observed, 'In their day-to-day work planners may rely more on intuition than explicit theory; yet this intuition may in fact be assimilated theory.' Theory and planning therefore go hand-in-hand. However, planning theory, and tourism planning theory in particular, is often regarded as having a soft theoretical base – if it is regarded as having a theoretical foundation at all. Nevertheless, planning theory has the capacity to inform practice and make explicit previous assumptions about the nature of tourism planning, thereby offering the opportunity for reflection and improvement of the planning process toward certain goals and objectives.

As Chapter 1 indicated, tourism planning has been characterised by a number of different approaches, each of which reflects a certain range of assumptions and values, utilises a limited range of methodologies, and defines problems in particular ways. Each of these we can argue is characterised by a particular theoretical orientation. There is not sufficient space to fully elucidate the way in which each of the planning approaches frames the world in a particular way. That would require a book in itself. Instead, this chapter examines one of the main theoretical constructs which underlies the developing sustainable approach towards tourism planning, that of systems and systems thinking.

Systems and systems thinking

A system is an object of study. A system comprises

1 a set of elements (sometimes also called entities)
2 the set of relationships between the elements
3 the set of relationships between those elements and the environment.

Systems analysis is valuable because simple linear relationships and casual chains, while being the realm of classical science which most of us learnt in high school and 'learn by numbers' management texts, cannot adequately describe or explain many of the complex situations encountered in either the physical or social sciences. Instead we are often faced with the problem of trying to explain the multiple and complex interactions which take place in everyday life. A system is therefore a means of abstracting from reality in a manner which makes it more understandable.

The structure of a system is composed of elements and the relationships between elements. Elements are the basic unit of a system. However, part of the art of systems analysis and definition will be the construction of a set of entities that form a relatively coherent object of study which has a well-defined relationship with its environment. Systems analysis cannot proceed without such abstraction. As Ashby (1966 : 16) observed, any real system will be characterised by 'an infinity of variables from which different observers (with different aims) may reasonably make an infinity of different selections'. Similarly, Wilson (1986 : 476) noted, 'while the definition of any particular system of interest obviously reflects the object of study, it is constructed by the analyst, and so different system definitions of the same object of study will be created by different people for different purposes'. For example, as Hall (1998b : 4) notes,

> one of the most frustrating things for a student starting a tourism course is that almost every text provides a different definition of tourism. This is not necessarily because authors are trying to be difficult and confuse the student, although some may have suspicions that this is indeed the case! Rather the author is trying to be specific about exactly where the text fits into the broad spectrum of tourism studies and is trying to delimit the boundaries of the book.

In other words, the definition is a convenient abstraction which can contribute to analysis. The above approach is fundamental to any subject. Each discipline and area of scholarship and research has as one of its first tasks the identification of the things which comprise the foci for study. By defining terms we give meaning to and provide a basis for the understanding of what we are doing. Moreover, we are able to give terms a specific, technical basis that can be used to help communicate more effectively and improve the quality of our research and management.

One of the most substantial problems in understanding the elements within a system is that of scale. Systems are embedded within systems. What we regard as an element of a system at one level of analysis may itself constitute a system at a lower level of analysis. For example, we often examine the flows of tourists within an international tourism system by analysing the flows of tourists between different countries, which are the elements of such a system. However, if we change our resolution we may then examine the flows of tourists within a country, by looking at the intra-regional flows of tourists. In the latter example it is the country which is the system and the regions the elements. How we define an element therefore depends on the scale at which we conceive the system, otherwise referred to as the resolution level.

> Every element is characterised by forming, from the point of view of the corresponding resolution level (at which the system . . . is defined), an indivisible unit whose structure we either cannot or do not want to resolve. However, if we increase the resolution level in a suitable manner . . . the structure of the element can be distinguished. In consequence, the original element loses its meaning and becomes the source of new elements of a relatively different system, i.e. of a system defined at a higher resolution level (Klir and Valach 1967 : 35 in Harvey 1969 : 454).

The other component in the structure of a system is the relationship or links between the elements that make up a system. Three basic forms of relationship can be identified: (1) a series relation (in which A leads to B), which is the characteristic cause-and-effect type relation of classical science; (2) a parallel relation in which two elements are affected by another element; (3) a feedback relation, which describes a situation in which an element influences itself. Both the elements and the relationships between them are part of the environment, which is most simply thought of as everything there is. However, when trying to model a system it is important to recognise the relevant elements in the environment which affect the operation of the system. Therefore, these are abstracted out from the environment and tied into a specific systems model for the purposes of analysis.

Another important element in systems analysis is defining the boundaries of a system. In mathematical terms this is extremely easy. However, in operational terms it can be extremely difficult. Sometimes the boundary of a system may be set by defining it in terms of something which is self-evident in terms of the questions being asked. For example, if one were examining a political systems problem then an appropriate boundary might be a government boundary. Similarly, a problem of water resource management may be dealt with in ecological terms through selecting a watershed as a boundary. Indeed, planning problems typically emerge when the different boundaries of different systems overlap, making management extremely difficult, a point which we will return to later. Many boundaries are not so easy to identify. Therefore, boundaries may be imposed through the application of judgement as to where a system begins and ends and in relation to the problem that we are trying to solve. This does not mean that such boundaries are arbitrary, rather they should be related to the goals of the study and experience of such systems, as clearly the selection of a boundary can have a major impact on research results. Nowhere has this been more clearly demonstrated in tourism than with respect to economic analysis.

A multiplier may be regarded as 'a coefficient which expresses the amount of income generated in an area by an additional unit of tourist spending' (Archer 1982 : 236). It is the ratio of direct and secondary changes within an economic region to the direct initial change itself. The size of the tourist multiplier is a significant measure of the economic benefit of tourism because it will be a reflection of the circulation of the tourist dollar through an economic system. In general, the larger the size of the tourist multiplier the greater the self-sufficiency of that economy in the provision of tourist facilities and services. Therefore, a tourist multiplier will generally be larger at a national level than at a regional level (e.g. state, province, county), because at a regional level leakage will occur in the form of taxes to the national government and importation of goods and services from other regions. Similarly, at the local level, multipliers will reflect the high importation level of small communities and tax payments to regional and national governments. As a measure of economic benefit from tourism, the multiplier technique has been increasingly subject to question, particularly as its use has often produced exaggerated results (Bull 1994), one reason being that the selection of the boundary of the economy being studied is so critical. The smaller the area to be analysed, the greater will be the number of 'visitors' and hence the greater will be the estimate of economic impact, while the selection of the boundary will also affect the extent to which there is leakage out of the system, for example, through the importation of goods and services for tourism. Boundary selection is therefore a key determinant in influencing the result of any analysis of an economic system (Burns and Mules 1986).

One area in which systems thinking has been especially influential and which will be familiar to most readers is in the biological and ecological sciences. For example, the concept of the 'web of life' conveys the idea that all life is interrelated in a network of relationships. The central organising idea of ecology is that of the ecosystem, a term developed by Arthur Tansley in 1935 to replace the more anthromorphic term 'community': 'All the parts off such an ecosystem – organic and inorganic, biome and habitat – may be regarded as interacting factors which, in a mature ecosystem, are in approximate equilibrium: it is through their interactions that the whole system is maintained' (Tansley 1935 : 207).

An ecosystem is therefore a model of interrelatedness in nature which includes a hierarchy of systems at different levels of complexity and extent. The ecosystem concept presents both the biological and non-biological aspects of the environment in one entity, with strong emphasis on the cycling of nutrients and the flow of energy in the system – whether it be a lake, a forest, or the earth as a whole (Worster 1977). Fosberg (1963 in Stoddart 1972 : 157) defined an ecosystem as

> a functioning interacting system composed of one or more living organisms and their effective environment, both physical and biological . . . The description of an ecosystem may include its spatial relations; inventories of its physical features, its habitats and ecological niches, its organisms, and its basic reserves of matter and energy; the nature of its income (or input) of matter and energy; and the behaviour or trend of its entropy level.

The ecosystem idea has been influential not just in ecology. Stoddart (1965, 1967), for example, argued that the ecosystem concept has four main properties that makes it suitable as a tool in geographic research, First, it is monistic, in that it brings together the environment, humans, plants and animals into a single framework, within which the interaction between components can be examined. Second, ecosystems are structured in an orderly, comprehensible manner. Third, ecosystems function, in that they involve the continuous throughput of matter and energy. 'In geographic terms, the system involves not only the framework of the communication net, but also the goods and people flowing through it. Once the framework has been defined, it may be possible to quantify the interactions and interchanges between component parts . . .' (Stoddart 1972 : 158). Fourth, the ecosystem is a general system thereby providing for application to a range of different situations where systems analysis may prove fruitful. However, while Stoddart's hope of systems analysis providing a methodological foundation for geography proved unfulfilled (see Johnston 1991), ecosystem and systems thinking did have substantial influence in related areas such as planning, management and, more recently, tourism (e.g. see Murphy 1985).

Within the planning tradition, systems models of planning have been particularly influential since the mid-1960s. For example, Chadwick (1971) in *A Systems View of Planning* which sought to integrate engineering, ecological and societal systems in a comprehensive theory of the urban and regional planning process, argued 'that planning is a process, a process of human thought and action based upon that thought – in point of fact, forethought, thought for the future – nothing more or less than this is planning, which is a very general human activity' (1971 : 24). Hall's explanation of what planning should do supports Chadwick's case: 'it [planning] should aim to provide a resource for democratic and informed decision-making. This is all planning can legitimately do, and all it can pretend to do. Properly understood, this is the real message of the systems revolution in planning and its aftermath' (Hall 1982 : 303). More recently, Peter Hall noted that fundamental to the idea of systems planning 'was the idea of interaction between two parallel systems: the planning or controlling system itself, and the system (or systems) which it seeks to control' (P. Hall 1992 : 230).

The systems influence has been equally significant in corporate planning and management thinking. In the late 1950s and early 1960s writers, such as Burns and Stalker (1961), began to stress more 'organic' modes of business organisation and management which highlighted the manner in which successful organisations are able to adapt and change to their environments. Organisations are therefore regarded as sets of interacting subsystems (e.g. strategic, technological, structural, human-cultural and managerial) operating within the business environment, receiving inputs in the form of human, financial, informational and material resources and producing goods and services as organisational outputs in the form of goods and services, ideally at an effective and efficient level of production which allows the organisational system to be maintained (Kast and Rosenzweig 1973). This 'contingency' approach to organisation is now the dominant perspective in contemporary organisational analysis (Morgan 1986). Indeed, it is now such a part of our everyday thinking and analysis about business and organisation that it is hard for us to appreciate how revolutionary the idea was and, perhaps, to reflect on the tremendous implications that such a systems analogy may have for understanding issues such as sustainability. As Morgan (1986 : 71) observed, 'By exploring the parallels between organisms and organizations in terms of organic functioning, relations with the environment, relations between species, and the wider ecology, it has been possible to produce different theories and explanations that have very practical implications for organization and management.' The organism metaphor therefore offers a number of strengths in terms of the insights it offers on organisations (Morgan 1986):

- It emphasises the importance of understanding relations between organisations and their environments. Organisations are best thought of as open systems continually adapting and changing, they are therefore an ongoing process rather than just a collection of parts.
- It draws attention to the importance off understanding the 'needs' which must be satisfied if an organisation is to survive. Therefore, the various demands of the strategic, technological, structural, human-cultural and managerial subsystems all need to be met.
- There are many different 'species' or types of organisation each with characteristics that may allow it to adapt or fit better into different environmental circumstances.
- Organic ideas of organisation which stress adaptation and innovation may provide a better mind-set, organisational culture and/or vision to actually provide for such innovation.
- The focus on ecology and interorganisational relations in terms of cooperation and competition may provide a far better foundation for creating organisational frameworks that provide for the development of cooperative structures in complex environments.

More recently the systems metaphor and systems thinking has been influencing the realms of business and organisation research through interest in ideas of organisations as self-reproducing systems and organisational evolution and change (Morgan 1986).

Process, flux and change are fundamental to a systems view of the world. One of the most influential writers in advancing this perspective has been David Bohm who argued that the world that we see at any given moment needs to be understood as but a moment within more fundamental processes of change and reality. Bohm describes this fundamental reality as being implicate (or enfolded) order, in contrast to the explicate (or unfolded) order which we see in our everyday view of the world. Explicate reality (or forms) can be likened to the eddies, waves and whirlpools that we see in fast-flowing rivers as the water rushes through rapids. Think of these eddies – while seemingly having a relatively stable form, they have no existence other than in terms of the movement of the flowing water in which they exist (the implicate order). Bohm therefore suggests that underlying explicate reality there are hidden processes and relations, termed by Morgan (1986 : 234) as 'logics of change', that help explain 'reality' at any given point of time. 'To discover these, we have to understand the movement, flux, and change that produce the world we experience and study' (Morgan 1986 : 234).

The idea of process and change has also become associated with systems thinking at the level of the individual. For example, writers such as Gergen (1991 : 170) emphasise the significance of relational psychology which recognises that

> We realize increasingly who and what we are is not so much the result of our 'personal essences' (real feelings, deep beliefs, and the like) but of how we are constructed in social groups . . . Relationships make possible the concept of self. Previous possessions of the individual self – autobiography, emotions, and morality – become possessions of relationships. We appear to stand alone, but we are manifestations of relations.

The identity of an individual involved in the planning process is therefore constituted by membership of particular sets of relational networks. Such an observation may have significant implications for the stewardship of resources, because resources are also part of network relationships as they are shaped and extracted from the environment through human perception and patterns of behaviour. Deep ecologists, for example, would argue that the relationship of individuals to resources may also be conceived as implying a moral relationship which would require the adoption of more sustainable ways of behaviour. While such a notion may be absurd to some readers, the ideas of relatedness to both others and the natural world is of increasing influence in the conservation movement around the world and underlies many of the policy developments which surround sustainability.

Systems analysis relates to the abstraction rather than the reality (Harvey 1969). However, this does not make systems thinking 'unreal'. We all have our ideas, models or theories about how the world or people operates. These are our abstractions which we use to understand the world, explain what is happening, and act accordingly in various situations. In the physical sciences

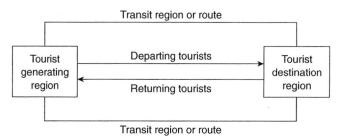

Figure 3.1 Geographical elements of a tourist system

or in engineering some of the systems models may be isomorphic, that is the abstracted model and the original system will be symmetrically related in terms of the elements within them and the relationships between such elements. The vast majority of abstractions though, particularly in the social sciences, are homomorphic, that is the relationship to the original system is asymmetrical. For example, imagine yourself on a walk in the countryside reading a map. Think of the relationship between the map (which is an abstraction) and the countryside (reality/the original system). Every element in the map can be assigned to an element in the countryside, yet the countryside contains many elements (or entities to use the terms above) which are not recorded on the map. The geometric relationships (physical distances) represented on the map also hold in the countryside, but there are also many geometric relationships around you in the countryside which cannot be portrayed on the map. 'We may treat the map as a model of the countryside, but we cannot treat the countryside as a model of the map' (Harvey 1969 : 471). Nevertheless, we may get easily lost without a map. So it is therefore that other abstractions based on systems modelling may be most useful for helping us find our way through the complexity of tourism and tourism planning.

Tourism systems

To Mill and Morrison (1985), as with many writers (e.g. Leiper 1989), tourism may best be conceived of as an interrelated system. As noted above, a system is an assemblage or combination of things or parts forming a complex or unitary role. Several different types of systems models have been utilised in tourism studies. For example, at a geographical level, three basic elements may be identified (Pearce 1995; Leiper 1989) (Figure 3.1):

- *Generating region*: this is the source region of the tourist and the place where the journey begins and ends.
- *Transit region or route*: this is the region which the tourist must travel through to reach his destination.
- *Destination region*: this is the region which the tourist chooses to visit and where the most obvious consequences of the system occur.

The basic tourism system model is useful for identifying the flows of tourists from the generating region to the destination region. Of course there may be more than one destination and therefore a whole pattern of destination regions and transit route regions may be built up. A more commercially oriented tourism system is that provided by Mill and Morrison (1985) (Figure 3.2) who argued that the system consists of four parts: market, travel, destination and marketing. The market segment highlights the decision of the individual to travel or become a tourist. The second segment of the model describes and analyses the where, when and how of the individual tourist's travel behaviour. The third segment of the model consists of the study of the destination mix, i.e. the attractions and services that are used by the tourist. The fourth component of the model highlights the importance of marketing in encouraging people to travel. As Mill and Morrison (1985 : xix) observed: 'The system is like a spider's web – touch one part of it and reverberations will be felt throughout.'

An alternative to the model of the tourism system provided by Mill and Morrison (1985) and Leiper (1989) are system models which emphasise the supply and demand dimensions of tourism. For example, Murphy (1985), Hall and McArthur (1993, 1996) and Hall (1998b) (Figure 3.3) have all developed models which focus on the importance of the tourist experience. As Murphy (1985 : 10) noted, 'the travel experience is this industry's product, but unlike other industries it is the consumer who travels and not the product'. Similarly, Krippendorf (1987 : 1) observed 'the behaviour and experience of travellers, the situation of the host population and their environment and the encounter between the visitors and the local', e.g. the key factors which determine the nature of the tourist experience, are of special interest in the study of tourism phenomenon.

Another approach to tourism systems at the level of the tourist destination has been developed by Le Pelley and Laws (1998) in a study of visitor management in Canterbury, England. According to the authors, 'the method focuses attention on the outcomes of the system's functioning for particular stakeholder groups during a given period of time' (Le Pelley and Laws 1998 : 89). The Le Pelley and Laws model divided the tourism system into

- a series of inputs (tourists' expectations, entrepreneurial activity, employee skills, investors' capital, local authority planning, residents' expectations and attitudes)
- components of what was described as the 'Canterbury Destination System' which included a series of primary (cathedral and historic city centre) and secondary elements (hotels, catering, retailing, attractions, information services, parking and infrastructure), along with external influences (transport developments, competition, tastes, legislation and currency exchange rates)
- outcomes in terms of impacts (economic, community, environment and ecology) and stakeholder outcomes.

As the reader will hopefully now realise, the concept of a tourism system can be conceptualised in a number of ways. Yet each of these may be regarded as appropriate in terms of the various emphases they give to the study of tourism. Such a situation is not uncommon in the analysis of a social phenomenon in which it is virtually impossible to model all of the elements

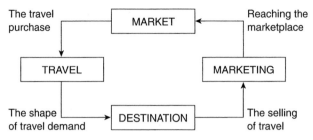

Figure 3.2 Mill and Morrison's tourism system (after Mill and Morrison 1985 : 2)

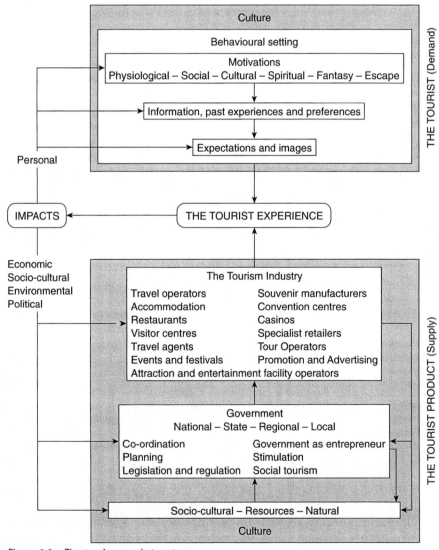

Figure 3.3 The tourism market system

which may be regarded as forming a part of the social system in question. In the case of tourism this situation is all the more complex because of the nature of tourism itself:

- it is hard to define, and is defined by different stakeholders in different ways
- it is 'diffuse' in the way it filters through economies and communities
- it is usually regarded as a service industry with the corresponding difficulties in dealing with the study of the intangible and perishable nature of services.

The concept of partial industrialisation is one attempt to describe the complex nature of tourism and the consequent problems of coordination, management and strategic development which are typically associated with it. According to Leiper (1989 : 25) partial industrialisation refers to the condition

> in which only certain organisations providing goods and services directly to tourists are in the tourism industry. The proportion of (a) goods and services stemming from that industry to (b) total goods and services used by tourists can be termed the index of industrialisation, theoretically ranging from 100% (wholly industrialised) to zero (tourists present and spending money, but no tourism industry).

One of the major consequences of the partial industrialisation of tourism is its significance for tourism development, marketing, coordination and network development. Although we can recognise that many segments of the economy benefit from tourism, it is only those organisations which perceive a direct relationship to tourists and tourism producers that become actively involved in fostering tourism development or in marketing. However, there are many other organisations such as food suppliers, petrol stations and retailers, sometimes described as 'allied industries', which also benefit from tourists but which are not readily identified as part of the tourism industry (Hall 1998). Therefore, in most circumstances, businesses which regard themselves as non-tourism businesses will often not create linkages with tourism businesses for regional promotion unless there is a clear financial reward. It will often require an external inducement, such as promotion schemes established by government at minimal or no cost to individual businesses, or regulatory action such as compulsory business rating tax for promotion purposes, before linkages can be established.

Although under-appreciated in the tourism literature, the concept of partial industrialisation is a powerful explanatory tool when trying to understand the nature of tourism, particularly when attempting to explain why coordination is so difficult with respect to the various components of tourism at the community, destination or even at the national level. Nevertheless, partial industrialisation provides only a partial insight into the complexities of tourism. Other aspects of trying to create a better foundation for understanding tourism, and tourism planning, also need to be considered. First, the issue of scale in tourism analysis. Second, the standpoint of the viewer or participant in the tourism planning process.

The issue of scale

Issues of scale of analysis have been given very little coverage in the tourism literature. For example, while Smith's (1995) excellent book on *Tourism Analysis* provides very good coverage on issues of regionalisation, there is no discussion on issues of scale. Similarly, other standard books on tourism research (e.g. Ritchie and Goeldner 1994), also fail to discuss issues of scale.

Scale is a critical element in social science research. Scale refers to the level at which we are representing reality in our research and our thinking. It can also be thought of as the level of resolution at which we are trying to understand things. Three basic questions have arisen with respect to scale (Haggett 1965; Harvey 1969):

1 *Scale coverage* – do we have regular and comprehensive monitoring of the world at all relevant scales? This issue is obviously clearly important with the collection of tourism statistics and the understanding of tourist flows.
2 *Scale standardisation* – do we have comparable data from equivalent sampling frames? This issue often arises when comparing the tourism statistics from one country or region to another. Not only do we need to know that the methodologies of collecting tourism statistics are the same but also the areas being investigated must be equivalent. Similarly, the collection of case study data from a number of different studies and then the aggregation of the information also creates difficulties of equivalency between the various cases.
3 *Scale linkage* – three different connections between the various scale levels can be identified (Harvey 1969):
   (a) same level – which refers to a comparative relationship
   (b) high to low level – which is a contextual relationship; e.g. tourism policy at the national level forms the context within which changes in tourist numbers at the local level can be analysed
   (c) low to high level – which is an aggregative relationship, e.g. tourist flows at the national level are the result of the activities of individual firms.

Substantial inferential problems arise in the last two cases because generalisations we make at one level may not hold for another. Indeed, the idea of emergence, i.e. that the whole is greater than the sum of the parts, makes this virtually a certainty. Such a situation creates substantial difficulties for explanation in tourism studies which the field has not addressed, especially as most tourism analysis often does not acknowledge the scale at which work is being undertaken, or the contexts of that scale, and the capacity to generalise from one scale to another. Issues of scale, if they are noted at all, tend to be dealt with in terms of the possibilities for comparison. The capacity to perceive or illustrate the linkages and relationships between scales is rarely acknowledged at all.

This last point is especially important for tourism planning. We acknowledged in Chapter 1 that tourism planning occurs at different scales – national, state/provincial, regional, local, yet how are those levels of analysis and levels of action linked? Moreover, how do we incorporate the supra-national level, e.g. organisations such as the European Union, or the role of the individual into the tourism planning equation? We recognise that tourism, like the environment, is a global issue which tends to be acted out at a local or place level by individuals and organisations who are aiming to satisfy their values and interests or, to use a well-worn environmental activist phrase which illustrates the connectivity between the individual and the local to the global – 'Think Globally, Act Locally'. Therefore, any conception of the tourism planning process needs to be able to accommodate the different scales or levels at which tourism planning occurs and the context of such planning in terms of the linkages and relationships between the various levels.

Standpoint

Another issue that has only received passing consideration in tourism is the standpoint of the viewer or participant in the tourism planning process. Where do we stand as students of tourism in terms of what we regard as appropriate in tourism? How do our work, interests and values influence such perspectives of tourism? How do we act on our values in our day-to-day lives through our involvement in tourism planning and tourism policy? There is no absolute standpoint in tourism planning. Our perspectives and actions will shift over time in relation to our changing experiences, knowledge base, values and ideologies, contact with different stakeholders, changed legislative and institutional frameworks, and changes in our desired environment, to name just a few factors. Our perspectives and actions will also change according to our position in the planning process. Are we working for a government agency, a private developer, or as a facility manager? Are we a member of an environmental interest group trying to preserve a building or save a species, or are we just wanting better facilities in our community, or just trying to stop yet another tower block being built which will block our view or change our streetscape? We may even occupy some of these roles simultaneously. However, these questions are not just academic. How we perceive tourism planning will depend on a particular intersection of factors at any given time and where we sit in the wider tourism planning system. Our place in, and ability to influence the planning system is therefore relational.

Such a perspective is not as radical as it seems. As Healey (1997 : 65) observed, 'it is now widely understood in the planning field that planning is an interactive process, undertaken in a social context, rather than a purely technical process of design, analysis and management'. This is a crucial point. Many textbooks relate planning as a technical process in which the writer is out of screen somewhere and the book seems to be written as a series of facts or statements which suggests that this is the way it must be. It isn't. As Chapter 1 illustrated, there are many different traditions of tourism planning, each having its own focus. Each tradition is not inherently wrong or right. We judge it as being wrong or right upon a particular set of criteria which in turn reflect what we believe tourism planning is and should be trying to achieve. This shifting base is a reflection of wider perceptions of the tourism 'expert' and the 'planner' in society. As Peter Hall (1992 : 248) noted, 'Whatever the planner's ideology, it appears that people are no longer willing, as once apparently they were, to accept his or her claim to omniscience and omnipotence.' Such a perspective does not mean that planning is obsolete or redundant as, 'almost be definition, . . . planners will never be completely ineffective, or completely omnipotent. They will exist in a state of continuous interaction with the system they are planning, a system which changes partly, but not entirely, owing to processes beyond their mechanisms of control. (P. Hall 1992 : 230). We therefore need to recognise that our position in tourism planning is relational to where we lie in the tourism system and the various stakeholders, interests and factors with which we interact. As Hall argued, we are constantly interacting with the people, institutions and environment around us which are in themselves in a constant state of change and flux.

> Planning in practice, however well managed, is therefore a long way from the tidy sequences of the theorists. It involves the basic difficulty, even impossibility, of predicting future events; the interaction of decisions made in different policy spheres; conflicts of values which cannot be fully resolved by rational discussion and by calculation; the clash of organized pressure groups and the defence of vested interests; and the inevitable confusions that arise from the complex interrelationships between decisions at different levels and at different scales, at different points of time. The cybernetic or systems view of planning is a condition towards which planners aim; it will never become complete reality (P. Hall 1992 : 246).

This relational perspective of planning is inherent in a systems view of society and of tourism planning, in that we acknowledge that we are part of, rather than separate from, the tourism planning process. When we espouse a particular course of planning action or interpretation of a planning situation we are not merely offering impartial, objective, technical advice but our advice is value- and interest-laden and has the power to have substantial social, economic, environmental and political impacts, some of which may be unintended. This applies as much to this author while in the act of writing this book which, as you read it and hopefully reflect on it, may influence your own notion of what tourism planning is, and what it can be, and how you might act, just as it does the person who is laying out the land use plans for a new resort.

As I write this section at about 1am on a November morning in a relatively small city in the South Island of New Zealand, I am surrounded by several piles of books, photocopies and field notes (and listening to Sunday's *Static and Silence* and KCRW's *Rare on Air 3*). I am conscious that I am arguing for a particular set of values and positions to be an appropriate structure for understanding tourism planning and perhaps achieving certain goals relating to sustainability that I regard as important. I am making such comments because I wish to encourage the reader to think about how they perceive tourism and how we both understand it and seek to achieve certain goals and objectives through tourism planning. You, me, people, actively construct their worlds. What world do we want to or are able to construct through tourism?

Knowledge is related to action. Knowledge and values are actively constituted through social, interactive processes. As Healey (1997 : 29) observed, public policy and planning are 'social processes through which ways of think-ing, ways of valuing and ways of acting are actively constructed by particip-ants'. Such an approach variously described as argumentative (Wildavsky 1979; Majone 1990, 1989; Fischer and Forester 1993; Hall 1994; Hall and Jenkins 1995), communicative (Healey 1992a, b, 1993, 1996; Sager 1994) or inter-pretive (Innes 1995) planning theory recognises:

- that all forms of knowledge, including policy and planning knowledge, are socially constructed
- that the development and communication of knowledge and reasoning takes many legitimate forms
- the significance of the social context and the interactions within that context which provides for the development of individual's interests and knowledge
- the role of power relations in influencing the social context and interactions of planning both at the level of decision making and non-decision making and at deeper levels of social relations and ideology
- that public policies and the development of the knowledge and reasoning which determine such policies need to be owned by all the stakeholders who are affected by the policy-making process, particularly when it is spatially organised around place needs and goals
- that the above observation means that greater emphasis needs be provided on collaborative consensus-building rather than competitive interest bargaining. In several polities this may require the formation of more participatory political cul-tures than exist at present
- that therefore planning, as part of the context of social relations within which decision making and policy development occurs, has the capacity to improve the context of social relations in order to develop more participatory and equitable practices (Healey 1997).

'Introducing' planning, then, means the introduction of ways and means to bring about changes that would otherwise not occur. 'The ongoing stream of life does not wait for planners to give it direction' (Friedmann 1973 : 347). Planners act upon social, physical and economic processes in order to guide society towards desired objectives. Tourism planning in this sense reflects the position of Friedmann (1973 : 346–347) that planning is 'the *guidance of change within a social system*. Specifically, this means a process of self-guidance that may involve *promoting differential growth* of subsystem components (sectors), *activating the transformation of system structures* (political, economic, social), and *maintaining system boundaries* during the course of change'. Friedmann's comments also reflect the essentially political nature of planning and policy. Cullingsworth's (1997 : 5) comment that 'Rational planning is a theoretical idea. Actual planning is practical exercise of political choice that involves beliefs and values. It is a laborious process in which many public and private agencies are concerned. These comprise a wide range of conflicting interests. Planning is a means by which attempts are made to resolve these conflicts', reinforces Peter Hall's (1992) observations on the political nature of planning. Similarly, the significance of politics, who gets what, when, where, how, and why is reflected by Wildavsky (1987 : 25), with respect to policy, when he argues, 'we must first exorcise the ghost of rationality, which haunts the house of public policy'.

Sustainability, Politics and Planning: Exorcising the Ghost of Technical Rationality

Sustainability is an 'essentially contested concept' (Gallie 1955–56); that is, a concept the use and application of which is inherently a matter of dispute. The reason for this is the degree to which the concept is used to refer to a 'balance' or 'wise use' in the way in which natural resources are exploited. The appropriateness of such an approach and the very way in which 'wise use' is defined will depend on the values and ideologies of various stakeholders. However, the history of natural resource management over the last century would suggest that sustainable development is another term which has emerged in an attempt to reconcile conflicting value positions with regard to natural resources and the environment and the perception that there is a crisis which requires solution (Hall 1998a). In a review of the historical antecedents of the concept of the sustainable development of natural resources, Hall (1998b : 22) made three observations regarding present-day issues which surround sustainability:

- debate over the sustainable development of natural resources in industrialised countries dates from the middle of the nineteenth century and cannot be seen as a new policy issue, at least at the local or national level
- tourism has long been a key factor in the justification for environmental conservation
- there has been no easy middle path in attempting to find a balanced use of natural resources. Political reality, rather than ecological reality, has been the order of the day.

Therefore, sustainability, and tourism planning as a mechanism of achieving more sustainable and appropriate forms of tourism, needs to be seen both within a political context in order to be able to understand the structure of planning issues and as a political goal in terms of their achievement. As Evans (1997 : 8) observed,

> sustainability is, at its very heart, a political rather than a technical or scientific construct, and the variety of interpretations of the notion reflect this. For this reason, there is unlikely to be a 'universal theory' of sustainability to inform or guide practice, and sustainability cannot be technicised or reduced to a series of indicators or standards, useful and necessary as these aids undoubtedly are.

One of the key issues in operationalising the concept of sustainability is the extent to which governments intervene in the market in order to achieve policy goals and initiatives which meet the sustainable vision. Public planning, of which tourism planning is usually a component, is by its nature interventionist. Planning seeks to reconcile individual interests in terms of arriving at decisions and actions which meet some notion of the public good. As Friedmann

(1959 : 329) noted, 'Planning is nothing more than a certain manner of arriving at decisions and action, the intention of which is to promote the social good of a society undergoing rapid changes.' Planning, and tourism planning, is therefore something we do in order to meet or satisfy the ideal of the public interest. However, unfortunately in my opinion, in recent years private preferences and economic measures, backed by the supposed legitimacy of 'the market', 'efficiency' and 'rational behaviour', have supplanted in many cases debate on political ideals and the idea of a common good (Saul 1995). According to de-Shalit (1997 : 96), 'this philosophy holds that society is an instrument for the benefit of individuals; all the more, therefore, should nature be subjugated by humans, who through its progressive transformation fulfill their individualistic desires'. In this idea of politics and governance, private interests, which are mediated in the market, hold sway of the public interest. Such a situation does not bode well for the environment or for notions of equity, which is one of the cornerstones of sustainability. As Porritt (1984 : 116) recognised,

> There may well have been a time, at the start of the Industrial Revolution, when Adam Smith's assertion that the sum of individual decisions in pursuit of self-interest added up to a pretty fair approximation of public welfare, with the 'invisible hand' of the market ensuring that individualism and the general interest of society were one and the same thing. But in today's crowded, interdependent world, these same individualistic tendencies are beginning to destroy our general interest and thereby harm us all.

Planning and markets are not necessarily in conflict or incompatible, indeed, appropriate public planning may provide a degree of certainty regarding government policy and the regulatory environment that can be welcomed in the marketplace. As Jacobs (1991 : 125) observes, planning 'stands in contrast to the operation of market forces, but it does not preclude the existence of markets'. As noted in Chapter 2, one of the central reasons for government intervention and public planning is the experience of market failure. In an ideal world the marketplace provides a mechanism for the continued readjustment of production in relation to consumer preferences and ability to pay. However, we do not live in an ideal world. Some markets may take the form of producer oligopolies and monopolies which may exclude new entrants into the marketplace (Healey 1997).

'The belief in market solutions has led to the vigorous search for economic instruments as a means of valuing environmental assets, giving signals to consumers and producers that will lead to resource conservation and lower pollution' (Blowers 1997 : 35). Nevertheless, business has long been resistant to environmental regulations, even in areas such as tourism in which supposedly businesses have a direct financial incentive to maintain the quality of the environment. Indeed, Schrecker (1991) characterised many businesses as being 'bitter' in their opposition to regulation of their activities, with the courts often being used to oppose the actions of public interest groups and government agencies. This is not to deny that individual businesses can act in an appropriate manner. However, if the marketplace alone sets the extent to which businesses utilise the physical and social environment, then history clearly suggests that the loss of environmental and social capital is inevitable.

Purely economic and self-interested individual preferences can easily lead to the continuing degradation and depletion of resources. One of the best examples of this idea, and one of the theoretical underpinnings of contemporary understanding of the problems of sustainability, is Garret Hardin's (1968) well-known 'Tragedy of the Commons'. According to Hardin, the state of the environment resembles an open pasture that is open to all. Each herder tries to keep as many cattle on the common land as possible. Each herder sees the utility of adding one more animal to his herd, with an advantage of +1. In contrast, the personal disadvantage to the herder of such a move is only a fraction of −1 as any effects of overgrazing will be shared by all the herders. The tragedy is that all herders who are seeking to economically maximise their position will arrive at the same conclusion and the herders as a collective then proceed to exceed the carrying capacity of the land.

Many issues regarding the sustainability of tourism resources, e.g. impacts of tourists in wilderness areas, accommodation or second home development without consideration of sewage disposal, air pollution in national parks or destruction of the ozone layer by jet aircraft, all illustrate that issues of sustainability are related to such concepts as 'collective action', the 'public good' and the 'public interest'. Therefore, as Ophuls (1977 : 186) recognised, 'environmental imperatives are basically matters of principle that cannot be bargained away in an economic fashion'. Clearly, 'not all of us think of ourselves primarily as consumers; many of us regard ourselves as citizens as well' (Sagoff 1988 : 27). Notions of public good or public interest are therefore to ideas of sustainability and tourism planning. Issues surrounding sustainability call for a politics of the common and consequently for interventionism, such a measure 'must make some assumptions about the idea of the good, since the argument rests on a theory of value, that is, on the idea of an intrinsic, noninstrumental. And such a theory value is simply a theory of the good' (de-Shalit 1997 : 98).

Intervention, often through public planning, is the mechanism that provides for the implementation of the public ideal. As Blowers (1997 : 35) stated, 'Intervention is needed that gives priority to the public or common interest and to the needs of future generations. There needs to be a shift from private to public interest.' However, notions of public good and the public interest shift over time according to processes of argument and debate within a civil society. The concept of sustainability and its applications are not a given, they have to be argued and fought for. Within academic circles there has clearly been some argument over the nature of sustainable tourism and how it can be operationalised (e.g. Butler 1990, 1991, 1992, 1998; McKercher 1993a, 1993b; Wheeller 1993; Wight 1993a, 1993b; Hall and Butler 1995; Clarke 1997; Lindberg and McKercher 1997). Yet such arguments, and recognition of the value and interest position of the author, have clearly not permeated into the tourism planning texts, where tourism planning is still presented as being primarily a technical issue and not a political problem (e.g. Inskeep 1991; Gunn 1994).

Yet, perhaps just as importantly in terms of public debate on the public interest with respect to tourism planning, the debate in the academic institutions has tended not to reach the wider public sphere. In part this is because universities 'are in crisis and are attempting to ride out the storm by aligning themselves with various corporatist interests. That is short-sighted and self-destructive. From the point of view of their obligation to society, it is simply irresponsible' (Saul 1995 : 177).

One of the difficulties of so-called postmodern approaches to the analysis of society, and tourism as a part of the wider social system, is that ideas of a public good on which action can be based has been severely undermined. All action is related to interest. The corporatist mentality, which dominates many institutions as well as ideas of governance at the various international, national, regional and local scales, and which gives sway to private interest in the ascendancy of 'the market' over the public interest of 'the public good' in government action or inaction, lies at the heart of the lack of debate.

> The citizen's great difficulty in making public debate work begins . . . with the crisis in our language. I have talked about the division between the powerless public language and the rhetoric, propaganda and dialects of corporatism. The resulting blockage in public debate is enormous. . . .
>
> The difficulty with many of the arguments used today to examine reigning fallacies is that they have fallen into the general assumptions of deconstructionism. They do not seek meaning or knowledge or truth. They seek to demonstrate that all language is tied to interest. The deconstructionists have argued against language as communication in order to get at the evils of rhetoric and propaganda. But if language is always self-interest, then there is no possibility of disinterest and therefore no possibility of the public good. The net effect has been to reinforce the corporatist point of view that we all exist as functions within our corporations.
>
> . . . the best hope for a regeneration of language lies not in academic analysis but in citizen participation (Saul 1995 : 174, 177).

Participation is a significant issue in tourism planning (e.g. Murphy 1985). However, participation and the shaping of the way communities manage tourism is a product of the institutional arrangements, individuals, power structures, interests and values that affect the decision-making process on different scales. The capacity of individuals and groups to participate in the tourism planning system is not just the result of cultural or democratic values, it is also a product of the structures of public governance and the extent to which such structures are genuinely open to participation and debate. Moreover, it is a product of the set of relationships that develop between those involved in the tourism planning and policy process. Participation is therefore a relationship within the tourism system. Indeed, the choice of techniques used in tourism planning, identification of indicators, selection of objectives and the production of outputs (what is conventionally recognised as a plan in the form of a document) are all determined by the set of relationships that exist between the various stakeholders and how exclusive or inclusive they are.

The nature of those relationships will determine who wins and who loses in the political system that is tourism planning.

In any system, there are large areas of indifference where political behaviour is possible without planned intervention. Nevertheless, the relative influence of the planning function in guiding the social and economic change which sustainability calls for will depend chiefly on five variables:

- the clarity of the system objectives
- the extent of consensus about them
- the relative importance that politicians attach to them
- the degree of variance relative to objectives expected in the performance of the system
- the extent to which a technical (as opposed to a purely political) approach is believed capable of making system performance conform to these objectives (Friedmann 1973 : 353).

It is to these issues that the following chapters will now turn in varying degrees.

Conclusions

This chapter has outlined some of the key issues and concepts underlying the development of some of the argumentative and collaborative approaches which are part of the emerging framework of non-technocratic sustainable tourism planning. This chapter is also rich in metaphor: concepts such as a system, ideas of scale, standpoint and relationships are powerful metaphors which can be used to help describe the complexity of tourism planning. As Morgan (1986 : 331) noted, 'The images or metaphors through which we read organizational situations help us describe the way organizations are, and offer clear ideas over the way they could be.' The chapter has also argued that it is the notion of the public good or interest which lies at the core of sustainable tourism planning. The next chapter will attempt to describe how the tourism planning system looks and prescribe how it might be improved in terms of the overriding vision of sustainability. Chapters 5 to 9 then look at the tourism planning system at various scales of operation and the interrelationships between those scales. Throughout all of these chapters the idea of relationship and the relational way in which we all 'see' tourism planning problems will serve as an important thread in the search for more sustainable forms of tourism.

Questions and further reader

What is the significance of the concept of partial industrialisation for tourism planning?
How do issues of scale affect tourism plannng?
Why is argument such an important component of tourism planning and policy?

On the importance of understanding the theoretical dimensions of planning and policy, see Pressman and Wildavsky (1973), Majone (1980a, b; 1989), Fischer and Forester (1993), and Healey (1996, 1997). The importance of organic and systems metaphors in management and planning is well covered by Morgan (1986), while Harvey (1995) provides an excellent introduction to dialectical analysis.

Chapter 4

The integrated tourism planning process: dealing with interdependence

Tourism planning is often highly complex, reflecting Peter Hall's observation that planning 'is merely an acute instance of the central problem of society' (1992 : 249). By this, Hall meant that problems in contemporary society have a habit of becoming 'interconnected', in that what was initially seen as a problem in one sphere, say unemployment, may then become connected to other policy and planning concerns such as the environment. Such planning and policy 'messes' (Ackoff 1974) may also be well described as metaproblems.

Tourism planning often poses metaproblems. Several reasons account for this. Most significant is the nature of tourism itself, difficult to define, diffuse through economy and society and, typically, with no clear control agency. Instead, tourism tends to cut across agency boundaries. Nevertheless, planning for tourism is still regarded as important because its effects are so substantial and potentially long-standing. Indeed, concern with making tourism, along with all development, sustainable has provided an even greater imperative for improved tourism planning.

As the previous chapter argued, systems approaches to tourism may provide valuable opportunities for the understanding of tourism and how it may be steered in one direction or another. Such a systems approach to planning, particularly one that consciously sets out to identify and articulate different sets of value choices, bears strong parallels to developments which are occurring in public planning. According to Peter Hall, 'The old planning was concerned to set out the desired future end state in detail, in terms of land-use patterns on the ground; the new approach . . . concentrated instead on the objectives of the plan and on alternative ways of reaching them, all set out in writing rather than in detailed maps' (P. Hall 1992 : 229) in the new planning 'the emphasis was on tracing the possible consequences of alternative policies, only then evaluating them against the objectives in order to choose a preferred course of action; and, it should be emphasized, this process would continually be repeated as the monitoring process threw up divergences between the planner's intentions and the actual state of the system' (P. Hall 1992 : 229). The current planning paradigm, which is heavily influenced by cybernetics and systems analysis, emphasises the pattern of: goals, continuous information, projection and simulation of alternative futures, evaluation, choice and continuous monitoring. For example, many readers will be familiar with the following steps in the planning process identified by Anderson (1995):

Table 4.1 Elements of a synergistic tourism planning approach

Goal oriented	Clear recognition of tourism's role in achieving broad community goals
Integrative	Including tourism planning issues in the mainstream of planning for the economy, conservation, parks, heritage, land use and infrastructure
Market driven	Planning for development that meets the needs of people and so will trade successfully in a competitive marketplace
Resource driven	Developing assets which build on the destination's inherent strengths while protecting and enhancing the attributes and experiences of tourism sites
Consultative	With meaningful community input to determine what is acceptable to the local population
Systematic	Drawing on, or undertaking research to provide conceptual or predictive support for planners. In particular, drawing on the experience of other tourism destinations

Source: Tourism South Australia (1991 : 28)

1 Identify issues and options.
2 State goals, objectives, priorities.
3 Collect and interpret data.
4 Prepare plans.
5 Draft programs for implementing the plan.
6 Evaluate potential impacts of plans and implementing programs.
7 Review and adopt plans.
8 Review and adopt plan-implementing programs.
9 Administer implementing programs, monitor their impacts.

Similar models have been applied in terms of planning for tourism. For example, the state government tourism agency in South Australia, Tourism South Australia, developed the most integrated planning model for a government authority for tourism in Australia in the early 1990s. Tourism South Australia (1991 : 28) noted that traditional approaches to tourism planning, as outlined in Chapter 2, were 'limited because they ignore research and evaluation of tourism demand (market needs and expectations) and tourism supply (resource utilisation consistent with demand preferences and environmental sustainability)'. Therefore, in order to provide the unique, satisfying tourism experiences which differentiate products and destinations in the marketplace, create long-term appeal, and sustain the resource base on which tourism products and destinations are based, they argued that tourism planning must integrate market- and resource-driven processes. According to Tourism South Australia (1991), such an approach provides for a 'synergistic' tourism planning process which is goal oriented, integrative, market driven, resource driven, consultative and systematic (Table 4.1).

A planning process for regional and local tourism which utilises a synergistic and integrated approach to tourism planning is illustrated in Figures 4.1 and 4.2 and Table 4.2. Such a process may not be applicable in all situations, instead the succession of stages indicate 'the investigative logic that is required for proper tourism planning' (Tourism South Australia 1990 : 28). The key

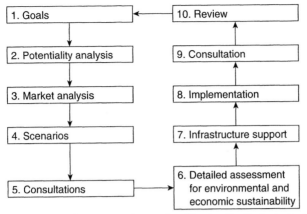

Figure 4.1   A regional planning process for tourism (Tourism South Australia 1991 : 29)

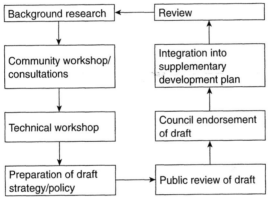

Figure 4.2   Local planning process for tourism (Tourism South Australia 1991 : 31)

elements identified in Table 4.2 are utilised in such a manner as to ensure that the planning process is systematic, pinpoints the needs of the various stakeholders in the tourism planning and development process, and incorporates an understanding of the market and the tourism resource base. This planning process was utilised in the preparation of regional tourism plans for Kangaroo Island (Tourism South Australia 1991), the Clare-Burra region (PPK Planning 1993b) and Victor Harbour (PPK Planning 1993a) in South Australia. However, while the model was well respected, particularly for the manner in which it sought to integrate sustainability issues into the planning process, its effectiveness was limited by developments at other levels. A change of government in South Australia meant that the goals of Tourism South Australia shifted to concentrate on tourism promotion so as to encourage greater visitor numbers. In this new policy setting, long-term sustainable planning goals became secondary to short-term increases in the number of tourists.

Table 4.2   Steps and outcomes in a regional planning process for tourism in South Australia

Step	Outcomes
1 Goals Within the tourism and conservation philosophies of the state, establish what is to be achieved by the process	Clear statement of purpose
2 Potentiality analysis Examine broad market trends Analyse area's tourism assets, strengths and weaknesses Undertake competitor analysis Determine community goals Determine the existing and potential role of tourism in the area's economy	Statement of tourism's potential and priority in community development
3 Market analysis Analyse the tourism market – trends, market segments, characteristics and needs, growth potential Identify fit between market forces and the area's assets and resources Determine market position Identify major product gaps	Target markets identified Statement of market positioning Major product gaps identified
4 Scenarios Identify preliminary 'primary values' Identify alternative future tourism scenarios Examine implications of growth Select preferred scenario Identify constraints to achieving preferred scenario Establish tourism objectives and strategies	Draft statement of desired future role and character of tourism in the area Statement of objectives and strategies

5 Consultations
Consult with key organisations and the community through interviews and workshops as appropriate
Present results of investigations and proposals
Identify community's primary values, key issues and problems

Vision or statement of an agreed 'Desired Future Character'

6 Detailed assessment for economic and environmental sustainability
Identify and evaluate natural and built tourism resources
Specify potential development opportunities consistent with positioning
Analyse environmental and landscape values
Identify conflicts and constraints to tourism development

Revise objectives and strategies
Tourism character areas identified specifying appropriate types and scales of development
Development principles and planning specifications for character units
Major development opportunities and performance criteria specified

7 Infrastructure support
Identify and detail infrastructure required to support investment and provide for visitor needs
Identify and detail infrastructure required to manage visitors' impact
Identify and describe opportunities for the interpretation of features of visitor interest

Prioritised programme of infrastructure works

8 Implementation
Devise implementation mechanism – programme of work, organisational responsibilities and timelines
Identify changes to existing legislation

Implementation strategy

9 Consultation
Consult with key organisations and the community

Concise document outlining stages 1 to 8
Draft Supplementary Development Plan as required
Amendment to tourism plan as appropriate

10 Review
Monitor and review implementation procedures

Periodic reports on implementation and recommendations for plan amendments

Source: Tourism South Australia (1991 : 29)

Such a situation is not unusual with respect to tourism planning. Indeed, within the public sphere it may even be the norm as governments, policies and institutional arrangements for tourism change. Yet such a situation also provides a valuable lesson for understanding tourism planning as it illustrates

- the multiscale nature of planning, in other words what occurs at one level may not be compatible with another. Furthermore, changes in policy will filter through the various levels of the planning system
- the implications of different sets of values affecting policy settings and planning processes
- how planning models and tools do not operate in isolation from the people who develop and implement them. You can have the best planning model in the world. However, unless you have the capacity to operate it, which may involve arguing your case to politicians and those to whom you are responsible, it is of little practical value, although it may still provide a stimulus for change elsewhere. Winning policy arguments, like sustainability itself, may take time.

As Cullingsworth (1997 : 25) observed, 'Planning is a process of formulating goals and agreeing the manner in which these are to be met. It is a process by which agreement is reached on the ways in which problems are to be debated and resolved.' This chapter will examine various aspects of the planning process and key issues which arise in trying to make planning and plans happen. The 'focus upon the processes of planning and land-use policy, rather than a concern with policy outcomes, might be viewed as irrelevant or even obsessional. However, it *is* important since the outcomes of policy are, in large part, a consequence of how that policy is framed, organised and implemented' (Evans 1997 : 5–6).

The policy, planning and decision-making process: the setting ——

As previous chapters have discussed, public policy making and planning are first and foremost political activities. Public policy is influenced by the economic, social and cultural characteristics of society, as well as by the formal structures of government and other features of the political system. Policy making therefore involves the economic, physical, social and political environments in a process of action and reaction over time (Barrett and Fudge 1981). Policy and planning are therefore consequences of the political environment, values and ideologies, the distribution of power, institutional frameworks, and of decision-making processes (Simeon 1976; Hall and Jenkins 1995; Elliot 1997). Policy analysis is a vital tool for understanding how tourism planning and policy operates. As Davis et al. (1993 : 16) observed,

'Policy is not a self-evident, independent behaviour fact. Policy acquires meaning because an observer perceives and interprets a course of actions amid the confusions of a complex world' [Heclo 1974 : 4]. If public policy is the choices (intended and unintended) acted upon within a society, then public policy analysis becomes a method for disentangling those decisions, for exploring why issues arise on the agenda, and how they are resolved. Public policy analysis therefore requires us to 'puzzle out' (to use another apt phrase from Heclo) this interaction of values, interests and resources, specify how they are shaped by prevailing organisational arrangements and explore the way politics can intervene to confirm or upset the expected result.

Policy analysis is multi-dimensional in examining the range of factors which affect the policy making and planning process. There are both different stages and different levels of analysis. Ham and Hill (1984 : 17–18) noted that

> Precisely how many levels are investigated is likely to vary according to the nature of the enquiry being undertaken, but it can be suggested that three levels will often be appropriate. These levels are: first, the micro level of decision-making within organisations; second, the middle range analysis of policy formulation [and implementation]; and third, macroanalysis of political systems including examination of the role of the state. It is the interaction between levels which is particularly significant and problematic.

What is often regarded in tourism as 'planning' refers to the first two levels, with questions of 'policy' often being consigned to the macro-level. However, as noted earlier, planning and policy may best be conceived as a continuum along the three levels. Nevertheless, the level of understanding of the three levels and the interactions between them is not particularly great. Hall and Jenkins (1995 : 96) argue that at the macro level there is widespread ignorance of institutional arrangements and, particularly, the role of the state in tourism public policy. At the meso level there is little understanding of how and why decisions are made and actions are taken, while at the micro level understanding of the relationship between individuals, their values and interests, and organisations and the state is lacking. While substantial progress has been made in understanding the various operation of these levels in different parts of the world, in overall terms our level of understanding is still relatively low.

One attempt to describe the relationship between the various levels in the context of heritage management was made by Hall and McArthur (1998) (Figure 4.3). While heritage was the focus of the model one could just as easily replace 'heritage' with 'tourism'. However, while the model may assist in conveying the manner in which interaction exists between the different levels of analysis of policy and planning, it still does not adequately express the multidimensional set of tourism policy and planning relationships that occur at different scales. Figure 4.4 seeks to illustrate the different dimensions of tourism planning that occur at different scales – from the local to the international. What is important to note is that the relationships between the various components of the planning and policy framework exist both vertically and horizontally. The tourism planning system therefore comprises the set of constant interactions between the various components of the system from the individual to the global. It is the analyst who draws the boundaries within the system in terms of trying to define and manage the planning problem.

One of the ways in which the implications of different scales for tourism planning can be seen is by examining the different levels of institutional arrangements that have been created to manage and plan tourism. For example,

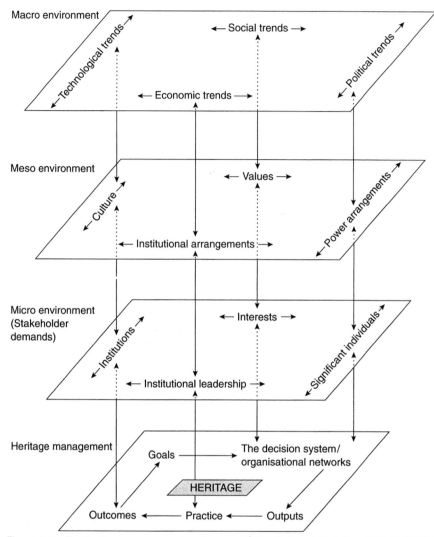

Figure 4.3 The heritage management environment (after Hall and McArthur 1998, Hall 1994 and Hall and Jenkins 1995)

tourism organisations have been established at the international level, e.g. the World Tourism Organization, the supranational level, e.g. European Community tourism organisations and through to national, regional and local tourism organisations (Table 4.3) (also see Pearce 1992).

The internationalisation of environmental issues also reveals the multiscale aspects of institutional arrangements which can be seen in the plethora of environmental legislation and regulation from the international (e.g. Agenda 21) through to the local scale (e.g. local government site regulations and planning schemes). There are very few legal agreements which deal specifically

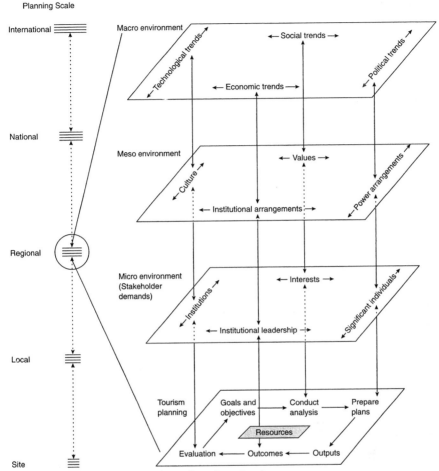

Figure 4.4 Factors and dimensions of tourism planning

with tourism and the environment. Instead, the relationship between tourism and the environment tends to be managed within general environmental and planning law. Table 4.4 identifies the various levels at which such legal frameworks operate from the international through to the national and the sub-national level, using South-east Asia and Malaysia and Singapore as examples.

A number of international conventions operate in the region. These conventions range from international agreements on oil pollution and the Law of the Sea, which is clearly of major importance to the cruise ship industry and marine tourism; to the World Heritage Convention, which serves to establish World Heritage listing for cultural and natural heritage sites of universal significance (e.g. Angkor Wat in Cambodia) which are typically of great significance as visitor attractions; and to provisions for the conservation of fauna and flora (e.g. the Ramsar Convention which governs habitat for migratory birds) which may also serve as important ecotourism attractions.

Table 4.3 Tourism and related organisations from the international to the local scale

	Government and intragovernment organisations	Producer organisations	Non-producer organisations	Single interest organisations
International	World Tourism Organisation; World Heritage Committee (UNESCO); Committee for the Development of Sport; OECD (Organisation for Economic Cooperation and Development)	World Travel and Tourism Council; International Air Transport Association; Tourism Sport International Council; International Olympic Committee	Tourism Concern; World Wildlife Fund (WWF); World Leisure and Recreation Association; Greenpeace; Friends of the Earth	World Congress Against the Commercial Sexual Exploitation of Children
Supranational	APEC tourism working group; Tourism Council of the South Pacific; ASEAN Promotion Centre on Trade and Investment; European Commission	Pacific Asia Travel Association (PATA); Baltic Sea Tourism Commission; Play Fair Europe; European Surfing Federation; National Olympic Committees	Sierra Club; International Downtown Association; Travel and Tourism Research Association	End Child Prostitution in Asian Tourism (ECPAT)
National	Indonesian Directorate General of Tourism; English Sports Council; Countryside Commission; Australian Tourist Commission; Irish Tourist Board (Bord Fáilte)	British Sports and Allied Industries Federation; Tourism Council Australia; Institute of Leisure and Amenity Management (ILAM); Irish Tourist Industry Confederation	National Trust; Australian Conservation Foundation; Australian Consumers Association	The Wilderness Society; Hispanic Association for Corporate Responsibility; ECPAT (Australia)
Regional (including provincial and state)	Tourism Alberta; Natal Parks Board; Western Australian Tourism Commission (WATC); Scottish Tourist Board; Tourism British Columbia	Tourism Council Australia (WA Division); Scottish Confederation of Tourism; Shannon Development; Coalition of Minnesota Business	Western Australian Conservation Council	Tasmanian Wilderness Society
Local	Local government involvement in leisure and tourism provision, e.g. Tourism Dunedin; Calgary Economic and Development Authority; Tourism Vancouver	Local chambers of commerce and industry associations; local sporting clubs and private sport and leisure centres	Ratepayers and resident associations, e.g. Waikiki Improvement Association	Single issue organisations such as a 'friends of a park' or a group which has been formed in order to prevent particular developments such as a hotel or airport

Table 4.4   Legal framework for tourism and the environment in South and South-east Asia

A. International conventions relating to tourism and the environment in South and South-east Asia

1969	International Convention on Civil Liability for Oil Pollution Damage (Brussels)
1969	International Convention relating to Intervention on the High Seas in Cases of Oil Pollution Damage (Brussels)
1971	Convention on Wetlands of International Importance especially as Waterfowl Habitat (Ramsar)
1972	Convention concerning the Protection of the World Cultural and Natural Heritage (Paris)
1972	Convention on the Prevention of Marine Pollution by Dumping of Wastes and Other Matter (London)
1973	Convention on International Trade in Endangered Species of Wild Fauna and Flora (Washington)
1973	International Convention for the Prevention of Pollution from Ships (MARPOL) (London)
1978	Protocol of 1978 relating to the International Convention for the Prevention of Pollution from Ships, 1973 (London)
1979	Convention on the Conservation of Migratory Species of Wild Animals (Bonn)
1982	United Nations Convention on the Law of the Sea (Montego Bay)
1985	Convention for the Protection of the Ozone Layer (Vienna)
1989	Convention on the Control of the Transboundary Movements of Hazardous Wastes and their Disposal (Basel)
1990	International Convention on Oil Preparedness, Response and Cooperation (London)
1992	Framework Convention for Climate Change (New York)
1992	Convention on Biological Diversity (Rio de Janiero)

B. Regional international conventions

1985   Agreement on the Conservation of Nature and Natural Resources (Kuala Lumpur)

Parties:
The Government of Brunei,
The Government of the Republic of Indonesia,
The Government of Malaysia,
The Government of the Republic of the Philippines,
The Government of the Republic of Singapore and
The Government of the Kingdom of Thailand,
Member States of the Association of South East Asian Nations (ASEAN)

C. National legislation and regulations

Malaysia	Environmental Quality Act, 1974 (127, Am.: A636) Fisheries Act, 1985 (317) Land Conservation Act, 1989 (385) Land Development Act, 1991 (474, Am.: 474,478, A818) National Forestry Act, 1984 (313, Am.: Pu(A) 82/86, A864) National Parks Act, 1980 (226, Am.: A571)
Singapore	National Parks Act Parks and Trees Act Preservation of Monuments Act State Lands Encroachment Act Urban Redevelopment Authority Act Water Pollution Control and Drainage Act Wild Animals and Birds Act

D. Provincial legislation and regulations

E. Local regulations

One of the most significant pieces of regional environmental international law in the region is the Agreement on the Conservation of Nature and Natural Resources signed in Kuala Lumpur in 1985. Signatories to the Agreement were the then member states of the Association of South East Asian Nations (ASEAN): Brunei, Indonesia, Malaysia, Philippines, Singapore and Thailand. The fundamental principle of the Agreement is that the signatories

> ... within the framework of their respective national laws, undertake to adopt singly, or where necessary and appropriate through concerted action. The measures necessary to maintain essential ecological process and life-support systems, to preserve genetic diversity, and to ensure the sustainable utilization of harvested natural resources under their jurisdiction in accordance with scientific principles and with a view to attaining the goal of sustainable development.
> ... To this end they shall develop national conservation strategies, and shall co-ordinate such strategies within the framework of a conservation strategy for the Region (Article 1).

The Agreement was also designed to encourage signatories to set aside protected areas. Under Article 13 the protected areas (national parks and reserves) were to be established for the purpose of safeguarding:

a. the ecological and biological processes essential to the functioning of the ecosystems of the Region;
b. representative samples of all types of ecosystems of the Region;
c. satisfactory population levels for the largest possible number of species of fauna and flora belonging to those ecosystems;
d. areas of particular importance because of their scientific, educational, aesthetic, or cultural interests; and taking into account their importance in particular as:
    i. the natural habitat of species of fauna and flora; particularly rare or endangered or endemic species;
    ii. zones necessary for the maintenance of exploitable stocks of economically important species;
    iii. pools of genetic material and said refuge for species, especially endangered ones;
    iv. sites of ecological, aesthetic or cultural interest;
    v. reference sources for scientific research;
    vi. areas for environmental education.

Furthermore, signatories undertook to develop plans of management, buffer zones (where appropriate), undertake impact assessment (Article 14), while protected areas established pursuant to the Agreement were to be regulated and managed in 'such a way as to further the objectives for the purpose of which they have been created. Contracting Parties shall, wherever possible, prohibit within such protected areas activities which are inconsistent with such objectives'. Nevertheless, while such a regional agreement is important and provides a useful declaration of intention with respect to conservation activity, it remains dependent on national legislation and, perhaps more importantly, a clear implementation regime for it to be effective.

At the national level, a number of legislative instruments may affect the relationship between tourism and the environment. For example, Table 4.4

notes some of the relevant laws in Malaysia and Singapore. However, tourism development will be influenced by an extremely wide variety of laws and regulations, particularly when national tourism organisations are usually responsible for tourism promotion and marketing rather than tourism's impacts. Nations with federal structures, such as Malaysia, will also have a range of provincial/state laws and regulations that will affect tourism, while within most countries decisions taken at the local level in the form of development permissions and local plans will also have a major effect on the environmental impacts of tourism development and tourist activities (Hall and Page 1999a).

The multiscale institutional arrangements which surround tourism and the environment are only one aspect of the difficulties of planning for tourism. The same pattern of multilevel institutional arrangements and policy relationships will usually exist in many other areas which affect tourism, e.g. employment, investment, trade, taxation, visa, and regional development incentives, adding to the complexity of the environment in which tourism planning occurs.

This section has discussed some aspects of the setting within which planning occurs. The environment for tourism planning and policy making is seen to be highly complex with multiple sets of vertical and horizontal relationships. Within this tourism planners develop planning procedures and plans, which are the output of such procedures. Having noted the setting within which planning occurs we will now return to the difficulties of establishing planning strategies within such an environment.

Strategic planning for tourism

As Chapter 2 noted, strategic planning is regarded as an essential component of sustainable tourism planning. A 'strategy' is a means to achieve a desired end. Porter (1980 : xvi) who focused on the idea of thinking competitively, stated that 'essentially, developing a competitive strategy is developing a broad formula for how a business is going to compete, what its goals should be, and what policies will be needed to carry out those goals'. Strategic planning is the process by which organisations effectively adapt to their environment over time by integrating planning and management in a single process and seeks to deal with the questions of

- where are we now? – check (monitor and evaluate)
- where do we want to get to? – plan
- how do we get there? – do (action)

The strategic plan is therefore the document which is the output of a strategic planning process and which serves to guide future directions, activities, programmes and actions. The outcome of the strategic planning process is the impact that the process has on the organisation, its activities and its environment, including the various stakeholders. Such impacts are then monitored and evaluated through the selection of appropriate indicators as part of the ongoing revision and readjustment of the organisation to its environment. Strategic planning therefore emphasises the process of continuous improvement as a cornerstone of organisational activity in which strategic planning is linked to management and operational decision making (Hall and McArthur 1998), with the three key mechanisms required to achieve this being (Gluck et al. 1980):

- a planning framework which extends beyond organisational boundaries and focuses on strategic decisions concerning stakeholders and resources
- a planning process that stimulates innovative thinking and provides a capacity to adapt to environments
- an organisational values system that reinforces commitment to the organisational strategy.

Strategic planning has been a part of business since the late 1950s and early 1960s, and the fact that it is 'oriented towards process rather than towards the production of one-shot (or end-state) plans' (P. Hall 1992 : 11) is a reflection of the wider influences of systems theory in the planning field. Strategic planning and the business ecology metaphor of the organisation responding and adapting to its environment in a state of constant interaction is a classic representation of the ideas of system thinking presented in the previous chapter. Strategic planning is therefore both a process, which leads to specific planning outputs, and a way of thinking about the world. As Ohmae (1983 : 79) stated:

> The drafting of a strategy is simply the logical extension of one's usual thinking processes. It is a matter of long-term philosophy, not short-term expedient thinking. In a very real sense, it represents the expression of an attitude to life. But like every creative activity, the art of strategic thinking is practiced most successfully when certain operating principles are kept in mind and certain pitfalls are consciously avoided.

Similarly, according to Primozic et al. (1991 : 15):

> Strategic thinking must be a continuous cycle. The cycle begins with formulating a strategic vision for the organization, proceeds through creating strategies that determine how the vision can be used to guide the organization's efforts, continues with developing appropriate tactics to implement the strategic plans, and leads to the implementation and operational steps that all members of the organization must carry out in the day-to-day running of the enterprise.

However, while perhaps being more conducive to sustainable thinking, strategic planning by itself will not necessarily lead to more sustainable forms of tourism. Instead, strategic planning may well be an important conceptual and practical tool that, given a set of sustainable objectives, may well be more suitable for actually achieving the objectives of sustainable tourism than non-strategic planning methods. According to Hall and McArthur (1998), there are a number of advantages in adopting a strategic approach to heritage management:

- it provides a sense of purpose and the foundation of criteria for the formulation of new projects
- it stresses the need for both short- and long-term objectives which can accommodate changing circumstances, e.g. a change in the level of government funding for tourism

- it gives stakeholders a clear indication of the current and long-term level of support required for tourism management programmes
- it provides for potential integration of stakeholder objectives into an organisational or program strategy, thereby increasing the likelihood of success
- it encourages strategic and increased receptiveness to opportunities in the external environment
- it can create a sense of ownership and involvement in planning processes and outputs with a consequent likely increase in performance and level of support
- it can make organisations more effective and efficient in attaining programme and/or organisational goals.

Furthermore, strategic planning always has an organisational focus. Even in the case of destination planning, for example, an organisation will still be responsible for the development, evaluation and implementation of the plan. The difficulty of course is for any destination's tourism organisation to be able to distinguish between a strategic plan for the organisation and a strategic plan for a destination for which it has responsibility. These are two different things. Unfortunately, the destination plan is often equated with the former.

Figure 4.5 outlines a model of a strategic tourism planning process which identifies key components of the process some of which, in turn, will correspond to some of the components of a formal planning document. The process is encompassed by the environment within which tourism planning and management operates. This includes, therefore, such factors as institutional arrangements, institutional culture, and stakeholder values and attitudes as well as broader economic, social, political and economic trends. Such factors are extremely important. For example, public sector tourism strategic plans will be developed and written in line with the legislative and regulatory powers and organisational structures of the implementing organisation(s), broader policy settings and, in some cases, ministerial directive. However, as Hall and McArthur (1998) observed, it may also be the case that once the strategic planning process is underway, goals and objectives formulated, and the process evaluated, the institutional arrangements, including legislation and organisational structures, may be recognised as inadequate for the successful achievement of certain goals and objectives. Indeed, strategic planning for tourism at the destination level often seems to give rise to new organisational structures and/or responsibilities in order to try and achieve more effective implementation of planning strategies. In order to be effective, the strategic planning process also needs to be integrated with the development of appropriate organisational structures and values, yet, at the destination level, such measures may give the impression that stakeholders are not adequately included in the planning process. In such situations the strategic planning process is as important as its output, i.e. a plan. By having an inclusive planning process by which those responsible for implementing the plan are also those who helped formulate it, the likelihood of 'ownership' of the plan and, hence, effective implementation will be dramatically increased (Heath and Wall 1992; Hall and McArthur 1996, 1998).

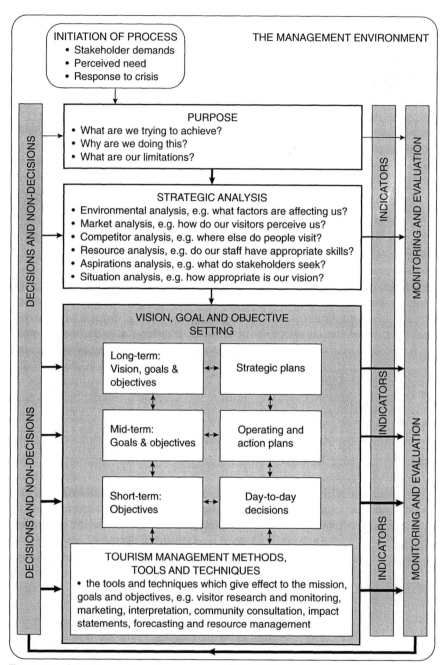

Figure 4.5   Strategic tourism planning process (after Hall and McArthur 1998)

A strategic planning process is usually initiated for a number of reasons (Hall and McArthur 1998), including:

- *Stakeholder demands* – demand for the undertaking of a strategic plan may come from the pressure of stakeholders, e.g. tourism industry, conservation groups or government.
- *Perceived need* – the lack of appropriate information by which to make decisions or an appropriate framework with which to implement legislative requirements may give rise to a perception that new management and planning approaches are required. This factor has become extremely important with respect to the need to develop new arrangements, structures, and strategies with which to develop sustainable tourism.
- *Response to crisis* – the undertaking of strategic planning exercises are often the result of a crisis in the sense that the management and planning system has failed to adapt to aspects of the management environment, e.g. failure to conserve a heritage site or a rapid decline in the number of visitor arrivals.
- *Best practice* – heritage managers can be proactive with respect to the adoption of new ideas and techniques. Therefore, a strategic planning process can become a way of doing things better including benchmarking destinations or developments with competitors.
- *Adaptation, innovation and the diffusion of ideas* – individuals within an organisation can encourage strategic planning processes as part of the diffusion of ideas within and between tourism planning and management agencies.

As Figure 4.5 indicates, the strategic planning process is hierarchically structured from a vision or mission statement, through to goals, objectives, and action statements. Each level expands on the other in terms of detail, direction and ability to be achieved. The hierarchical structure also reflects the various layers or scales of the planning system within which planning problems are 'solved'. For example, as McLoughlin (1969 : 105) stated with respect to physical planning in the urban environment:

> It follows from the hierarchical or tree-like nature of choices and alternatives that lower-level decisions tend to require higher-order choices to be clarified. For example, it is often found that a particular proposal such as the rebuilding of a row of older shops and houses cannot be resolved without consideration of the question of the future width and alignment of the street, which itself cannot be decided until the circulation and access system for that part of the city (and thus perhaps the whole city) is decided upon; this in turn forces attention onto the land use patterns which the transport system is to be designed to serve.

Once underway, strategic planning is also designed to be iterative. That is, planning systems should be able to adapt and change to the internal and external forces with which they interact, that is, they *learn* how to be effective in terms of the most appropriate set of goals, objectives, actions, indicators, institutional arrangements, and practices. As the environment changes so the planning system, and the components within it, also change.

Figure 4.5 illustrates the process dimensions of current planning paradigms which we noted at the start of the chapter. However, while we typically talk of 'stages' of the planning process, and we write them up as such in books such as these, one should always remember that the process is never purely linear (i.e. A leads to B leads to C leads to D and returns to A). There is constant feedback, adjustment and change between all the components of the process; sometimes this is formal, e.g. when new legislative arrangements are established in order to meet the goals and objectives of a plan, but often such accommodation occurs informally during the process, e.g. objectives emerge over a period of behind-the-scenes negotiation between stakeholders as to what is acceptable and required. Indeed, one of the biggest frustrations in reading about planning is that one often comes across the phrase of 'establish objectives' or similar, as if it is a perfectly rational and self-evident process. Yet in reality there tends to be a whole series of, often heated, interaction between various stakeholders and interests over objective setting, because such a process sets the direction of planning in motion, determines what the planning problems are, how they might be solved and who is responsible (see Santter and Leisen 1999). Most significantly, by clearly stating the purposes of planning it becomes possible to state

- what an organisation is trying to achieve
- why an organisation is undertaking the planning process
- what the limitations of the process are.

Where do we want to go?

The first step in the strategic planning processes is to identify the purposes which the planner seeks to achieve, to order them in terms of their importance, and to consider how far they are reconciliable each with the other. As Peter Hall stated, 'unless objectives are made explicit, no one can be sure that they are shared by the people they are being planned for; nor is it possible rationally to prefer one plan to another' (1992 : 233).

Mission, goal and objective formulation is therefore a critical component of strategic tourism planning. An organisation's mission or vision, goals, objectives and targets are highly interdependent (Byars 1984). The formulation of mission statements and the development of goals and objectives needs to be conducted hand-in-hand with the strategic analysis and vision setting, i.e. a statement as to what we are trying to achieve. As Heath and Wall (1992 : 63) noted with respect to strategic tourism marketing, management strategies 'grow out of and reflect the environmental analysis, resource analysis and goal formulation steps. Unless . . . goals have been set to be accomplished, there is no purpose in strategy formulation.'

The mission statement describes what the organisation is trying to accomplish in the longer term. Goals generally emphasise long-range intentions of the organisation and are not usually quantified; they are abstract and tend to express areas of organisational concern. Objectives are measurable goals which are capable of being carried into action and which have been made more specific with respect to magnitude, time and responsibility and which are judged to be attainable within a specific time. Objectives therefore also imply an element of competition for scarce resources. Targets represent specific programmes in which criteria of performance are set against target dates (P. Hall 1992; Heath and Wall 1992). The selection of goals, objectives and targets is also important in terms of sustainable tourism because they lead to the selection of indicators by which success in meeting objectives, and therefore the overall goal of sustainability, can be evaluated.

Nevertheless, the selection of goals, objectives, targets and indicators is not easy. The problem emerges of seeking to integrate individual programmes into a coherent plan. This operates not only at the level of what is contained within the planning document but also with respect to organisational structures and values held by those who are responsible for both the formulation and implementation of planning strategies. Indeed, as noted earlier, the process itself, by which different interested parties, groups and individuals come together to communicate different options and possibilities, is as important as what the plan eventually looks like. Communication and involvement in planning processes can lead to ownership of any plan therefore leading to increased possibilities of successful implementation. In tourism planning this becomes extremely important because at the destination level it is the sum of all the components which make up the destination product, which therefore includes the local community, rather than just members of the destination promotion organisation or even the members of the tourism industry. Such a situation means that one of the key tasks of any tourism planner is seeking the involvement and collaboration of the various stakeholders in the tourism planning process from outside of the organisation context within which they work.

'The task of reconciliation is the essence of the job of the ... planner' (P. Hall 1992 : 10). However, such a task helps explain why tourism planning is so difficult in terms of the amount of information and expertise that is required and 'the need to frame and then weigh up different objectives' (P. Hall 1992 : 10) which may be sought by different interests and stakeholders in the planning process – although it should be noted that there is no necessary relationship between the scale and expense of a planning programme and the complexity of the objectives behind it (P. Hall 1992).

Integrated approaches towards tourism planning are therefore neither *top-down*, 'where goals at each level in the organisation [or spatial area] are determined based on the goals at the next higher level' (Heath and Wall 1992 : 69), or *bottom-up*, where the goals of individual units are aggregated to become the strategic plan. Instead, integrated tourism planning is an *interactive* or *collaborative* approach which requires participation and interaction between the various levels of an organisation or unit of governance and between the responsible organisation and the stakeholders in the planning process (Hall and McArthur 1998).

How do we get there?: The problem of coordination

Finding creative solutions in a world of growing inter-dependence requires envisioning problems from perspectives outside our own. We need to redesign our problem-solving processes to include the different parties that have a stake in the issue. Achieving creative and viable solutions to these problems requires new strategies for managing interdependence (Gray 1989 : xviii).

The lack of single authorities responsible for tourism development has meant that local authorities and private industry have often been confused by the tourism development and planning process. Furthermore, the diverse structure of the industry has meant that coordination of the various elements of the planning process has been extremely difficult. However, perhaps paradoxically, it is the very nature of the industry which makes planning so important. As Gunn (1977 : 85) observed, because of the fragmented growth of the tourism industry 'the overall planning of the total tourism system is long overdue . . . there is no overall policy, philosophy or coordinating force that brings the many pieces of tourism into harmony and assures their continued harmonious function'.

The need for coordination has become one of the great truisms of tourism planning and policy (Hall 1994). For example, Lickorish et al. (1991 : vi) argued that 'There is a serious weakness in the machinery of government dealing with tourism in its co-ordination, and co-operation with operators either state or privately owned. Government policies or lack of them suggest an obsolescence in public administration devoted to tourism . . . Political will is often lacking.' One therefore has to ask why?

' "Co-ordination" usually refers to the problem of relating units or decisions so that they fit in with one another, are not at cross-purposes, and operate in ways that are reasonably consistent and coherent' (Spann 1979 : 411). Coordination for tourism occurs both horizontally, e.g. between different government agencies which may have responsibilities for various tourism related activities at the same level of governance (i.e. national parks, tourism promotion, transport), and vertically, e.g. between different levels of government (local, regional, provincial, national) within an administrative and policy system. Two different types of coordination are covered under Spann's definition: administrative coordination and policy coordination. The need for administrative coordination can be said to occur when there has been agreement on aims, objectives and policies between the parties that have to be coordinated but the mechanism for coordination is undecided or there are inconsistencies in implementation. The necessity of policy coordination arises when there is conflict over the objectives of the policy that has to be coordinated and implemented. The two types of coordination may sometimes be hard to distinguish as coordination will nearly always mean that one policy or decision will be dominant over others. Furthermore, perhaps the need for coordination only becomes paramount when it is not occurring. Most coordination occurs in a very loose fashion that does not require formal arrangement. In addition, some conflict can also be productive in the formulation of new ideas or strategies for dealing with problems (Hall 1998). Nevertheless, coordination is a political activity and it is because of this that coordination can prove extremely difficult, especially when, as in the tourism industry, there are a large number of parties involved in the decision-making process. As Edgell (1990 : 7) observed, 'there is no other industry in the economy that is linked to so many diverse and different kinds of products and services as is the tourism industry'.

In a collaborative or interactive approach towards tourism planning the emphasis is on planning *with* rather than planning *for* stakeholders. The approach reinforces the complex nature of tourism destination products, by recognising that the opinions, perspectives and recommendations of external stakeholders are just as legitimate as those of the planner, or the 'expert', or of industry. Such an approach may well be more time-consuming than a top-down approach but the results of such a process will have a far greater likelihood of being implemented because stakeholders will have a degree of ownership of the plan and of the process. Furthermore, such a process may well establish greater cooperation or collaboration between various stakeholders in supporting the goals and objectives of tourism organisations, and also create a basis for responding more effectively to and for change (Hall and McArthur 1996, 1998).

Coordination refers to formal institutionalised relationships among existing networks of organisations, interests and/or individuals, while cooperation is 'characterized by informal trade-offs and by attempts to establish reciprocity in the absence of rules' (Mulford and Rogers 1982 : 13). Often, the problem of developing common approaches towards tourism planning and policy problems, such as the metaproblem of sustainability, is identified in organisational terms, e.g. the creation of new ones or the allocation of new responsibilities to old ones. However, such a response does not by itself solve the problem of bringing various stakeholders and interests together. Instead, by recognising the level of interdependence that exists within the tourism system, it may be possible for 'separate, partisan interests to discover a common or public interest' (Friedmann 1973 : 350).

Collaboration is one important means to advance the collective good of stakeholders in tourism. Collaboration is essentially an emergent process rather than a prescribed state of organisation (see Table 4.6) (Gray 1989; Wood and Gray 1991). According to Gray (1989 : 15), 'Typically, collaborations progress from "underorganized systems" in which individual stakeholders act independently, if at all, with respect to the problem . . . to more tightly organized relationships characterized by concerted decision making among the stakeholders,' with stakeholders being defined as 'all individuals, groups or organizations that are directly influenced by actions others take to solve the problem' (Gray 1989 : 5). Under conditions of interdependence the range of interests associated with any particular problem is wide and therefore often controversial. Depending on the scale of analysis and the issue being examined, the number of stakeholders which an organisation has to contend with may be extremely large. For example, in terms of agreements with stakeholders, the United States Forest Service has developed more than 12,000 agreements with other agencies at all levels of government, universities and colleges, rural communities and organisations, and other outside interests (Ungar 1994). In the state of Vermont alone, the Forest Service has working agreements with the Abenaki Nation, the Catamount Trail Association, the Nature

Table 4.5 Steps in the stakeholder audit

1 Identification of stakeholders.
2 Determination of stakeholder interests, goals, priorities and values.
3 Review of past stakeholder behaviour in order to assess their strategies relating to issues and the likelihood of their forming coalitions with other stakeholders.
4 Estimation of the relative power (legal authority, political authority, financial, human and physical resources, access to media) of each stakeholder and stakeholder coalitions.
5 Assessment of how well your organisation is currently meeting the needs and interests of stakeholders.
6 Formulation of new strategies, if necessary, to manage relations with stakeholders and stakeholder coalitions.
7 Evaluation of effectiveness of stakeholder management strategies, with revisions and readjustment of priorities in order to meet stakeholder interests.

Source: After Roberts and King (1989); Hall and McArthur (1996).

Conservancy, Lyndon State College, the University of Vermont, the Vermont Association of Snow Travelers, the Ecotourism Society, the Green Mountain Club, Tree Talk, Inc., the Vermont Department of Forests, Parks and Recreation, the Vermont Department of Fish and Wildlife, Division of Water Quality, County Sheriffs, and the Youth Conservation Corps, and numerous other stakeholders (Ungar 1994). Large numbers of stakeholders can clearly make satisfactory outcomes difficult to achieve, but if legitimate stakeholders are excluded or ignored the quality and degree of acceptance of any recommendations will be highly suspect. As Healey (1997 : 70) noted, 'unless all stakeholders are acknowledged in the [planning] process, policies and practices will be challenged, undermined and ignored'. Indeed, there are a number of interrelated judgements that stakeholders weigh up when deciding whether or not to collaborate:

• Does the present situation fail to serve my interests?
• Will collaboration produce positive outcomes?
• Is it possible to reach a fair agreement?
• Is there parity among the stakeholders?
• Will the other side agree to collaborate? (Gray 1989 : 59).

Stakeholder audits are one mechanism which can assist planners in identifying the interests, groups and individuals that are stakeholders in the tourism planning process as well as help in understanding and confronting the complex web of relationships that surround tourism planning and management (Roberts and King 1989). Hall and McArthur (1996) identified seven steps in the undertaking of a stakeholder audit (Table 4.5). The audit is a useful tool for managers as it provides a framework for the identification of the various interests and values which impinge on the successful undertaking of organisational objectives. Managers and staff of organisations often have a mental map of the individuals and groups which affect their work and act accordingly in relations with them. Stakeholder analysis is therefore a more systematic way of identifying the range of interests in a particular tourism planning issue and their ability to affect planning processes and actions (Hall and McArthur 1998).

'A legitimate stake means the perceived right and capacity to participate in the negotiations. Those actors with a right to participate are those impacted by the actions of other stakeholders. They become involved in order to moderate those impacts. However, to be perceived as legitimate, stakeholders must also have the capacity to participate' (Gray 1985 : 922). Collaboration therefore operates on a model of shared power which is in keeping with the idea of the existence of a shared or public interest (Wood and Gray 1991). Nevertheless, for the planner, 'successfully advancing a shared vision, whether in the public or the private sector, requires identification and coordination of a diverse set of stakeholders, each of whom holds some but not all of the necessary resources' (Gray 1989 : 9). Collaboration is a highly dynamic process consisting of a number of elements:

- stakeholders are interdependent
- solutions emerge by dealing constructively with differences
- joint ownership of decisions is involved
- stakeholders need to assume collective responsibility for the future direction of the domain
- collaboration is an emergent process.

Collaborative planning approaches have been extensively used with respect to multi-party environmental disputes, e.g. land and water use, natural resource management and public land use issues (Bingham 1986) and are becoming increasingly recognised as significant for tourism (Selin and Beason 1991; Selin 1993; Selin and Chavez 1994, 1995; Jamal and Getz 1995; Selin and Myers 1995, 1998; Buhalis and Cooper 1998, Bramwell and Sharman 1999). Gray (1989) identified a number of benefits of collaboration

- broad comprehensive analysis of the domain improves the quality of solutions
- response capacity is more diversified
- it is useful for reopening deadlocked negotiations
- the risk of impasse is minimised
- the process ensures that each stakeholder's interests are considered in any agreement
- parties retain ownership of the solution
- parties most familiar with the problem, not their agents, invent the solutions
- participation enhances acceptance of solution and willingness to implement it
- the potential to discover novel, innovative solutions is enhanced
- relations between the stakeholders improve
- cost associated with other methods are avoided
- mechanisms for coordinating future actions among the stakeholders can be established.

The emphasis on sharing power and participation means that collaborative approaches fulfil one of the social pillars of sustainability, namely the requirement for equity. As Blowers (1997 : 42) noted, 'Inequality is about power relationships.' Collaboration therefore becomes a means of involving all affected parties to search for common interests and outcomes (see Table 4.6). 'Instead of trying to restrict participation, a common tactic, the professional

Table 4.6 The collaborative process

Phase 1: Problem setting
- common definition of problem
- commitment to collaborate
- identification of stakeholders
- legitimacy of stakeholders in terms of both internal and external acceptance
- convenor characteristics
- resource identification and availability for participation and collaboration

Phase 2: Direction setting
- establishing ground rules
- agenda setting
- organising subgroups, e.g. task forces
- joint information search
- exploring options
- reaching agreement and closing the deal

Phase 3: Implementation
- dealing with constituencies
- building external support
- structuring
- monitoring the agreement and ensuring compliance

Source: After Gray (1989).

manager gains more control over the situation by ensuring that all the necessary parties are there at the table, recognizing that parties in a dispute often engage in adversarial behaviour because no other approach is available to protect their interests' (Carpenter and Kennedy 1988 : 26). Furthermore, 'joint ownership means that the participants in a collaboration are directly responsible for reaching agreement on a solution' (Gray 1989 : 13). Waddock and Bannister (1991; see also Selin and Myers 1998) found the following factors to be significant predictors of partnership effectiveness:

- partners need to trust other partners
- partner representatives need to have adequate power to make decisions for their organisations
- appropriate partner organisations need to be identified and included in the partnership
- partners need to sense that there will be benefits to all members of the partnership from their efforts
- partners need to recognise that they are interdependent
- issues being dealt with need to be salient to partners
- partners need to feel that they add value to the partnership
- power needs to be balanced among partners
- objectives for the partnership should be clear and well defined
- competent staff are required for successful implementation of the partnership
- feedback to partners is important
- a strong vision of the partnership must be articulated by leaders
- strong leadership is required to maintain the partnership.

Waddock and Bannister's (1991) observations were borne out in further research by Selin and Beason (1991) and Selin and Chavez (1994) on tourism partnerships, with the latter study also noting the significance of several organisational and operational characteristics for successful partnerships. Organisational characteristics included:

- administrative support
- flexible protocols
- staff continuity
- mediator roles

and operational characteristics such as

- a written plan
- meeting environment
- cooperative agreement
- the setting of new goals.

Selin and Chavez (1994 : 59) observed that 'partnerships form a complex system of interrelationships between agencies and interests that is constantly changing'. Table 4.7 illustrates the types of agencies that American government tourism agencies collaborate with in respect of ecotourism policy. One of the conclusions that Edwards et al. (1998) drew from this survey was that even though some tourism agencies may not have policies or activities that are ecotourism-related, they may work closely with other government agencies that do. Table 4.7 also demonstrates the importance of the environment, natural resources, and fish and wildlife to tourism, as these categories received a third (34%) of the mention of collaborating American government agencies (Edwards et al. 1998). Nevertheless, significant barriers to collaborative planning also exist. Selin et al. (1997) in a study of collaborative planning in the US Forest Service noted that the four greatest perceived barriers to collaboration were

- initiatives constrained by personal agenda
- the Federal Advisory Committee Act
- the lack of full support of line offices
- initiatives becoming too politicised.

In the case of the Forest Service 'many managers were skeptical of collaborative forums characterized by shared decisionmaking, joint ownership, and collective responsibility; their concept of collaborative planning contradicts Gray's (1989). Most preferred to see collaborative planning as an advisory function, with the Forest Service retaining primary control over final decisions' (Selin et al. 1997 : 27). Furthermore, in a wider setting, protracted conflict between stakeholders which has led to substantial mistrust, the vesting of power in elite organisations and a lack of incentives to participate may all constrain the effectiveness of collaborative strategies (Selin 1998).

In a more positive vein we can also note that collaborative planning approaches also encourage planners, and others, to reflect on the manner in which planning and implementation represent two sides of the same coin.

Table 4.7   Types of collaborating government agencies in USA and Canada

No. of times mentioned ($n = 277$)	Percentage (rounded)	Type of agency
41	15	Natural Resources/Forestry/Conservation
35	13	Transportation
31	11	Environment/Parks
25	9	Culture/Heritage/Film
23	8	Fish and Wildlife/Game
22	8	Government (federal, local, legislature, etc.)
19	7	Economics/Commerce/Labour
18	6	Other/focus not possible to determine
15	5	Collaborate with all agencies, sometimes depending on issue
14	5	Agriculture
11	4	Education
7	3	Development/Planning
6	2	Budget and Finance
5	2	Law Enforcement/Police
5	2	General Tourism/other tourism offices

Note: Collaborating agencies were placed in categories by the authors. Placement was done according to the name of the collaborating agency. Agencies with more than one category in their names were placed in the category that corresponds to the first mentioned (for example, the Ministry of Agriculture and Forestry was placed in 'Agriculture').

Source: Edwards et al. (1998 : 23).

As Friedmann (1973 : 359) observed, '*the kind of implementing mechanism adopted will itself influence the character of the plan and the way it is formulated.* The formulation and implementation of plans are closely interdependent processes, so that the choice of one will in large measure also determine the second.' The inclusiveness of collaborative approaches may therefore help assist in dealing with some of the key problems of problems of implementation:

1 Many policies represent compromises between conflicting values.
2 Many policies involve compromises with key interests within the implementation structure.
3 Many policies involve compromises with key interests upon whom implementation will have an impact.
4 Many policies are framed without attention being given to the way in which underlying forces (particularly economic ones) will undermine them (Barrett and Hill 1993 in Ham and Hill 1994).

The importance of having those stakeholders who will be responsible for implementing the solution which emerges from the planning process cannot be emphasised enough. Acceptance of and support for a solution is enhanced when those who must abide by it are included in designing the solution

(Delbecq 1974); such a situation may be extremely important in such areas as codes of environmental practice by tour operators or developers, for example. Furthermore, insufficient consideration of implementation of outputs within the planning process, 'may result in settlements that create devastating precedents that may result in reluctance to negotiate in the future; damage interpersonal relationships; and financial, time or resource loss' (Moore 1986 : 248).

How do we know we've got there? The role of evaluation and indicators

Through evaluation and performance monitoring, governments and agencies seek to establish whether public sector activities are achieving their goals or objectives, or are achieving them to an increased extent over time, and to determine whether objectives are being pursued as efficiently as possible. Evaluation can also seek to establish why public planning activities do or do not achieve their objectives, allowing lessons from successes to be applied elsewhere and failures to be dealt with (O'Faircheallaigh and Ryan 1992).

Evaluation is increasingly becoming a significant component of tourism planning and policy as they are undertaken on a more strategic basis. Nevertheless, 'The word "evaluation" needs careful definition. To most lay observers, it conveys a connotation of economic criteria . . . But essentially, *evaluation consists of any process which seeks to order preferences*' (Hall 1982 : 288). Peter Hall's definition of evaluation is insightful for two principal reasons. First, many other definitions of evaluation confine evaluation to the 'what happened after the policy was implemented' phase (e.g. Dye 1992). Although evaluation tends to be more focused on determining performance for outcomes such as impact assessment; justification; accountability; planning and resource allocation; improvement; and continued support (Cauley 1993), there is no reason as to why evaluation cannot be undertaken before a policy is put into effect. Indeed, it makes good sense to include an objective whereby responses to policy proposals are evaluated, 'Because errors are to be expected projects should be planned to facilitate early detection and correction' (Hollick 1993 : 125). Similarly, Hall and Jenkins (1995) argued that constant monitoring of the tourism policy process can alert decision-makers and policy-makers to situations in which public officials carry out different activities from those envisaged, or perhaps when policies fail to reach intended clients. In other words, to simply 'evaluate the programme in terms of its original objectives might lead to a conclusion that the policy was a failure, yet this might be misleading since the policy as originally envisaged might not actually have been put into effect' (Hogwood and Gunn 1984 : 220). Policy failure or success could be the result of various aspects of policy design (e.g. ambiguous statements of objectives and intent), policy implementation (e.g. bureaucratic discretion or uncontrollable global forces), or from unforeseen forces (e.g. economic, political and social) creating changes in public need (Hall and Jenkins 1995). Second, Hall's (1982) definition acknowledges that 'evaluation is not simply concerned with carrying out technically correct evaluations; it

Table 4.8   Roles of evaluation and monitoring in the tourism planning and policy-making process

---

- Assessing the degree of need for government intervention and policy.
- Continuous function of the policy-making process to enlighten, clarify and improve policy. Evaluation allows for the testing of assumptions regarding the way in which the process operates, the nature of outcomes and the effectiveness of programmes.
- Conceptual and operational assistance to decision-makers, planners and policy-makers, particularly as shifts in implementation and target needs and expectations occur. Evaluation allows access and integration of relevant information that improves the quality of decision making in areas such as resource allocation and other policy and programme directions.
- Specification of policy outcomes and impacts.
- Review of performance indicators through consideration of whether the original objectives or desired outcomes remain realistic and appropriate.
- Assessing or measuring the efficiency and cost-effectiveness of tourism policies and plans in terms of the financial, human and capital resources.
- Accountability reporting for resource allocation, distribution and redistribution, through assessment and demonstration of the degree to which a policy or programme is meeting its objectives.
- Symbolic reasons (to demonstrate that something is being done).
- Political reasons (to use the results of evaluation for political ends in order to win policy and planning arguments).

Source: Hall and Jenkins (1995); Hall and McArthur (1998).

has to be concerned with how evaluation results are consumed and utilized' (Hogwood and Gunn 1984 : 220). Tourism planning and policy evaluation should therefore be concerned with who requested the evaluation, why the evaluation was requested, the estimation, assessment or appraisal of policy, including its development, content, implementation and effects, and the manner in which that evaluation will be consumed and utilised. Evaluations of policy must consider why who got what and where, and the outcomes and impacts of policy. That said, goals and objectives may be ambiguous or covert and therefore difficult to detect. This in itself means policy evaluation must go beyond simply measuring outcomes and impacts with respect to goals and objectives (Hall and Jenkins 1995).

Evaluation involves making judgements about the results of some sort of measurement against specific objectives. This is typically done by collecting and analysing information, judging the worth of something and making informed decisions for the future. Table 4.8 outlines some of the reasons for which evaluation and monitoring is undertaken in tourism planning and policy. However, evaluation rarely occurs for a single reason and the roles which evaluation undertakes are multiple and interrelated. According to Hall and McArthur (1998), some of the principles that should be kept in mind when undertaking evaluation are:

- what needs to be measured is determined before the measurement technique
- the only aspects assessed are those that will provide the necessary critical information

- stakeholders clearly understand the rationale and nature of the evaluation programme
- what is to be evaluated already has some form of measurable objectives or performance criteria
- relevant information can be collected
- results are balanced and reliable, and recommendations are relevant, feasible and timely
- information is presented in a way that increases the possibility of acceptance
- the right information reaches the right people
- the programme is delivered to stakeholders in a way that reflects their interests and abilities (e.g. comprehension and cognitive).

Evaluation is both an ongoing task of strategic planning and is a key element of strategic thinking. If we accept Lindblom's (1980 : 64) notion that 'Most, perhaps all, administrative acts make or change policy in the process of trying to implement it,' then this observation in itself justifies the need for monitoring and evaluation. By incorporating monitoring and evaluation at the very beginning and throughout the tourism planning and policy-making process, the type of information required from monitoring and evaluation can be specified during the formation of the plan/policy and in advance of the plan's/policy's implementation. Moreover, the policy analysis approach to evaluation, which acknowledges the politics of tourism planning and public policy, is not simply concerned with carrying out technically correct evaluations; it has to be concerned with how evaluation results are ordered, consumed and utilised (Hogwood and Gunn 1984). In other words, the planner needs to be aware of the power of argument and the communication of ideas to the various stakeholders who receive them. 'The process of critical evaluation . . . requires that we explore competing explanations and arrive at judgments regarding the way that they fit together' (Morgan 1986 : 331). Interpretations need to be played off against each other and, when necessary, choices need to be made between them.

Although monitoring, auditing and evaluation are closely related concepts there are significant differences between them. Monitoring is a process of repetitive observation of one or more elements or indicators according to prearranged schedules in time and/or space. Auditing is the comparison of predicted outcomes with those outcomes that have already occurred. Evaluation research is at the other end of a spectrum of evaluative activity from auditing with evaluation referring to the systematic assessment of the effectiveness, efficiency, (or) appropriateness of a policy, programme or part of a programme (Hall and McArthur 1998) (see Table 4.9). Auditing and monitoring are therefore a component of the wider field of evaluation.

Environmental auditing has become a well-recognised technique within environmental planning and, increasingly, within tourism planning as well (e.g. World Travel and Tourism Council 1990). Nevertheless, with respect to the conduct of auditing of environmental impact statements (EIS), Selman (1992 : 140) notes

Table 4.9 Characteristics and purposes of audit and evaluation

Audit	Evaluation
• Typically the agent of an external third part (e.g. parliament); focused on accountability, with a consequent strong emphasis on independence of the area under review.	• Pursued in collaborative relationship with programme managers; scope includes accountability, but main areas of concern are the appropriateness and effectiveness of programme activities.
• Generally attempts to assess performance against established (i.e. well-documented if not statutory) standards; focus is on internal processes.	• Aims to assess the impact of programmes in terms of policy objectives/program goals; focus is on stakeholders.
• Takes policy settings and strategies as given.	• Critically examines existing policy settings and strategies within programmes and may recommend change.
• Confined to an examination of what is already done or has been completed.	• Can be used to form a judgement about the appropriate design of policy for future implementation as well as to review work in progress or completed.
• Strong focus on accountability and control.	• Focus on program improvement with accountability being a secondary consideration.
• A well-defined profession based in accountancy.	• An emerging profession drawn from a wide range of academic backgrounds.

Source: After Douglas (1992).

... often it is impossible to conduct an adequate audit because of the vague wording of predictions. Auditing of many impacts can only be undertaken when monitored data allow statistically valid interpretations of cause-effect relationships to be derived for projects with a long operational life ... monitoring may be required for long periods before trends can be identified.

One of the great difficulties, therefore, with assessment of tourism's impacts, along with other forms of evaluation of tourism, is the creation of appropriate baseline data along with reliable monitoring practices. With respect to tourism–environment relationships, for example, Mathieson and Wall (1982 : 94) identified several significant methodological problems as requiring urgent attention:

• the difficulty of distinguishing between changes induced by tourism and those induced by other activities
• the lack of information concerning conditions prior to the advent of tourism and, hence, the lack of a baseline against which change can be measured

- the paucity of information on the numbers, types and tolerance levels of different species of flora and fauna
- the concentration of researchers upon particularly primary resources, such as beaches and mountains, which are ecologically sensitive.

Nevertheless, environmental auditing for tourism is becoming increasingly important as businesses and organisations seek to ensure that they are complying with regulations and legislation (e.g. with respect to pollution) and evaluate their performance in relation to membership of voluntary environmental programmes (e.g. Green Globe) and more broadly assumed environmental responsibility. Relevant types of environmental audits that may be undertaken include:

- *compliance audits*, which ensure that regulations are not being breached
- *site audits*, comprising sport checks of known problem areas
- *corporate audits*, which examine the performance of an entire business or agency, and more positively, ensuring that technical and advisory support on environmental matters is available throughout the organisation
- *issues audits*, which are a response to specific environmental issues (such as energy use, recycling, or use of rainforest timber)
- *associate audits*, in which vetting of environmental action is extended to an organisation's contractors, agents and suppliers in order to ensure that they are operative in appropriate ways
- *activity audits*, which evaluates policies in activities which cut across business boundaries, such as distribution and transport networks (after Selman 1992).

Whether it be auditing or part of a broader evaluation process, indicators play a major role in measuring success in meeting goals and objectives. Sustainable development indicators measure sustainability or sustainable development performance. 'Sustainability indicators need to take account of economic linkages, quality of life and perhaps future welfare aspects, as well as environmental quality . . . The challenge is to strike a balance between having a small number so that the main messages are clear, while not oversimplifying the issues or omitting significant areas, or suppressing significant geographical variations' (HMSO 1994 : 220).

Development of sustainable indicators provides a theoretical and practical framework for defining the meaning of sustainability at various scales, from global to the community, and for measuring progress towards that goal. Sustainability indicators serve as a 'reality check' to ensure that strategic, planning and management processes are moving in desired directions and that agencies and individuals are held accountable for their decisions and actions. Sustainable indicators also enable comparison between different regions, but are most valuable when measuring a nation, region, community or place against itself over time.

The role of an indicator is to make complex systems understandable or perceptible, 'those things which a decision-maker needs to know to reduce the risk of unknowingly taking poor decisions' (World Tourism Organization 1993 : 8). As Jacobs (1991 : 237) noted, 'without accurate and systematic information about the state of and changes in the environment (which many countries surprisingly lack) it is impossible to set sustainability targets and to direct policy to meet them'. An effective indicator or set of indicators helps nations, regions, communities and organisations determine where they are, where they are going, and how far they are from chosen goals. Indicators of sustainability also provide information on long-term viability based on the degree to which economic, environmental and social systems are efficient and integrated. To measure the degree of efficiency and integration, a set of numerous indicators is often required. At the community level, for example, these indicators may incorporate several broad categories such as economy, environment, society/culture, government, resource consumption, education, health, housing, transportation and quality of life. The usefulness and accuracy of indicators of sustainability depends on their ability to create a 'snapshot' of economic, environmental and social systems at a given scale. This 'snapshot' must be appropriate to the scale at which the evaluation is occurring and for which goals and objectives have been developed. In addition, the indicators used at one scale should be related to the indicators which are used at other scales in order to ensure integration of objectives for and evaluation of sustainability. Choosing the appropriate indicators and developing a program is a complex process requiring collaboration between many sectors including government agencies, the public, research institutions, civic and environmental groups, and business. Indicators should be developed in accordance with the following criteria:

- recognition of scale and relationship between various scales
- relevant to the main objective of assessing progress towards sustainable development
- understandable in that they are clear, simple, and unambiguous
- realisable within the capacities of governments, organisations and communities, given their logistic, time, technical and other constraints
- conceptually well founded
- limited in number, remaining open-ended and adaptable to future developments
- broad in coverage of all aspects of sustainable development
- representative of an international consensus, to the extent possible
- where possible, dependent on data which are readily available or available at a reasonable cost/benefit ratio, of known quality and updated at regular intervals; where this is not the case new data will be required.

Indicators for sustainable tourism are most often used to provide information for tourism planners and managers at various scales of operation ranging from individual businesses through to national agencies and even international businesses in some cases. According to the World Tourism Organization (1993), the type of indicators that tourism sector managers need to know include:

- *warning indicators* which sensitise decision-makers to potential areas of concern and the need to act to anticipate and prevent problems, e.g. visitor numbers
- *measures of pressures or stresses* which measure key external factors of concern or trends which must be considered in any management response, e.g. changing community expectations or changing levels of visitor satisfaction
- *measures of the state of the natural resource base (product) and measures of level of its use*, e.g. changing use levels, measures of biodiversity, or pollution levels for a given site

- *measures of impacts*, usually related to measures of physical, social and economic impact, which examine the cause and effect relationships between the decisions and actions and the external environment, e.g. changing attitudes to tourism due to changes in visitor numbers or days of beach closures due to unacceptable pollution levels
- *measures of management effort/action* which examine the question of 'is enough being done?', e.g. extent of area declared as national park or conservation reserve or amount of funds spent on visitor management strategies
- *measures of management impact* which evaluate the effectiveness of management decisions and actions, e.g. levels of visitor-related degradation in areas set aside as national parks or conservation reserves.

Undoubtedly the selection of indicators is fraught with difficulties. They must meet the criteria noted above, must be appropriate to measuring the efficiency and effectiveness of goals and objectives and must also provide a clear indication of cause and effect relationships. However, the use of indicators has also been criticised at a deeper level for its 'managerial' approach towards sustainability (Bayliss and Walker 1996), in which indicators are used to measure environmental assets to ensure that the total stock of assets is not diminished between generations (the principle of intra-generational equity). In this setting 'the environment is likened to a stock of natural capital yielding a flow of services to the economic system (i.e. its essential economic functions), then sustainable development of that system involves maximising the net benefits of economic development, subject to maintaining the services and quality of the stock of natural resources' (Pearce et al. 1989 : 42).

Bayliss and Walker (1996) criticise this approach as they note that not only have there been inconsistencies in gathering data, difficulties in selecting criteria and high levels of variability and uncertainty throughout the process of monitoring sustainability but that there are inherent problems in such a positivistic/scientific approach to sustainability in the first place. Indeed, McConnell (1981) criticised such positivistic comprehensiveness in planning by noting that theory without being spatially, temporally and stakeholder group specific, cannot be falsified, leaving a lack of any basis to establish the reliability of the claims it makes to producing reliable knowledge (Bayliss and Walker 1996). Such a powerful critique reflects wider concerns as to the way in which the concept of sustainability and its implementation cannot be separated from the political arena (e.g. see Sachs 1993). However, as this book has consistently pointed out, policy and planning outputs, such as the selection of indicators and monitoring results, should not be taken as a given. They should be part of a contested public domain in which their selection, suitability, operation and outputs are subject to debate and discussion in order to ensure that they meet the widest possible notion of the public interest at that level. Indicators and the evaluation process need to be as much a part of the process of argument and debate as any other component of planning. This does not mean that indicators are without value, far from it; appropriate indicators can be invaluable in determining the value of policy settings and the efficiency and effectiveness of planning processes. If well done, they provide a basis for policy renewal and targeting which is even more appropriate to the task in hand. However, like any planning tool, their use needs to be seen within the wider political context of interests, values and power.

Strategic planning is a powerful conceptual tool and approach. It puts in operational terms the dynamic nature of tourism systems and the wider set of interrelationships and interdependencies that operate in the human and physical environment. It is also ongoing and seeks to both respond and stimulate appropriate change. However, as noted earlier, it does not by itself automatically lead to sustainable outcomes in the environment external to the organisation which is undertaking such activities. Indeed, again as previously observed, there is a common tendency in tourism to assume that strategic planning processes undertaken by destination organisations are automatically the same as a strategic plan for a destination. They are not; the objectives, stakeholders, interests, values and outcomes which are related to such a process will be different. There is a difference between determining the long-term survival of a tourism organisation and the long-term sustainability of a destination.

The idea of interdependence in planning has run very strongly through this chapter. Before moving on to examine the policy and planning process at various scales we shall discuss the role of dialectical analysis which underpins much of the thinking about the importance of relational and communicative planning theories and strategies.

Understanding interdependence: the importance of dialectical analysis

One of the most critical problems facing the analysis of the tourism phenomenon, and the construction of the tourism landscape in particular, is the relationship between process and form. Unfortunately, much analysis of tourism merely accounts for form with there being little attention to the processes by which such forms have been created. In addition, where processes are considered they are often examined from a positivist ontological perspective. However, positivism is only one of several possible ways of understanding the human condition and the spaces within which human life unfolds. One alternative to positivism is that of dialectical thinking.

Dialectical analysis has recently been noted by a number of authors (e.g. Hollinshead 1992; Roche 1992; Hall 1994; Hall and Jenkins 1995) as a valuable tool in examining tourism, particularly in the area of tourism policy. Indeed, Hall (1994 : 200) argued that 'The process of dialectical inquiry would appear to be essential to the study of the political dimensions of tourism,' given that 'the vast majority of tourism research is one-dimensional and fails to adequately account for *both* tourism as a complex social phenomenon and the theoretical frameworks that are being utilised' (1994 : 199). Similarly, Roche (1992 : 591) argued that dialectical forms of conceptualisation are needed

> to appreciate the difference and interdependence between social facts and social values, between theory and description, and between theory and policy. But further

it requires [students of tourism] to appreciate the unity-in-difference in social reality of such complex phenomena as action and structure, continuity and change, consciousness and material conditions, micro and macro levels and so on.

However, despite the potential significance of dialectical analysis for broadening the scope of tourism knowledge there has been little detailed discussion of the nature and relevance of dialectical thinking. Therefore, the remainder of this section outlines the key elements of dialectical thinking along the lines of principles identified by Ollman (1993) and Harvey (1995), and their application to tourism.

Relations and flows

Dialectical analysis emphasises the understanding of processes, relations and flows over the analysis of elements, things, structures and organised systems. The self-evident world of things identified within a positivistic framework is transformed through dialectical inquiry into a more confusing world of relations and flows manifested as things. Ontologically, dialecticians hold that 'elements, things, structures and systems do not exist outside of, or prior to, the processes and relations, that create, sustain, or undermine them' (Harvey 1995 : 4). Such a step may be too bold for many readers; as Ollman (1993 : 34) observed, it is extremely difficult for social scientists to abandon the 'common sense view' that 'there are things and there are relations, and that neither can be subsumed in the other'. Nevertheless, it should be emphasised that such a way of viewing the world is increasingly gaining support in other areas of academic endeavour including physics (e.g. Bohm 1980), biology (e.g. Capra 1997), psychology (e.g. Gergen 1991) and Christian theology (e.g. Cupitt 1987).

Dialectical analysis which emphasises the role of process, of continually becoming, is therefore explicitly denying the validity of Cartesian, positivistic modes of enquiry. In a manner which recalls the analyses of Hewison (1987, 1991) and Hollinshead (1992) in heritage tourism, Harvey (1995 : 5) observed that 'The more we treat the world as being made up of finished products separate from the continuous flow of experience out of which such products are created, so we reduce everything to the past.' Conventional tourism analysis therefore explores relations between things rather than the continuous processes of formation, maintenance and dissolution of things which therefore has substantial implications for the manner in which culture tends to be represented in tourism research. Students of tourism should take heed of Williams' (1997 : 128) excellent commentary:

> In most description and analysis, culture and society are expressed in an habitual past tense. The strongest barrier to the recognition of human cultural activity is this immediate and regular conversion of experience into finished products. What is defensible as a procedure in conscious history, where on certain assumptions many actions can be definitively taken as having ended, is habitually projected, not only into the always moving substance of the past, but into contemporary life, in which relationships, institutions and formations in which we are still actively

involved are converted, by this procedural mode, into formed wholes rather than forming and formative processes. Analysis is then centred on relations between these produced institutions, formations, and experiences, so that now, as in that produced past, only the fixed explicit forms exist, and living presence is always, by definition, receding.

Wheels within wheels

Things (elements) are constituted out of flows, processes and relations operating within bounded fields which constitute structured systems, yet from a dialectical approach both individual things and the system itself 'rests entirely on an understanding of the processes and relations by which they are constituted' (Harvey 1995 : 5–6). Dialectical analysis therefore sees systems within systems, patterns within patterns, in a sort of Mandelbrot set of the social sciences. 'Things' are 'internally heterogeneous [contradictory] at every level' (Levins and Lewontin 1985 : 272). 'Any "thing" can be decomposed into a collection of other "things" which are in some relation to each other' (Harvey 1995 : 6) (also refer to the discussion of systems in Chapter 3). While analysis may be focused on the destination, for example, dialectical analysis emphasises the problematic nature of reduction by noting the significance of relationships to processes occurring at further meta and micro scales and relationships to things outside of the destination although at the same scale of analysis. Destinations and their analysis are therefore perceived to be embedded within a complex web of socio-cultural, economic, political and environmental relationships within which the social scientist also crafts their understanding of such relationships. These, in turn, can be decomposed into the various things which make up a destination: businesses, communities, infrastructure and environments. This is not to say that destinations or individuals are merely a passive product of external processes. As Mellor (1991 : 114) noted with respect to analyses of heritage by melancholic postmodernists who have assumed:

> . . . that people are not in active negotiation with their symbolic environment, but are passively shaped by it. The problem with this wretched scenario that it has been devised by people who are compulsive readers of texts. They pay close attention to their semiotic surroundings and believe that others do too . . . The alternative is to treat people as active agents interacting with real structures. People make their own cultures, albeit not in circumstances of their own choosing. Amongst those circumstances – within and towards which their activity is directed – are structures of representation; but so too, are structures of class, ethnicity, and gender, along with deliberate economic and political strategies that bear upon these. These things are real. They do not merely exist in discourse. Their reality and their consequences exceed their representation. But people are not merely passively constructed by them. Even in leisure, people act intentionally; although in doing so they may slice the world along a different grain to that expected by the melancholic intellectual.

As Harvey (1995) noted, there are several implications that arise from the heterogeneity of things. First, every thing is decomposable – there is no basic unit. It is therefore legitimate to investigate 'each level of organization without having to search for fundamental units' (Levins and Lewontin 1985 : 278).

Nevertheless, as Harvey (1995 : 7) also observed, 'critical practice in the human-ities is very much guided these days, perhaps overly so, by concerns to dis-solve fixed categories within conflicting fields and fluxes of socio-linguistic and representational practices'. Second, given that all things are heterogeneous the only way we can understand the attributes of things is to understand the processes and relations which they internalise. Third, and following on from the second, there is no fixed or *a priori* boundary to the system within which a thing is located. This therefore raises the important problem of where one sets boundaries in analysis. Changes in boundaries will change not only the nature of theories but also answers. This problem has already been well recog-nised with respect to economic analysis in tourism in terms of where one sets the boundary of the economic region but also with respect to issues of pollu-tion and sustainability, e.g. what is sustainable at one level may not be sustain-able at another (Hall and Butler 1995). This does not mean that one should stop setting boundaries. Such a venture would make analysis impossible. Rather it means that the arbitrary nature of boundary setting needs to be made more overt in the process of research and evaluation (see Majone 1980b for a further exposition of this problem from within a dialectical framework). Similarly, Morgan (1986 : 337) in his excellent discussion on the nature of organisational analysis observed, 'People who learn to read situations from different (theoretical) points of view have an advantage over those committed to a fixed position. For they are better able to recognize the limitations of a given perspective. They can see how situations and problems can be framed and reframed in different ways, allowing new kinds of solutions to emerge.' Significantly, in an implicit reference to dialectical modes of thinking, Morgan then went on to note, 'the trick is to learn how to engage in a kind of conversation with the situation one is trying to understand. Rather than impose a viewpoint on a situation, one should allow the situation to reveal how it can be understood from other vantage points . . . as one develops the art of reading situations, critical analysis and evaluation becomes a way of thinking' (1986 : 337). What does this mean for some of the key concepts which we face in examining tourism planning?

Space and time

Space and time are not absolute. Instead, they are actively constructed by various processes. Dialectical thinking emphasises that there are multiple spaces and times which are contingent and contained within different biological, physical and social processes. Space and time are therefore relative properties, awareness of which has already partially infiltrated into tourism studies from research into the different space–time conceptions of many indigenous peoples.

Parts and wholes

'Parts and wholes are mutually constitutive of each other' (Harvey 1995 : 8) – an observation which anticipates the work of Giddens (1984) on structuration theory, in which agency makes structure and structure makes agency. This holistic approach to the analysis of social systems has been particularly influ-ential in human geography and cultural studies. However, it has had barely little substantive impact on mainstream tourism studies, although it was clearly influential in the work of Britton (1989, 1991) in his efforts to get capital recognised as a key concept in the geography of tourism (also see Hall and Page 1999a).

Cause and effect

Given the nature of the relationship between parts and the whole in dialectical analysis, it also follows that cause and effect, subject and object are also interchangeable. This therefore means that dialectical thinking makes only very limited reference to cause and effect type argument.

Contradiction and creativity

The heterogeneity that exists in things and systems gives rise to contradictions (a well-known characteristic of dialectical analysis) out of which creative tensions or, as Harvey (1995 : 9) described them, 'transformative behaviours'. Such dialectical relationships between opposing forces and concepts is therefore held to be the basis of the tensions which give rise to the evolving social (Levins and Lewontin 1985) and personal world. Through dialectical analysis one learns about others through oneself, and oneself through others.

Change

In dialectical analysis change is a constant. Change and instability are the norm not the exception. Nevertheless, in research we tend to focus on the 'moments' and 'forms' which are embedded within processes. The critical issue, though, is to be aware of the mechanisms and transformations that may give rise to those forms rather than just the form itself. In tourism studies the emphasis has generally been on the latter.

Argument

Dialectic analysis does not lie outside of its own form of argumentation but remains subject to it. It is a process which produces things in the form of concepts and theories which in themselves will be supported or undermined in terms of the ongoing process of critique and enquiry. The observer is not outside of the process he or she is examining. As soon as a researcher begins to examine a process, she or he has entered into a relationship with that process and has become part of the process itself. Observation is intervention. Similarly, the success or otherwise will be judged by other constituents of processes and systems of which the researcher is a part. The success of any argument therefore does not rely on any objective criteria. Instead, it is founded on the shifting criteria of particular groups and individuals which change over time. Several authors have focused on the role of argument, particularly with respect to tourism planning and policy which are themselves very process driven (see Hall 1994; Hall and Jenkins 1995).

Eduction – the search for possibilities

Finally, let us deal with eduction, which is 'the exploration of potentialities for change, for self-realization, for the construction of new totalities (for example, social ecosystems) and the like, rather than deduction or induction – the central motif of dialectical praxis' (Harvey 1995 : 10). Praxis is totalisation, totalisation is praxis. Dialectical analysis highlights the role of values in social processes, e.g. tourism policy and planning, and sees the constructed knowledge which result as discourses situated in a realm of power and interests. Values are not universal truths or abstractions but this does not mean that value choice is unimportant. Far from it. Dialectical reflection forces the researcher to confront the implicit and explicit nature of values in the development and reporting of academic research. Unfortunately, a wander through the increasing number of tourism journals and books which weigh down the library shelves would suggest that such reflection, if it does exist, remains well hidden in the confines and strictures of academic writing which has tended to reinforce the fact-value dichotomy of Cartesian views of the world within which the researcher appears to lie outside of the world he or she studies. The relevance of much academic research in tourism could well be questioned – relevant to what and to who? Results tend to be produced and reproduced for the greater benefit of narrow industry and personal interests (e.g. promotion, greater status within the walls of academia) rather than actually seeking to improve the lot of the individuals who are most affected by the vagaries of tourism.

The act of tourism planning and research, as with the subject matter of such research, needs to be located within the continuous flows of processes, relationships and systems from which it is constituted and which it informs. Dialectical thinking, for this author at least, is a crucial component of tourism analysis which needs to put at the forefront of tourism knowledge, rather than cast to the rear. The unfolding and becoming of one's life is the search for possibilities. To paraphrase Harvey (1995): the search for such possibilities is embedded within, rather than articulated after, the research process, and it is to the discussion of some of these possibilities that this book now turns.

Conclusions

This chapter has emphasised the importance of systems thinking in tourism planning and the corresponding role of strategic planning in tourism. Strategic tourism planning is designed to be holistic, integrated and comprehensive. Integration in tourism planning and management refers to an awareness that tourism is a system of interrelated social, economic, physical and political variables and the corresponding establishing of a series of institutional arrangements and planning processes which reflect such a system. At an organisational level, to be comprehensive, three conditions must be met:

1 Functional programmes and activities must be in keeping with the wider values, mission, principles, goals and objectives of the management organisation.
2 Any programme or activity must be monitored and evaluated in terms relevant to the wider values, vision, mission, goals and objectives.
3 All relevant variables must be considered in the design of individual programmes and activities (Hall and McArthur 1998).

This chapter has also outlined a process of strategic tourism planning. It has emphasised the significance of the reasons for the initiation of strategic planning and the construction of an integrated set of goals, objectives and actions which can then be implemented and evaluated over time horizons ranging from the day-to-day to the long term. This chapter has also provided a strategic planning process that is geared towards stakeholders. As Colenutt (1997 : 109) observed, 'The participation of local residents makes a difference to how the local authority conducts itself and can also affect how the developers and landowners act'. However, such a philosophy applies throughout the planning process. As Colenutt went on to argue in the context of town planning:

> The purpose of planning, its values and vision should, therefore, be redefined. Communities and their needs should be at the centre not simply responding to the demand (or lack of it) of the property market. If we move down this path, it then becomes possible within the framework of planning consultation to debate explicitly how to create and protect jobs, house the homeless, create a decent healthy environment, ensure adequate public transport and reduce crime. These issues are real, and, if they are not brought into the planning system, town planning will die as an instrument of social policy, leaving it to be manipulated by rich and powerful corporate elites (Colenutt 1997 : 115).

Such sentiments apply equally to tourism planning. If the creation of sustainable places is a goal of tourism planning, then tourism planning must be a process which is geared not only to government, industry and tourist satisfaction but to a broad notion of stakeholders which is inclusive of the local community and the public interest.

Questions and further reading

How might a concern with the policy and planning process improve outcomes?
What are the key elements of a strategic approach to tourism planning?
Why is a strategic planning process usually initiated?
Explain the similarities and differences between the concepts of coordination and collaboration?
What are the differences between conducting an audit and undertaking an evaluation?

Peter Hall (1992) provides a good account of strategic planning in the public context. Hall and McArthur (1998) detail a strategic approach to heritage management which can be easily applied to tourism planning, while Heath and Wall (1992) provide an excellent outline of strategic destination marketing. Gray (1989) provides the classic work on collaboration. Valuable recent examples on collaboration in the tourism context are provided by Selin and Chavez (1994, 1995), Jamal and Getz (1995), Selin and Myers (1995, 1998), Buhalis and Cooper (1998) and Bramwell and Sharman (1999). The use of indicators in tourism policy and planning is discussed by the WTO (1993), Hall and Jenkins (1995), Hall and McArthur (1998) and Wight (1998). For readings on systems approaches to tourism planning see the recommended readings from Chapter Three.

Chapter 5

Tourism planning and policy at the international and supranational level

> The concept of the absolute sovereignty of states will have to make concessions as never before in face of today's emerging environmental crisis. There will have to be a high degree of willing subordination of national sovereignty in favour of the common good of all nations.
>
> This new common interest lies in the preservation, for the peoples of the globe and for their future generations, of a world no less habitable than it is today, while at the same time rehabilitating those parts of it that man is making, or has already made, relatively uninhabitable. (Stephen 1991 : 185)

For a field as international in scope as tourism there are surprisingly few international agreements and regulations which are directly concerned with managing tourism activity. Tourism is a significant component of international relations and diplomatic activity, with the ease of access between countries often being an indirect measure of the degree of positive relations between them. As Derek Hall (1991 : 53) observed:

> The numbers, and to a lesser extent nature, of tourist flows can be comprehensively influenced by administrative and bureaucratic controls and impositions. These can cover such areas as visa regulations, currency exchange controls and proscriptions, on tourist movements and activities. In other words, constraints may be imposed before, at and subsequent to the tourist's point of entry.

Despite the existence of a number of international tourist organisations, the most notable being the World Tourist Organization, there is 'little in the way of supranational regulation of tourism services' (Williams and Shaw 1988b : 231) except for the area of air transport where there are a number of conventions covering landing rights and safety. Tourism has also received little attention in international trade conventions, such as the General Agreement on Trade and Tariffs (GATT), although the overall liberalisation of the services area agreed to in the 1993 conclusion to the Uruguay Round of GATT and the subsequent efforts to liberalise trade in services and overseas investment will undoubtedly have a substantial effect on tourism development. Despite the relative paucity of international agreements related directly to tourism, there is a significant institutional framework for tourism policy and planning at the international level consisting of international organisations with direct and indirect interests in tourism, and a range of international laws related to cognate areas, including the environment, heritage, trade, labour relations and transport. In addition, there has been substantial development of supranational institutional arrangements for tourism, that is, arrangements which, though not global in scope, create a series of arrangements between a number of countries, often within a regional context.

This chapter will examine a number of aspects of tourism planning and policy making at the international level. It will discuss the nature of 'hard' and 'soft' international law and discuss the role of international organisations, such as the World Tourism Organization, in tourism planning and policy. It will also look at the role of international conservation and environment law in tourism planning with specific reference to the World Heritage Foundation. The chapter will then discuss the role of supranational organisations, such as the Organisation of American States and the European Community in influencing tourism planning and policy.

'Hard' and 'soft' international law

One of the most important components of institutional arrangements for tourism at the international level is that of international law. International law helps proscribe the extent to which agreements undertaken between nations at the international level affect domestic arrangements. International law may be described as either 'hard' or 'soft'. Hard international law refers to firm and binding rules of law such as the content of treaties and the provisions of customary international law to which relevant nations are bound as a matter of obligation. Soft law refers to regulatory conduct which, because it is not provided for in a treaty, is not as binding as hard law. Examples of soft law include recommendations or declarations which are made by international conferences or organisations (Lyster 1985). For example, the Convention on Biological Diversity adopted at the United Nations Conference on Environment and Development (UNCED) in June 1992 in Rio de Janeiro may be regarded as hard international law. The recommendations of the same conference are examples of soft international law.

Soft law is particularly important in the area of international conservation and environmental law because treaties and conventions often require parties to attend regular meetings which make recommendations for implementation. For example, the World Heritage Convention has annual meetings of its members to discuss the progress of the implementation of the treaty. Agreed procedures under the Antarctic Treaty, the Man and the Biosphere Programme, and the World Conservation Strategy are all examples of soft environmental law that arose out of United Nations conferences and which have affected tourism development, planning and policy in various countries throughout the world.

One of the central issues in the enactment of treaties and conventions is the obligation that the international agreement places on the signatory. International law cannot be enforced in the same manner as domestic law, because nations can only rarely be compelled to perform their legal obligations, i.e. through the use of force. However, the moral obligations that accrue to members of the international diplomatic community and the norms of international relations are usually sufficient to gain compliance from nations. Soft law fixes norms of behaviour which nations should observe, but which cannot usually be enforced. As Lyster (1985 : 14) observed, 'states [i.e. nations] make every effort to enforce a treaty once they have become party to it: it is in the interests of almost every state that order, and not chaos, should be the governing principle of human life, and if treaties were made and freely ignored chaos would soon result'. Matters of international concern, for example, those covered by soft international law, do not necessarily have to be the subject of international treaties. However, the existence of a treaty, a convention or an agreed declaration may serve to provide evidence for such concern in domestic political life. For example, the World Heritage Convention (discussed below), does appear to oblige signatories to protect World Heritage property on their territory.

In contrast, implementation of the World Conservation Strategy (WCS), a forerunner to UNCED, was promoted by the IUCN which issued progress reports on the various requirements and actions. Implementation was not marked by the same set of legal obligations that characterise the World Heritage Convention. Instead, it rested upon the moral urgency that surrounds environmental problems and the priorities created by the strategy within the international community of nations. However, the WCS (IUCN 1980: Sec. 15.3) noted that 'perhaps the most important form of international action is the development of international conservation law and of the means to implement it' and specifically noted the 'four main global conservation conventions' (Sec. 15.4): the Convention on Wetlands of International Importance, Especially as Waterfowl Habitat (Wetlands Convention), Convention Concerning the Protection of the World Cultural and Natural Heritage (World Heritage Convention), Convention on International Trade in Endangered Species of Wild Fauna and Flora (CITES) and the Convention on Conservation of Migratory Species of Wild Animals (Migratory Species Convention). These have since been complemented by the Convention on Biological Diversity. In this way soft international law may act as a forerunner to the establishment of hard international law.

Trade

Probably the most significant series of international agreements for tourism policy at the macro level of policy making are those which are concerned with trade. International tourism trade issues are usually dealt with on either a bilateral or multilateral basis, although unilateral action may be taken by governments when they feel that their interests are being impeded. Many bilateral trade agreements relating to tourism are usually in the area of transport (e.g. air transport agreements) or investment (e.g. protection for foreign investment under most-favoured-nation status). Multilateral negotiations are often conducted under the auspices of international organisations. Three international trade organisations with an interest in tourism are the International

Monetary Fund (IMF), the Organisation for Economic Cooperation and Development (OECD), and the World Trade Organization (WTO). Organisations with a more specific interest in tourism activities include the World Tourism Organization (WTO), the International Civil Aviation Organization (ICAO), the International Maritime Organization (IMO), the Customs Cooperation Council (CCC), and regional bodies such as the Tourism Council of the South Pacific (TCSP) and the Tourism Program of the Organization of American States.

At the global level the United Nations Conference on International Travel and Tourism in Rome in 1963 was perhaps the first to highlight the role of tourism in economic development and in improving international relations, with the conference considering 'that it is incumbent on governments to stimulate and coordinate national tourist activities' (1963 : 17). Despite the economic significance of tourism to many countries and to the global economy as a whole, the establishment of trade regimes for tourism has not had the high profile of the agricultural or manufacturing sectors. This is most likely because of tourism's position as a service industry and as an 'invisible' export or import in many countries' trade balances. Such a situation has meant that, for many years, tourism has not been taken seriously as a priority area for policy development, particularly in developed countries (Williams and Shaw 1988a; Kearney 1992; Hall 1994; Davidson and Maitland 1997). However, economic restructuring of traditional industries and the recognition of service industries, including telecommunications and finance, as potential growth poles for economic development and employment purposes in Western economies has increased interest in tourism. Indeed, the Uruguay round of GATT, concluded in December 1993, gave substantial attention to mechanisms to encourage freer trade in the area of services.

The organisation which has probably focused most on trade liberalisation in the area of tourism services is the Organisation for Economic Cooperation and Development (OECD) based in Paris. Created in 1961, the OECD groups 29 member countries in an organisation that, 'provides governments a setting in which to discuss, develop and perfect economic and social policy. They compare experiences, seek answers to common problems and work to coordinate domestic and international policies that increasingly in today's globalised world must form a web of even practice across nations' (OECD 1999). OECD countries produce two thirds of the world's goods and services and account for about 70% of the world's international tourism trade. However, the OECD does not perceive itself as an exclusive club, instead regarding membership as limited only by a country's commitment to a market economy and a pluralistic democracy.

Although the OECD provides economic statistics and forecasts, the latter of which may be particularly influential in affecting investment flows and currency exchange rates, it is as a policy forum that the OECD has had the most significant long-term effect on tourism policy. At an informal level the policy debate within the OECD leads to 'policy learning' between countries, by which we mean that elements of policies and institutional arrangements in one country are modelled on another country's experiences. This has been particularly important with respect to the organisation of tourism at the national, and even state/provincial level in Australia, Canada and New Zealand, for example. In formal terms policy discussion can lead to the development of formal agreements, e.g. by establishing legally binding codes for free flow of capital and services.

Although the OECD has produced comparative information on tourism statistics and policy between member nations, its major contribution to tourism has been in the area of international tourist trade liberalisation (Davidson and Maitland 1997). The Ad Hoc Working Party on Obstacles to International Tourism for the OECD's Committee on Tourism identified 40 specific obstacles to international travel and tourism in five different areas (Table 5.1): first, those affecting companies providing services to facilitate travel (e.g. travel agents). Second, those affecting companies providing transportation (e.g. airlines, coach operators). Third, those affecting companies providing reception facilities (e.g. hotels). Fourth, obstacles affecting the individual intending to travel (e.g. currency restrictions, restrictions on overseas travel). Fifth, other obstacles such as discriminatory regulations (Ascher 1984; OECD 1991).

In examining obstacles to international travel and tourism, Ascher (1984 : 3) has identified a number of government-imposed restrictions which affect tourist trade:

- Government attention to tourism is focused more on promotion of inbound tourist business rather than on a more general approach that deals with reduction or removal of restrictions to tourism on a worldwide basis.
- Governments have not fully assessed the 'tourism impact' of their laws and regulations.
- Government policies concerning international relations – political, economic, monetary, financial – often conflict with, and override, tourism policy.
- For the most part, the international organizations that address problems of tourism deal with them mainly in piecemeal fashion and not with tourism as an integral unit.
- Although there is some coordination among international organizations on tourism matters, greater cooperation would improve their effectiveness.
- There is a lack of general internationally accepted rules and principles for dealing with new problems as they arise, as well as a mechanism for dispute settlement.

Obstacles to tourism can further be classified as to whether they constitute tariff or non-tariff barriers. Non-tariff barriers include travel allowance restrictions, restrictions on credit card use, limitations on duty-free allowances, and advance-import-deposit like measures (e.g. compulsory deposits prior to travel). Tariff barriers include import-duty measures, airport departures or airport taxes, and subsidies, for example, a consumer-subsidy measure such as an official preferential exchange rate for foreign tourists or price concessions. Although tourism tariff barriers may be lowered by specific tourism agreements, tariffs are usually dealt with under broader multilateral negotiations on tariff reductions on trade in goods and services, e.g. the World Trade Organisation, or negotiations within a specific trading bloc such as the European Community, the Association of South East Asian Nations (ASEAN) or the North American Free Trade Agreement (NAFTA) between Canada, Mexico

Table 5.1   Types of obstacles to international tourism

I. Obstacles affecting the individual intending to travel

1   Imposed by the home country:
    (a) Currency restrictions imposed upon residents.
    (b) Conditions and procedures for issue of travel documents.
    (c) Customs allowances for returning residents.
    (d) Restrictions on overseas travel.

2   Imposed by the host country:
    (a) Currency restrictions imposed upon visitors.
    (b) Entry visas, identity documents, limitations on duration of stay.
    (c) Formalities concerning entry of motor vehicles, pleasure boats or other craft.
    (d) Formalities concerning applicability of drivers licences, car insurance, etc.
    (e) Restrictions on acquisition of property by non-nationals (e.g. holiday flats).
    (f) Taxes on foreign visitors.

II. Obstacles affecting companies providing services to facilitate travel (e.g. travel agents, tour operators)

3   Limitations on foreign investment/equity participation.
4   Restrictions on the establishment of foreign owned entities (branches and subsidiaries).
5   Requirements for qualifications for operating professionally which are either directly discriminatory or more difficult for non-nationals to acquire.
6   Restrictions on non-national personnel and employment (e.g. visas, work permits).
7   Difficulties in obtaining licences to operate.
8   Relevant restrictions on transfer of funds in and out of the country (not covered under I above).
9   Restrictions upon the ability of non-established foreign companies to solicit for custom, advertise or sell direct to clients without locally established intermediaries.
10   Distinction in EEC countries between EEC and non-EEC nationals with regard to the above items.

III. Obstacles affecting companies providing transportation (e.g. airline, railways, coach operators, cruise liners)

11–18 Categories as under II (3–10).
19   Restrictions on non-national airlines, coach operators or cruise liners.
20   Limitations on movements of passengers by foreign airlines or cruise ships.
21   Discriminatory landing dues, taxes or port charges.
22   Lack of reciprocal recognition of qualifications (e.g. air crew, site guides, coach drivers).
23   Requirements for government employees to use national airlines/ferry services.
24   Discriminatory access to special terms from state enterprises (e.g. airlines, railways), including differential commissions.
25   Limitations on access to reservation systems.

Table 5.1 (cont'd)

IV. Obstacles affecting companies providing reception facilities (e.g. hotels, resorts, car hire firms)

26–33 Categories as under II (3–10).

34 Restrictions on imports of essential goods.

35 Requirements for placing of contracts (e.g. for site development) with local enterprises.

36 Discriminatory tax regimes for foreign entrants (including tax holidays not available to nationals).

37 Restrictions on ownership by non-nationals (e.g. leasing only permitted) and problems related to security of tenure or repatriation of investments.

38 Limitation on access to reservation systems.

V. Other obstacles

39 Discriminatory regulations on health inspection/consumer protection, etc.

40 Compulsory use of centralized governmental/municipal organizations or middlemen.

41 Others.

Source: Ad Hoc Working Party on Obstacles to International Tourism for the OECD's Committee on Tourism in Ascher (1984 : 14).

or the United States; or through bilateral agreements, e.g. the Closer Economic Relations (CER) agreement between Australia and New Zealand (Hall 1994). In addition, attempts to liberalise international trade in tourism services are also encouraged through the action of international organisations such as the World Tourism Organization and the World Travel and Tourism Council.

The World Tourism Organization

The World Tourism Organization (WTO) is the leading international policy organisation in the tourism field, being particularly influential in less developed nations and in the United Nations system of organisations of which it is a member. In 1998 its membership included 138 countries and territories and over 350 Affiliate Members representing local government, tourism associations, private sector companies, and educational institutions. 'Through tourism, WTO aims to stimulate economic growth and job creation, provide incentives for protecting the environment and heritage of destinations, and promote peace and understanding among all the nations of the world' (WTO 1999).

Although a member of the United Nations system its origins predate the establishment of the UN. The WTO was originally formed in 1925 as the International Union of Official Tourist Publicity Organizations based at The Hague in the Netherlands. After the Second World War it was renamed the International Union for Official Tourism Organizations (IUOTO) and moved to Geneva. As international tourism and the corresponding complexity of inter-governmental relations with respect to tourism grew in the 1960s, IOUTO sought to have a stronger role in international tourism and the United Nations system in a similar fashion to the World Health Organization (WHO), UNESCO and the International Civil Aviation Organization (ICAO). In December 1969 the UN General Assembly passed a resolution which recognised such a role, with the resolution being ratified in 1974 by 51 of the nations whose official tourism organisations were members of IUOTO.

In 1975 IUOTO was renamed the World Tourism Organization with its first General Assembly being held in Madrid where the Secretariat was also installed in the following year at the invitation of the Spanish government, which provided a building and other financial assistance for the organisation. In 1976, WTO became an executing agency of the United Nations Development Programme (UNDP) and in 1977, a formal cooperation agreement was signed with the United Nations itself. Although full (national) and affiliate membership have grown over the years, it is noticeable that a number of OECD member countries, such as Australia, Canada, New Zealand and the United States, are not members of the WTO. In part this is because officials from these countries, while cooperating with the WTO, rightly or wrongly do not perceive the organisation as 'providing value for money' and, perhaps, do not have the influence on the direction of WTO policies and undertakings as they might wish.

The funding basis for the WTO is also interesting. WTO is primarily financed by members' contributions. Full Members pay an annual quota calculated according to the level of economic development and the importance of tourism in each country. Associate Members pay a fixed annual contribution of US$20,000 and Affiliate Members pay US$1700 a year. Associate and affiliate members have the opportunity to participate in WTO policy fora and may also be in a better position to enter into partnership arrangements with the WTO in development projects. WTO's budget for the two-year period 1996–97 totalled US$18,099,000, membership dues accounting for about 90% of the budget, with the remainder coming from UNDP support costs, consultancies, investment income and sales of publications and electronic products (WTO 1999). Indeed, one of the greatest challenges facing the WTO is the generation of funding to finance its activities, which is leading to an increasing focus on partnerships with industry and, possibly, changes in the focus of WTO organisational philosophies.

At the policy level the activities of the WTO have been substantial. Although the outputs of the WTO may be regarded as soft international law their influence is still significant. For example, former WTO secretary-general Antonio Enrìquez Savignac attended the Rio Earth Summit in 1992 and was instrumental in getting tourism included in Agenda 21 as one of the only industries capable of providing an economic incentive for preservation of the environment (WTO 1999). Although sustainable development has been one focus of WTO policy activity, other areas such as trade liberalisation (WTO 1998a, 1998b), public–private partnerships (WTO 1998c, 1998d), health and safety have also been important. Examples of such policy measures include the development of

- Tourism Bill of Rights and Tourist Code (1985, resolution of Sofia conference)
- Recommended Measures for Safety
- Creating Tourism Opportunities for Handicapped People
- Health Information and Formalities in International Travel
- WTO Statement on the Prevention of Organized Sex Tourism
- The Manila Declaration on World Tourism (1980)
- The Hague Declaration on Tourism (declaration of the Inter-Parliamentary Conference on Tourism, jointly organised with the Inter-Parliamentary Union) (1989)
- The Bali Declaration on Tourism (1996).

Such is the importance of public–private partnerships that in 1998 the WTO announced the composition of a Strategic Group to advise the WTO Secretary-General on implementation of an active public–private partnership within WTO. The members of the Strategic Group were announced as being, representing the government sector: EMBRATUR President Caio Luiz de Carvalho; Egyptian Tourism Minister Mamdouh El Beltagui; Maldives Tourism Minister Ibrahim Hussain Zaki; Honorary WTO Secretary-General Antonio Enriquez Savignac; Swiss Tourism Chief Peter Keller; and the Tunisian Tourism Minister Slaheddine Maâoui. Representing the private sector are: Martin Brackenbury, chairman of the WTO Business Council and President of the International Federation of Tour Operators; Geoffrey Lipman, President of the World Travel and Tourism Council; Isao Matsuhashi, Chairman of the Japan Travel Bureau and the Japan Association of Travel Agents; Bill Norman, President and CEO of the Travel Industry Association of America; and Stefano Torda, Deputy Secretary-General of CONFCOMMERCIO and formerly tourism director of Italy (WTO 1998e). The composition of the group is interesting as it conveys an appreciation of the networks that exist both within the WTO and between the WTO and other organisations.

In addition to its policy function, the WTO also has substantial influence on national and regional tourism development and plays an important role as a land use and tourist resource planner. This function is significant not only for its direct impact on tourism development, particularly in developing countries, but also because it illustrates the manner in which the activities of international bodies operate at lower scales of the tourism policy and planning process all the way through to the regional and local level, affecting various stakeholders at all these levels. The WTO acts as an executing agency of the United Nations Development Programme (UNDP), while other planning and development activities are secured through consultancies and financing from other national and international agencies. According to the WTO (1999), US$4.4 million worth of development activities was undertaken in 42 countries in the operating period 1996–97. Example of WTO planning and development projects include:

- strategy for environmentally sustainable development of India's Andaman Islands (1996)
- tourism master plan in Ghana (1996)
- reconstruction and development plan in Lebanon (1997)
- action plan for sustainable tourism development in Uzbekistan (1997).

Although the WTO has a significant role to play in tourism at the international level, the growth in international tourism has also led to the development of international organisations with interests in tourism, particularly at the supranational level. Private sector organisations such as the World Travel and Tourism Council, the OECD and supranational organisations such as the European Community and the Organization of American States are all competing for policy ascendancy in influencing international tourism policy debate and the subsequent development of international agreements on tourism matters. Substantial policy shifts have occurred in recent years, including within the WTO, where greater emphasis has been given to liberalisation of trade and encouragement of further development. As Burns 1994 (in Davidson and Maitland 1997 : 119) observed, 'it is clear . . . that WTO is actively promoting the expansion of tourism at a global level. WTO survives not so much through its membership fees (governments and affiliates) but through spin-off activities such as consulting and project management. It therefore actually needs more tourism!' A sustainable WTO therefore requires tourism to continue to exist and grow. That the WTO perceives itself as assuming the leadership role in world tourism is beyond doubt. As the WTO Secretary-General, Francesco Frangialli, stated, 'In the absence of the European Union's capacity to make itself felt in the tourism sphere, the World Tourism Organization remains today the principal body concerned with tourism cooperation between European countries' (WTO 1998f). With the Secretary-General adding that it was unfortunate that the world's two most important tourist areas, Europe and the United States, lack overall strategies and vision for tourism development (WTO 1998f). Nevertheless, as we shall see later on in the chapter both Europe and the Americas both have significant supranational bodies developing strategies for tourism development.

The development of international conservation and environmental law

The institutional arrangements surrounding conservation and the environment clearly have substantial impact on tourism planning and development. It is not as easy to define the precise boundaries of environmental law as it is to define a traditional area such as criminal law. Since World War II environmental law has expanded as concerns over environmental quality have arisen not only on a domestic level but also in the international sphere. Ecological processes do not recognise legal boundaries. Acid rain, the ozone layer, the greenhouse effect, sea level rise and the Chernobyl disaster are all testimony to the transnational basis of environmental problems. Issues of pollution, wildlife protection, conservation of biodiversity and the preservation of cultural and natural heritage have become international in scope.

Environmental law may be defined as: 'any regulation which affects the natural environment *per se*; or which declares the right of any person to take action to develop or protect it; or which might affect the scenic, historical, artistic or cultural beauty or appreciation of man's efforts to harmonize the built and natural environments' (Bates 1983 : 2). Environmental law may be broadly categorised as having two components: 'protective' and 'exploitative'. 'Protective' rules protecting the natural environment from human activity and conserve the built and cultural environments, and 'exploitative' rules control the disposition of natural resources and facilitate development. Legislation may combine both components, but conceptually it may be useful to separate them.

Although the setting aside of areas, such as national parks, wilderness areas and reserves, which are also significant tourist attractions, for the protection of species and biodiversity is an important part of international strategies for sustainable development, such a protective component is not new at the international level. For example, the Convention for the Preservation of Wild Animals, Birds and Fish in Africa was signed in London in May 1900. The first convention to refer to the preservation of wilderness areas was the 1940 Convention on Nature Protection and Wildlife Preservation in the Western Hemisphere, which was restricted to members of the Organization of American States (formerly the Pan American Union). This Convention defines in Article 1(4) the expression 'Strict Wilderness Reserve': 'A region under public control characterized by primitive conditions of flora, fauna, transportation and habitation wherein there is no provisions for the passage of motorized transportation and all commercial developments are excluded.' This definition is complemented by Article 4 which states: 'The contracting governments agree to maintain the strict wilderness reserves inviolate as far as practicable except for duly authorized scientific investigations or government inspection or such uses as are consistent with the purposes for which the area was established.'

As Lyster (1985 : 96) commented, the Convention 'was a visionary instrument, well ahead of its time in terms of the concepts it espouses'. It preceded the United States Wilderness Act by some 24 years. Its great weakness was that it did not establish an administrative structure to implement its terms. This may be compared with the World Heritage Convention, which we shall examine below, which has a World Heritage Bureau and a mechanism with which to implement its terms. Nevertheless, the objectives of the Western Hemisphere Convention set an important precedent in the field of international conservation and environment agreements. The Convention's preamble states that it is the desire of the parties to:

> protect and preserve in their natural habitat representatives of all species and genera of native flora and fauna, including migratory birds, in sufficient numbers and over areas extensive enough to assure them from becoming extinct through any agency within man's control.
> . . . protect and preserve scenery of extraordinary beauty, unusual and striking geologic formations, regions and natural objects of aesthetic, historic or scientific value, and areas characterized by primitive conditions in those cases covered by this Convention.

These goals were to be achieved through the establishment of national parks, reserves, nature monuments and strict wilderness reserves. Although the Convention has become something of a 'sleeping treaty' (Lyster 1985 : 111), in terms of its implementation throughout much of the Americas, it still remains a significant agreement in international conservation. The precedent established by the Convention has also had implications in domestic disputes surrounding the preservation of wilderness areas. For example, Guilbert (1973, in Coggins and Wilkinson 1981 : 785) argued that the convention places an obligation on the United States to keep wilderness areas inviolate. However, 'no court has yet accepted or even seriously considered Mr Guilbert's unique thesis' (Coggins and Wilkinson 1981 : 787). In Australia, the convention was referred to in the Franklin Dam case (Coper 1983) in the High Court in establishing the degree of international concern surrounding the preservation of the world's heritage. Therefore, international institutional arrangements, such as those of conservation law and regulation, can substantially influence domestic conservation policies from the national through to the local level, an issue which is discussed with respect to the implementation of the World Heritage Convention.

The World Heritage Convention

> The philosophy behind the Convention is straightforward: there are some parts of the world's natural and cultural heritage which are so unique and scientifically important to the world as a whole that their conservation and protection for present and future generations is not only a matter of concern for individual nations but for the international community as a whole (Slatyer 1983 : 138).

> World Heritage Sites are contemporary tourism magnets and national icons that continue to influence present values. They are treasures in the fullest and deepest sense. They must be managed in such a way that they are preserved for future generations and at the same time presently made accessible to the public for its education and enjoyment. Finding the proper balance between these two demands is the difficult and important task of World Heritage Site managers (ICOMOS 1993 : 1).

The Convention for the Protection of the World's Cultural and Natural Heritage (WHC), to give it its full name, was adopted by a United Nations Scientific, Education and Cultural Organisation (UNESCO) Conference on 16 November 1972. The convention came into force in December 1975, when 20 nations had ratified it. The convention is 'an innovative legal instrument' (Slatyer 1984 : 734) designed to enable nations to cooperate in the protection of cultural and natural sites of outstanding value to humanity. 'The Convention provides a permanent legal, administrative and financial framework for international co-operation for the safe guarding of the cultural and natural heritage of mankind' (Australian Heritage Commission 1983 : 5.1) and may be regarded as one of the pinnacles of world conservation (Eidsvik 1980; McNeely and Miller 1983; Hales 1984; McNeely 1984).

The signatories commit themselves to assist in the identification, protection, conservation and preservation of World Heritage properties. They undertake to refrain from 'any deliberate measure which might damage directly or indirectly' cultural or natural heritage (Art. 6(3)), and to 'take appropriate legal,

Plate 5.1   Proposed site of the Franklin Dam, Tasmania, Australia. Australia's accession to the World Heritage Convention provided the necessary legal basis to stop the dam from being built and reducing the high wilderness qualities of the region.

scientific, technical, administrative and financial measures necessary for [its] identification, protection, conservation, presentation and rehabilitation' (Art. 5d).

The convention is administered by the Intergovernmental Committee for the Protection of the World Cultural and Natural Heritage, commonly referred to as the World Heritage Committee, which is composed of 21 states elected at a general assembly of State Parties to the convention every two years. The committee is the key policy and decision-making body. It is responsible for all decisions pertaining to nominations to the World Heritage List and the World Heritage in Danger List, and to requests for assistance under the World Heritage fund. As the operational guidelines for the implementation of the convention noted, the committee has three essential functions:

(i) to identify, on the basis of nominations submitted by State Parties, cultural and natural properties of outstanding universal value which are to be protected under the Convention and to list those properties on the 'World Heritage List';

(ii) to decide which properties included in the World Heritage List are to be inscribed on the 'List of World Heritage in Danger';

(iii) to determine in what way and under what conditions the resources in the World Heritage Fund can most advantageously be used to assist State Parties, as far as possible, in the protection of their properties of outstanding universal value (World Heritage Committee 1984 : 3).

The committee elects a bureau which is responsible for detailed examination of new nominations and requests for funding. The bureau consists of a chairperson, a rapporteur and five vice-chairpersons elected from World Heritage Committee membership. The committee and the bureau receive technical advice for 'cultural' sites from the International Council for Monuments and Sites (ICOMOS) and the International Center for Conservation in Rome (ICCROM), while for 'natural' properties the advisory body is the International Union for Conservation of Nature and Natural Resources (IUCN). UNESCO provides a secretariat to help implement the decisions of the committee. A World Heritage Fund has also been established to provide financial and technical assistance to those nations which otherwise would not be in a position to fulfil their obligations under the convention.

All signatories to the convention are invited to identify and submit nominations of outstanding universal value to the World Cultural and Natural Heritage List. This is a 'select list of the most outstanding' cultural and natural properties 'from an international viewpoint' (World Heritage Committee 1984 : 4). Cultural property nominated to the World Heritage List (WHL) should:

21(a) (i) represent a unique artistic achievement, a masterpiece of the creative genius; or

(ii) have exerted great influence, over a span of time or within a cultural area of the world, on developments in architecture, monumental arts or town-planning and landscaping; or

(iii) bear a unique or at least exceptional testimony to a civilization which has disappeared; or

(iv) be an outstanding example of a type of building or architectural ensemble which illustrates a significant stage in history; or

(v) be an outstanding example of a traditional human settlement which is representative of a culture and which has become vulnerable under the impact of irreversible change; or

(vi) be directly or tangibly associated with events or with ideas or beliefs of outstanding universal significance (the Committee considers that this criterion should justify inclusion in the List only in exceptional circumstances or in conjunction with other criteria); *and*

(b)   meet the test of authenticity in design, materials, workmanship or setting (the Committee stressed that reconstruction is only acceptable if it is carried out on the basis of complete and detailed documentation on the original and to no extent on conjecture) (World Heritage Committee 1984 : 7–8).

Natural property nominated to the WHL should:

24 (i)   be outstanding examples representing the *major stages of the earth's evolutionary history*; or
   (ii)   be outstanding examples representing *significant ongoing geological processes, biological evolution and man's interaction with his natural environment*; as distinct from the periods of the earth's development, this focuses upon ongoing processes in the development of communities of plants and animals, landforms and marine areas and fresh water bodies; or
   (iii)   contain *superlative natural phenomena, formations or features*, for instance, outstanding examples of the most important ecosystems, areas of exceptional natural beauty or exceptional combinations of natural and cultural elements; or
   (iv)   contain *the most important and significant natural habitats where threatened species of animals or plants of outstanding universal value* from the point of view of science or conservation still survive (World Heritage Committee 1984 : 8–9).

Nominations need to provide a detailed account of the characteristics of each site (World Heritage Committee 1984). Each nomination must be endorsed by the national government, and be signed by the government authority which is responsible for the implementation of the convention. Following endorsement, the nomination is sent to the UNESCO secretariat via the UNESCO National Commission of the nominating signatory. The Secretariat passes nominations for cultural properties to ICOMOS or ICCROM and for natural properties to IUCN (World Conservation Union). These bodies rigorously analyse the nomination to determine whether the property concerned meets the World Heritage criteria and is of outstanding universal value. The World Heritage Bureau, acting upon the advice of ICOMOS, ICCROM or the IUCN, can make three types of recommendations to the World Heritage Committee. Nominations may be accepted, rejected or deferred until further information is available.

The commitment of the World Heritage Committee to ensure that the WHL retains the criterion of universal significance in the assessment of nominations is indicated in its willingness to reject or defer unsuitable nominations. The acceptance of nominations to the list which are clearly not of World Heritage standard is regarded as devaluing the purpose of the convention and the protection that it provides for the world's cultural and natural heritage. Through the international and national attention which is focused on the nomination process, 'the inclusion of a property on the World Heritage List should give added protection to the site' (Slatyer 1983 : 142). In addition to the prestige attached to a World Heritage site, a degree of protection under international law, and a possible increase in the attraction of the site as a tourism destination may be expected. Yet, the WHL is not necessarily unchanging.

Table 5.2   World Heritage List sites by status, December 1998

Category	Number of sites	Percentage of sites (%)
Cultural	445	76.5
Natural	117	20.1
Mixed	20	3.4
Total	592	100

Source: UNESCO, www.unesco.org/whc.

Properties which have been degraded through either human or natural causes may be deleted from the WHL and placed on the World Heritage in Danger List. It is hoped that the prospect of a site being placed on the latter list will focus enough attention to save it before the 'symbolic fate' of deregistration occurs. Furthermore, the World Heritage Committee is constantly seeking to update the procedures by which nominations are reviewed in order to ensure that nominated properties fit the criteria for World Heritage listing.

The sites of the WHL can be classified into cultural, natural or mixed sites depending on which criteria they meet. Table 5.2 reports the numbers and percentages of cultural, natural and mixed heritage sites on the WHL as of December 1998. Cultural listings far outnumber natural sites, in spite of the fact that the Operational Guidelines recommend a balance between the two categories. However, according to von Droste (1995), Director of the World Heritage Centre and editor of the World Heritage Newsletter, despite the continuous expansion of properties on the WHL each year, it does still not fully reflect the world's cultural and natural diversity. Pocock (1997) is also critical of the greater attention given in the Operational Guidelines to the inscription criteria for cultural properties compared to natural properties. The Committee has recommended that measures be taken to improve the balance between cultural and natural heritage. One way they hope to achieve this is by offering assistance in the preparation of nominations of types of properties under-represented in the WHL (http://www.unesco.org/whc; www.unesco.org/whc (accessed 19.08.98). There have been a number of suggestions as to why the existing imbalance has occurred, including the fact that there are few parts of the natural world untouched or influenced by humankind in some way, and nominations for often larger natural areas can be associated with controversy and opposed at a local level for commercial and economic reasons. For example, the nomination of Australia's Wet Tropics World Heritage area resulted in conflict between environmentalists and professional scientists with logging companies and the Queensland Government (Hall 1992; Mercer 1995).

The nomination process and the additional prestige gained by receiving World Heritage status can only serve to increase the attraction of a site as a tourist destination for both domestic and international tourists. Furthermore, given the qualities possessed by World Heritage Sites it is not surprising that they are popular tourist attractions and destinations. For example, Shackley observes that, 'such sites are magnets for visitors and the enrollment of a new

Plate 5.2   Mount Cook National Park, New Zealand. The Park is part of the South Westland World Heritage Area and is a major attraction for visitors interested in natural history and the environment.

property on the World Heritage List, with the concomitant publicity, is virtually a guarantee that visitor numbers will increase' (Shackley 1998, preface). Similarly, Cook (1990 in Drost 1996 : 481) observes, 'It appears that designation does increase visibility through public information generated by the World Heritage Committee, the host State and the private sector,' while Ashworth and Tunbridge (1990) take a more jaundiced view, noting, 'The coveted UNESCO designation of World Heritage Site is used for national aggrandizement and commercial advantage within the international competition for tourists, more often than it is a celebration of an international identity.'

Although tourism is a beneficiary of World Heritage listing, the benefit is clearly not all one way. Tourism is a way to help ensure the conservation of World Heritage sites through revenue generation and creating awareness of their significance and, possibly, encouraging the application of principles of sustainable development to site management and planning (Drost 1996). The philosophy underlying the Convention also has implications with respect to tourism. The Convention states that a site is to remain open to visitors so that heritage identities can be strengthened in the public mind. The obligation to promote World Heritage sites is complemented by an obligation to protect these sites; however, promotion often threatens the site protection. Under the Convention, protection should take precedence over promotion, as is indicated in the full title of the Convention (Drost 1996). Nevertheless, World Heritage sites offer many practical advantages to the tourism industry as they possess many of the features that create a successful tourism attraction. World

Plate 5.3   Cliff Palace World Heritage Site, Mesa Verde National Park, Colorado, USA.

Heritage listing offers a clear and recognisable brand with an international profile. The listing processes identifies the characteristics that makes the site unique, while also reinforcing ideas of authenticity. In addition, the reservation process clearly identifies the boundaries of any listing which can then correspond to the space that tourists may seek to occupy.

The WHC therefore clearly has implications for tourism. To reiterate the theme picked up earlier in the chapter – decisions and actions taken at the international level clearly have the capacity to reverberate through the national, regional and local levels in a manner which has substantial implications for tourism planning and policy. Hales (1984) in discussing the status and direction of the WHC noted that 'Conventions, like babies, must crawl before

Plate 5.4   Acropolis, Athens, Greece. Accorded World Heritage status, the Acropolis is under substantial pressures from both visitor impact and the affects of air pollution.

Plate 5.5   Tour group at the Acropolis, Athens, Greece.

Plate 5.6 Streetscape, Roros, Norway. The World Heritage area includes this streetscape which is a major attraction to visitors.

Plate 5.7 Smelter turned museum, Roros, Norway. This award winning museum interprets the industrial heritage of the World Heritage site to visitors.

they can walk, and walk before they can run. This Convention is both preco-
cious and far from recognizing its potential.' McMichael and Gare (1984 : 262)
noted that international conventions, such as World Heritage, 'will be used to
give status, and therefore additional protection, to important protected areas'.
While increased protection is a possibility created, the relationship between
World Heritage listing and tourism may also create substantial tension between
local and global policy goals and institutions:

> Many World Heritage Sites are in countries that simply do not have the money or
> the expertise to meet international conservation standards. Even when there is
> a national awareness, financial support for even minimal conservation is 15 or
> 20 years away. There are too many other needs on the national agenda. These
> countries need an interim plan that will initiate basic conservation steps. They
> need to match this plan with a tourism plan that promotes their World Heritage
> Site as magnets for only limited tourism. Such a plan of action would help conserve
> the sites for future generations, allow access and appreciation among the present
> generations. Such a plan of action would help generate income for the national
> economy without endangering the national patrimony. In the future, World Heritage
> Sites may become the high-priced, hard-to-get-into attractions in the tourism
> world (ICOMOS 1993 : 3–4).

However, a difficult balancing act will need to be undertaken:

> The World Heritage convention requires that nations not only protect, conserve
> and rehabilitate World Heritage sites; it also requires that these sites be given a
> function in the life of the community. The point is not to place these treasures
> under lock and key but to make them safely part of the fabric of life. There is a
> dilemma here that re-emphasises the need for balance: old sites, residents, new
> numbers of visitors (ICOMOS 1993 : 4).

The tension between the global and the local, between different conceptions of use and value, operating within the context of the Convention has
probably been seen more in federal systems, such as Australia and Canada,
which accentuates the political goals of different levels of governance, than
anywhere else. Indeed, few arrangements of international and domestic law
can have been so misunderstood and distorted as the operation of the WHC
in Australia in the 1980s (e.g. Davis 1985, 1989a, 1989b; P. Hall 1992:
Mercer 1995). 'Insofar as calculation is possible, Australia has probably had
more litigation and political challenges to the Convention than all other states
party to the Convention combined' (Suter 1991 : 4). In commenting on the
1983 Franklin Dam case, Davis (1984 : 186) noted that it was 'apparent that
many politicians and the lay public had a rather confused view of what the
World Heritage Convention entailed and how the nomination procedure
operated. In particular few people appeared to know what Australian institutions were involved in World Heritage activities and how such bodies related
to UNESCO in Paris'. Nevertheless, it can be noted that similar controversy
occurred in New Zealand in the case of the nomination of South Westland to
the WHL with respect to perceptions that local land was going to be under
UNESCO control and concerns over the lack of recognition of local cultural
values (Kirby 1993).

The local impact of World Heritage listing is in fact substantial it proscribes appropriate and inappropriate activities in terms of maintenance of the integrity of the World Heritage values, it requires the conduct of a management plan while, with respect to natural values, section 44(b)(vi) of the Operational Guidelines states that the site 'should have adequate long-term legislative, regulatory or institutional protection. The boundaries should include sufficient areas immediately adjacent to the area of outstanding universal value in order to protect the site's heritage values from direct effects of human encroachment and impacts of resource use outside of the nominated area' (UNESCO, http://www.unesco.org:80//whc/opgutoc.htm (accessed 11 January 1999)). It is not the intention to discuss the manner in which tourism planning for World Heritage sites should be done. Instead, let us reiterate the highly visible relationship, between global policy and institutional arrangements and local resource use and development, that exists in the case of WHC. International agreements, policies and laws therefore act both to directly affect local land use as well as circumscribe the planning and policy processes that are occurring at the local level. Many hard international laws, as with a number of global conservation conventions, typically have spatial outcomes which are clearly discernible, e.g. the creation or recognition of a reserve such as a national park, while others are not so immediately visible, such as those which affect business practice. Nevertheless, they are real, they exist and they may have enormous implications for tourism planning and policy. The next section will look at some of these connections at the supranational level.

The supranational scale

The scope of supranational tourism policy and planning has grown substantially in recent years. The increased internationalisation of the world's economy and policy making has led to the development of regional trade alliances and groupings, e.g. NAFTA, APEC (Asia Pacific Economic Cooperation), while international groupings have developed in all manner of human affairs. Indeed, one of the outcomes of economic globalisation has been not only increased awareness of the importance of the local but also increased attention to regional groupings of nations within which problems, which are now recognised as being international in scope, e.g. economic development, pollution, natural resource management, can be addressed. Tourism has also been strongly influenced by the development of such international bodies. However, the scope of such organisations is substantial, ranging from government membership only (e.g. ASEAN (Association of South East Asian Nations)) through to public–private partnerships, e.g. Baltic Sea Tourism Commission, and fully private-oriented international organisations, e.g. End Child Prostitution in Asian Tourism (ECPAT). Furthermore, the goals of supranational organisations may range from being solely concerned with tourism, e.g. the Pacific Asia Tourism Association, through to a policy portfolio of which tourism is only a small part, e.g. European Union. Nevertheless, the actions of such organisations may be extremely significant in tourism policy and planning terms. While policy and planning occurs at the supranational level, the effects of policy decisions will often be enacted at the local, leading to significant outcomes for the processes of tourism development and for local communities. This section will discuss two examples of tourism within supranational organisations, the European Union and the Organisation of American States.

European Union

Tourism is an area of great economic significance to the European Union (EU). Tourism accounts for approximately 5.5% of GDP, around 5% of export earnings and over 6% of total jobs. Although Europe's market share, in terms of both arrivals and revenue, of international tourism is tending to diminish in relation to other world regions, notably the Asia-Pacific region, Europe is still a major force in world tourism, with increased ease of travel between the EU member countries encouraging ongoing tourism growth. Indeed, the Mediterranean basin alone accounts for 35% of the international tourist trade and is the world's leading tourist area. The number of tourists in the Mediterranean region could grow to as many as 380–760 million per year in 2025, depending on the economic growth rates. This development would be in addition to predicted demographic changes in the area. 160 million of these tourists in the year 2000 and 260 million in the year 2025 would visit Mediterranean coastal areas, as compared to 55 million in 1984 and around 100 million in 1990, with up to 90% of any increase accruing to EU member states in the region (EU 1993).

Although the European Parliament has been relatively slow in establishing policies for tourism relative to other economic, social and environmental areas of interest (e.g. see Barnes and Barnes 1993), the extent of EU involvement in tourism is not as insubstantial as may be suggested by the comments of the WTO Secretary-General quoted earlier in this chapter. Indeed, as we shall see, the EU has a substantial impact on tourism development in Europe.

Tourism has become a significant part of EU planning and policies for a number of reasons.

- Tourism is now recognised as an important economic activity.
- The transnational character of some tourism businesses has necessitated the development of a European-wide policy framework.
- The cultural impacts of tourism have raised concerns over the retention of cultural identity while at the same time attempting to promote the concept of Europe.
- The movement of pollution across national boundaries and the possible movement of capital to locate where environmental standards and costs are lowest. Indeed, the environmental dimensions of tourism have developed as a major EU concern in the tourism area (European Commission 1995; Bramwell et al. 1996).
- Concerns over the social dimensions of poverty and unemployment, particularly in disadvantaged regions, given impetus to the use of tourism as a tool for employment generation and economic development at a regional level (Jenkins et al. 1998).

Nevertheless, as early as the early 1980s, the European Parliament and the Council had adopted resolutions concerning the development of a policy for tourism. However, the EU's first tangible action in favour of tourism was the Council Decision of 21 December 1988 declaring 1990 the 'European Year of Tourism'. The objective of the EYT was to exploit the integrating role of tourism in the creation of a citizens' Europe and to stress the economic and social importance of the tourism sector (EU 1998: Sec. 8). ECU 7.74 million was spent on the EYT from the Community budget. Independently of the EYT, appropriations were granted by the EU for measures in the field of tourism, which increased from ECU 3 million in 1989 to ECU 4.9 million in 1992, and for the promotion of European tourism in non-member states which amounted to ECU 1.75 million in the 1992 to 1993 period (EU 1998, Sec.10). Since the Treaty on European Union has come into force, tourism has been included in the Treaty establishing the European Community (EU 1998).

In 1994, the European Court of Auditors based in Luxembourg carried out a horizontal audit of tourist policy and the promotion of tourism. On the occasion of its first on-the-spot audit at the Commission, the Court found that there had been serious irregularities, leading to the suspension of two members of DG XXIII's staff (Directorates-General XXIII which is responsible for enterprise, trade, tourism and social economy policy), and that the Commission had not released any information on this matter. However, the report by the Court (EU 1998) provides a valuable account of EU tourism, particularly with respect to expenditure and problems of coordination, which will be referred to below.

EU tourism measures can be divided into direct measures which are provided for in the general budget and indirect measures in which tourism plays an instrumental role towards the realisation of other objectives. However, the financial volume of the direct measures represents less than 1% of total EU expenditure on tourism (EU 1998), with priorities being work undertaken with respect to rural, cultural, educational and environmental tourism and measures designed to increase Europe's appeal as a tourist destination (EU 1998: Sec. 11).

The importance of tourism in relation to indirect expenditure is primarily reflected in EU funds allocated to implement regional development and social cohesion policies. As the EU has enlarged so the extent of regional disparities within the Community has also expanded. According to the European Commission (1996), the ten most prosperous regions in the EU are three times as wealthy, and invest three times as much in their economic fabrics, as the ten poorest. In response to such problems of regional disparity the EU established a series of 'structural' funds. One of the main structural funds is the European Regional Development Fund (ERDF) which was established in 1975 following the accession of Britain, Denmark and Ireland to the then European Community. However, the development of single market and the establishment of economic and monetary union in 1999 provided even greater impetus to encourage regional development, with a new fund, the Cohesion Fund, being established to channel financial assistance to the four poorest member states: Spain, Portugal, Greece and Ireland (Jenkins et al. 1998). Regional development is a collaborative effort between the EU; national, regional and local authorities; and the private sector. Areas qualifying for EU regional aid programmes are defined according to the nature of their economic problems. Four categories are identified which have regional emphasis:

- Objective 1: promoting the development and structural adjustment of the regions whose development is lagging behind;
- Objective 2: converting regions or areas seriously affected by industrial decline;
- Objective 5b: facilitating the development and structural adjustment of rural areas; and
- Objective 6: promoting the development and structural adjustment of regions with an extremely low population density (European Commission 1996).

The Community Support Frameworks (CSFs) for the 1989 to 1993 period made explicit provision for tourism to the amounting of ECU 2305.9 million in connection with Objectives 1, 2 and 5b. This figure represented some 4% of all Community assistance. For the 1994 to 1999 period, the EU contribution to tourism under Objectives 1, 2, 5b and 6 amounted to ECU 7284.9 million (EU 1998: Sec. 12). This figure represented some 6% of all assistance (EU 1998: Sec. 76). In addition, direct European Investment Bank (EIB) EIB financing (individual loans and loans from global loans) in the 'tourism-leisure' field amounted to ECU 1014.2 million over the 1990 to 1994 period (EU 1998: Sec. 13), while other monies allocated under other Objectives, initiatives and funds although substantial, are regarded as too hard to provide exact figures for (EU 1998: Sec. 12).

One of the most significant European strategies for rural development is LEADER (Liason Entre Actions de Développement de l'Économie Rurale). LEADER is a 'Community initiative' launched in 1991 as part of the major 'cohesion' policies of the EU, by the Directorate General for Agriculture of the European Commission. As LEADER acknowledges, the 'drive among government administrations and the various . . . operators to promote rural tourism . . . is undoubtedly a response – in some cases prompted by a guilty conscience – to economic crisis and the need to find solutions to it, to the negative effects of reforms of farm structures and to the eradication of basic structures in many rural areas' (LEADER II 1995b, np). LEADER principally funds local action groups which are a combination of public and private partners who have jointly devised a strategy and a set of public and private innovations for the development of a rural area at a community scale, which is defined as being less than 100,000 people. Other rural collective bodies, public or private, e.g. local authorities, business associations or chambers of commerce, can also be funded provided that their activities are related to a local rural development plan (LEADER II 1995c). However, overall responsibility for the management of the LEADER programme lies with national and/or regional authorities (Jenkins et al. 1998). The first phase (LEADER I) ended in December 1994. The second phase (LEADER II) covers the period 1995–99 (LEADER II 1995a). Within the framework of the LEADER I initiative

(1991 to 1994), rural tourism measures represented some 40% of the ECU 400 million of assistance available (EU 1998).

In LEADER II the EU's participation was set at ECU 1.4 billion of which ECU 900 million has been allocated to the regions of Objective 1, although the final level of tourism-related financing is not yet known, 'but it may be assumed that it will not diminish' (EU 1998). LEADER II money may be matched with private and public sector funding. The goals of LEADER II are:

- to ensure that support for exemplary local initiatives involving local development continues from LEADER I
- to support operations that are innovative, suitable as a model and transferable, and that illustrate the new directions that rural development may take
- to step up exchanges of experiences and the transfer of knowhow through a European rural development network
- to back transnational cooperation projects developed by local bodies in rural areas which reflect their solidarity (LEADER II 1995c).

Four types of measures are eligible to meet the goals of LEADER II:

- skills acquisition, e.g. local rural needs analysis, training programmes and strategies
- rural innovation programmes – model and transferable programmes which are usually promoted by local action groups that can include: technical support for rural development, vocational training, support for rural tourism, support for small businesses, local exploitation and marketing of agricultural, forestry and fisheries products, and preservation and improvement of the environment and living conditions
- transnational cooperation, e.g. joint projects between groups from member states
- contributions to the European network for regional development (LEADER II 1995c).

The projects developed under the LEADER project are extremely diverse ranging from the development of a communications strategy for 'Cathar Country' in Toulouse, France, to the development of 'Via Mediterranea' (a Mediterranean cultural tourism network comprising tourist trails, the construction of numerous visitor interpretation centres, resource centres museums and walkways), to direct assistance for small business development (Jenkins et al. 1998). Again, what is significant for the purposes of the present chapter is not just the undertaking of regional development projects with a tourism component. It is the series of linkages from the supranational to the local which actually provide for such undertakings. Under the EU monies are being reallocated for development purposes as a result of policies which are being pursued at the supranational level and which, in turn, interact with policy settings at the national and regional level. Tourism planning at the local level in the EU member states is therefore clearly embedded within institutional arrangements and interests at higher levels. Indeed, the power to act is also constrained by the authority which lies not only at the national and regional level, but also at the supranational level of the EU. To many people living in the EU area, such a statement may be regarded as reasonably self-evident given the very visible range of EU regulations and development programmes. However, supranational institutions also play an important role in areas where the supranational organisation does not have the degree of legislative power accorded to it by member states, which is the case for the EU. This next section will look at the role that the Organization of American States plays in tourism planning and policy in the Americas.

The Organization of American States and Tourism Planning and Policy

The American parallel to the European Union is the Organization of American States (OAS). The OAS is the world's oldest regional organisation, dating back to the First International Conference of American States, held in Washington, DC, from October 1889 to April 1890, which approved the establishment of the International Union of American Republics. The Charter of the OAS was signed in Bogota in 1948 and entered into force in December 1951. The Charter was subsequently amended by a number of protocols. The OAS currently has 35 member states with Permanent Observer status granted to 37 states, as well as the European Union. The basic purposes of the OAS are:

- to strengthen the peace and security of the continent
- to promote and consolidate representative democracy, with due respect for the principle of nonintervention; to prevent possible causes of difficulties and to ensure the pacific settlement of disputes that may arise among the Member States
- to provide for common action on the part of those States in the event of aggression
- to seek the solution of political, juridical and economic problems that may arise among them
- to promote, by cooperative action, their economic, social and cultural development
- to achieve an effective limitation of conventional weapons that will make it possible to devote the largest amount of resources to the economic and social development of the Member States.

In the Declaration of Principles and in the Plan of Action from the 1996 Miami summit, the OAS also agreed to establish the Free Trade Area of the Americas, in which barriers to trade and investment will be progressively eliminated, and to guarantee sustainable development and conserve the natural environment for future generations.

A body with similar functions to the WTO within the OAS is the Inter-Sectoral Unit for Tourism, which is responsible for matters directly related to tourism and its development in the hemisphere. The Unit was created in June 1996, in recognition of the growing importance of tourism in the hemisphere, and in order to strengthen the tourism group of the Organization of American States and their activities. The functions of the Inter-Sectoral Unit for Tourism are to:

- provide support to the Inter-American Travel Congress forum for formulating hemispheric tourism policy
- provide support in the area of sustainable and integral tourism development
- provide support to other sectors of the General Secretariat engaged in activities related to sustainable and integral tourism development

- provide support to hemispheric and subregional conferences, workshops and seminars
- to formulate, evaluate, and undertake execution of selective technical cooperation projects and promote public/private sector cooperation
- to facilitate the exchange of information related to sustainable and integral tourism development in the region
- conduct research and analysis of tourism issues
- and promote cooperation with international, regional and subregional tourism organizations (http://www.oas.org/EN/PROG/TOURISM/tr_back.htm).

At a development and land-use planning level the Unit has been responsible for a range of technical cooperation activities and projects within the developing countries of the region. Indeed, the unit is directly charged with facilitating and supporting national and regional tourism development programs and activities, and promoting mechanisms for external support and horizontal collaboration between member states. Examples of the Unit's planning and development activities are contained in Table 5.3. What is significant in looking at the development activities of the Unit is, again, the extent to which decisions and undertakings at the supranational level with respect to tourism planning and development will have a regional and local impact. Similarly, the resolutions of the conferences and meetings of the OAS although being examples of soft international law may have substantial influence on overall international policy direction. For example, the Declaration of San José from the XVII Inter-American Travel Congress, San José, Costa Rica (Organization of American States 1997) (Table 5.4), not only refers to sustainable development as an important element in tourism but, as with the WTO, also makes reference to the significance of public–private partnerships and trade liberalisation. Such measures become important stepping stones in the world of international diplomacy and negotiation towards more formal agreements while, with the gradual development of a free trade zone throughout the Americas, tourism is also being signalled as a significant component of international trade in the area through such measures as an 'open-sky' policy with respect to international aviation.

Conclusions

This chapter has discussed some of the institutional arrangements surrounding tourism planning and policy making at the international and supranational level. It has concentrated on the organisational component to illustrate the role and influence of hard and soft international law on the various levels of governance which lie below the international scale. Examples have also been provided of the activities of the World Tourism Organization, the European Union and the Organization of American States as well as the role of international conservation law through the World Heritage Convention. The key theme of the chapter has been the extent to which spatial outcomes at the local scale, what most people conceive of tourism planning in terms of land

Table 5.3 Selected examples of the tourism planning, policy and development activities of the OAS Inter-Sectoral Unit for Tourism, 1998

Plan	Goal
• Integrated National Tourism Development Plan (Guyana).	For the preparation of an integrated national tourism development strategy.
• Heritage Tourism Project (St. Vincent & The Grenadines).	For the development of heritage sites, implementation of heritage awareness program, training of craft persons and organisation of national craft fairs.
• Caribbean Small Hotel Assistance Program (Regional Project)	To develop a recovery and strategic plan and organise seminars on management operations and marketing
• Inter-American Technical Meeting on the Effects of Free Trade Agreements on Tourism (Regional Activity).	For the analysis of the positive and negative effects on tourism by the reduction and/or elimination of trade barriers.
• National Consultation on Draft OECS Sustainable Tourism Strategy (Regional Activity).	For the preparation of a draft OECS tourism development strategy.
• Integrated Planning and Development Program of the Tourism Product of Central America (Regional Project).	For the preparation of an integrated tourism development strategy for Central America.
• Caribbean Environment and Tourism Public Attitudes and Awareness Program (Regional Project).	To support attitudes and awareness activities in six member states.
• Program of Conservation, Upgrading, and Revitalization of Caribbean Tourism Heritage Sites (Regional Project).	The project will support the development of an action plan for the conservation upgrading and revitalization of three heritage sites in the Dominican Republic Haiti, and Jamaica.

Source: Organisation of American States, http://www.oas.org/EN/PROG/TOURISM/tr_tech.htm (accessed 11 January 1999).

Table 5.4   Declaration of San José, 1997

We, the ministers of tourism, gathered in San José, Costa Rica, on April 10 and 11, 1997, on the occasion of the Seventeenth Inter-American Travel Congress,

Convinced of the increasing importance of public/private sector collaboration in ensuring the sustainable development of tourism in the Hemisphere; and

Recognizing the Inter-American Travel Congresses as the principal hemispheric forum for discussing all tourism-related issues as well as strategies to address future tourism challenges and opportunities,

DECLARE:

1 Our firm commitment to the sustainable development of tourism in the Hemisphere, in accordance with the initiatives adopted by our leaders at the Summit of the Americas in Miami in December 1994.

2 Our recognition of the need to play an active role in ensuring the sustainable development of the member states, in accordance with the Declaration of Rio and Agenda 21, adopted at the United Nations Conference on Environment and Development, held in Rio de Janeiro in 1992.

3 Our commitment to the decisions adopted in the Declaration and the Plan of Action adopted at the 1996 Summit of the Americas on Sustainable Development, held in Santa Cruz de la Sierra, Bolivia, which emphasized that development strategies need to include sustainability as an essential requirement for the balanced, interdependent, and integral attainment of economic, social, and environmental goals.

4 Our agreement to promote the development of sustainable tourism, in accordance with the commitments undertaken at the United Nations Global Conference on the Sustainable Development of Small Island Developing States, held in Barbados in 1994.

5 Our recognition of the Regional Plan of Action for Tourism Development, approved at the XVIII Summit of Central American Presidents, held in Montelimar, Nicaragua, in 1996, which identifies tourism as a high-priority and strategic economic activity for the sustainable development of the region.

6 Our commitment to the agreements reached on tourism at the Association of Caribbean States (ACS) Summit, held in Port-of-Spain, Trinidad and Tobago, in 1995, and to the mandate agreed on by its members at the meeting of the Special Committee on Tourism held in Santo Domingo in March 1997, to create a sustainable tourism zone.

7 Our recognition of the work initiated by the Confederation of Latin American Tourism Organizations (COTAL) in the area of public/private sector collaboration at the Third Meeting of Latin American Tourism Ministers in 1996.

8 Our firm commitment to the principles of the Charter of the Organization of American States, in which we, the member states, decided to make every effort to promote private initiative and investment in harmony with action in the public sector.

9 Our recognition of the primary role tourism can play in economic development strategies and its role in poverty alleviation in the Hemisphere.

10 Our need to respond collectively to the natural disasters which impede sustainable tourism development and are extremely injurious to the economies of the Hemisphere.

11 Our acknowledgement of the importance of the role of the private sector in the development and promotion of tourism in our countries, and the corresponding need to strengthen and promote collaborative activities at the national, regional, and hemispheric levels.

Table 5.4 (cont'd)

12 Our confidence in the Inter-American Travel Congresses as the principal vehicle for the
    creation and strengthening of mechanisms for cooperation between the public and
    private sectors at the local, national, and regional levels.
13 Our recognition of the need for the international financial organizations to promote, as
    a matter of priority in their operating plans, projects that support sustainable tourism
    and development through active participation by the public and private sectors.
14 Our commitment to facilitate dialogue with the private sector in order to develop
    integrated civil aviation policies that will facilitate intraregional, interregional, and
    international air travel.
15 Our commitment to encourage regional agreements to simplify and standardize
    immigration and customs formalities in order to facilitate the free movement of travelers
    between countries of the region.
16 Our acknowledgement of the important contribution made by local communities to the
    development of sustainable tourism, and our resolve to encourage their full participation
    in the formulation of tourism strategies and policies.
17 Our interest in promoting horizontal cooperation in the Hemisphere in accordance with
    the policies of the Organization of American States, especially in the area of human
    resource development and training.
18 Our recognition of the need to adopt an open skies policy in order to increase the
    supply of air transportation in terms of frequency and capacity, thereby increasing
    tourism flows and hence tourism earnings.

Source: Organization of American States (1997).

use, are the outcome of policy and planning decisions which have occurred at
the international and supranational scale. However, it should be noted that
the relationship is not just top-down. There is instead a flow of information,
influence and desire to affect outcomes between stakeholders from the local
through to the global. The next chapter will look at the national level in this
ongoing process of relationship and interaction.

Questions and further reading

What are the implications of differences between 'hard' and 'soft' international law for
    tourism planning and policy?
How does international trade policy affect tourism?
How has the development of international conservation and environmental law
    affected tourism planning and policy?
Identify the various international and supranational tourism organisations of which
    your country is a member. Discuss their significance for tourism planning and
    policy.

The best sources of information on the main international organisations which influence tourism planning and policy are their respective web sites. There are few critical appraisals of international tourism policy. Edgell (1990) provides a prescriptive approach, while Hall (1994) and Elliot (1997) approach the subject from a political science and public policy background.

Chapter 6

Tourism planning and policy at the national and sub-national level

Although processes of globalisation are dramatically affecting the role of the state in contemporary society, any comments that the state is dead are well and truly premature. International and supranational organisations are clearly playing a major role in tourism planning and policy. However, although international law provides some basis for regulation and organisational authority, it carries nowhere near the weight of domestic law, particularly with respect to how laws are enforced. Undoubtedly, pressures for free trade, an apparent desire for smaller government in many western democracies witnessed through reduced government intervention in the economic and the public spheres and a move away from the collective consumption of social services (Knox and Agnew 1989), and the reawakening of interest in regional governance have all given impetus to the possible claim that the role of the state has declined. Instead, we should perhaps note that the role of the state has changed, as it has always been doing, in relation to global economic, political and social processes. Yet the state is still extremely significant.

The state can be conceptualised as a set of officials with their own preferences and capacities to effect public policy, or in more structural terms as a relatively permanent set of *political institutions* operating in relation to civil society (Nordlinger 1981). The term 'state' encompasses the whole apparatus whereby a government exercises its power. It includes elected politicians, the various arms of the bureaucracy, unelected public/civil servants, and the plethora of rules, regulations, laws, conventions and policies which surround government and private action. The main institutions of the state include: the elected legislatures, government departments and authorities, the judiciary, enforcement agencies, other levels of government, government-business enterprises and corporations, regulatory authorities, and a range of para-state organisations, such as labour organisations (Hall and Jenkins 1995). Although the boundaries of the state are becoming increasingly blurred in many jurisdictions as emphasis is increasingly placed on the creation of public–private partnerships and reducing government intervention in the economy it should be noted that the state still set the regulatory framework within which public and private activity occurs.

The functions of the state will affect tourism planning, policy and development to different degrees. This chapter will discuss the various roles that government assume in tourism and their effect on tourism policy, the organisation of government involvement in tourism, the changing nature of intergovernmental relations, and the increasing significance of sub-national governments in tourism planning and policy at both the international and domestic level.

The role of government in tourism

Although tourism is often regarded as a private sector activity, 'government agencies at every level from the international down to small towns have adopted a progressively more active role in the use of tourism as a development tool . . . government agencies currently promote tourism as a panacea for under-employment in economically depressed areas' (Smith 1989b: x–xi). Government helps shape the economic framework for the tourism industry although international economic factors relating to exchange rates, interest rates and investor confidence are increasingly important, helps provide the infrastructure and educational requirements for tourism, establishes the regulatory environment in which business operates, and takes an active role in promotion and marketing. In addition, tourism may be politically and economically appealing to government because it can potentially give the appearance of producing results from policy initiatives in a short period of time in terms of visitor numbers and/or employment generation (Hall 1998b). For example, the European Union argued that 'The importance of tourism in a region's development is due in particular to its job-creating capacity, to its contribution to the diversification of economic regional activities and to various indirect effects of expenditure by tourists' (EU 1998: Sec. 74).

A number of roles of government in tourism can be identified, although there will be variation from place to place in terms of the extent to which they apply. The forerunner to the WTO, the International Union of Travel Organisations (IUOTO) (1974), in their discussion of the role of the state in tourism identified five areas of public sector involvement in tourism: coordination, planning, legislation and regulation, entrepreneur, and stimulation (also see Jenkins and Henry 1982; Mill and Morrison 1985). To this may be added two other functions, a social tourism role, and a broader role of interest protection (Hall 1994). A discussion on these seven roles of government in tourism follows.

Coordination

Coordination is necessary both within and between the different levels of government in order to avoid duplication of resources between the various government tourism bodies and the private sector, and to develop effective tourism strategies. Given the large number of public organisations which have an interest in tourism matters one of the main challenges for government is being able to bring the various organisations and agencies together to work for common policy objectives. Furthermore, in several jurisdictions government has often served to help coordinate private sector activities as well.

Planning

As stated in the first chapter, public planning for tourism occurs in a number of forms (e.g. development, infrastructure, land and resource use, promotion and marketing); institutions (e.g. different government organisations) and scales (e.g. national, regional, local and sectoral) (Hall 1994). In several nations, such as Israel, and in several regions, notably the island states of the Pacific (Hall and Page 1997), national tourism development plans have been drawn up in which government identifies which sectors of the industry will be developed, the appropriate rate of growth and the provision of capital required for expansion. Throughout many parts of the world regional tourism development plans are also a common government initiative, particularly where such regions are seeking to utilise tourism as a response to problems of economic restructuring (Jenkins et al. 1998). Nevertheless, while planning is recognised as an important element in tourism development, the conduct of a plan or strategy does not by itself guarantee appropriate outcomes for stakeholders, particularly as issues of implementation and the policy-action relationship need to be addressed. Indeed, as has already been noted, one of the major problems for public tourism planning is the extent to which tourism-specific agencies, which usually have a very limited legislative base of responsibility, have the authority to direct other government organisations to meet tourism specific policy goals.

Legislation and regulation

Government has a number of legislative and regulative powers which directly and indirectly impinge on tourism. Government involvement in this area ranges from authority on passport and visa matters, through to environmental and labour relations policy. However, substantial issues for tourism often emerge because of the extent to which tourism policy needs to be integrated with other policy areas. With the possible exception of island microstates which are highly economically dependent on tourism, tourism policy tends to be only a relatively minor area of government policy initiatives. Nevertheless, policy decisions undertaken in other policy jurisdictions, e.g. economic policy, and environmental and conservation policy, may have substantial implications for the effectiveness of policy decisions undertaken in tourism. For example, general regulatory measures such as industry regulation, environmental protection, and taxation policy will significantly influence the growth of tourism (Hall 1998b).

The level of government regulation of tourism tends to be a major issue for the various components of the tourism industry. Undoubtedly, while industry recognises that government has a significant role to play, particularly when it comes to the provision of infrastructure, marketing or research, the predominant argument by industry throughout most of the world is that the industry must be increasingly deregulated. However, government simultaneously has calls for increased regulation of tourism, especially with respect to the desire for environmental protection (Bramwell and Lane 1993), and, increasingly, human rights and social justice, especially with respect to the rights of indigenous peoples (e.g. Smith and Eadington 1992).

The issue of regulation in the context of tourism and the environment has been well described by McKercher (1993a). As a predominantly private sector driven industry, development decisions by tourism enterprises must be geared to function at a profit, resulting 'in preference for investment in profit centres (such as swimming pools) rather than in cost centres (such as sewage systems) . . . Mitigation protection programmes will receive lower priorities, unless there is an opportunity for profit generation or a legislative imperative forcing such investment' (McKercher 1993a : 10). According to McKercher (1993a : 10), 'The very nature of the tourism industry makes voluntary compliance with environmental programmes virtually impossible,' therefore creating a regulatory vacuum in which government most operate in order to establish clear environmental guidelines. Given this situation, conservation groups will often seek the extension of government regulation to ensure that tourism remains 'controlled', particularly in environmentally and politically sensitive areas such as national parks or the coastal zone. In many cases, especially when companies are using the environment as part of their branding and competitive strategy, the regulatory conflict is perhaps not so much whether controls should be in place but rather what the nature of the controls should be, with industry often seeking to place the locus of control on themselves, e.g. self-regulating, while conservationists will usually seek to have control placed in a government body, such as an environmental protection authority, which is distinct from the tourism industry (Hall 1998b).

Government as entrepreneur

Government has long had an entrepreneurial function in tourism. Governments not only provide basic infrastructure, such as roads and sewage, but may also own and operate tourist ventures including hotels and travel companies. Governments at all levels have had a long history of involvement in promoting tourism through bureaus, marketing ventures, development of transport networks through national airline and rail systems, and the provision of loans to private industry for specific tourism-related developments. According to Pearce (1992 : 11), 'because of the scale of development and the element of the common good, provision of infrastructure is a widely accepted task of public authorities and one which can greatly facilitate tourist development and selectively direct it to particular areas'. However, the entrepreneurial role of government in tourism is changing in a climate in which less government intervention is being sought. This has meant the development of increasing public–private arrangements in tourism-related redevelopment projects and the conduct of such developments on a commercial basis where substantial direct economic return is being sought for government authorities rather than development occurring for the notion of a wider public good.

The role of the state as entrepreneur in tourism development is closely related to the concept of the 'devalorisation of capital'. The 'devalorisation of capital' (Damette 1980) is the process by which the state subsidises part of the cost of production, for instance by assisting in the provision of infrastructure or by investing in a tourism project where private venture capital is otherwise unavailable. In this process what would have been private costs are transformed into public or social costs. The provision of infrastructure, particularly transport networks, is regarded as crucial to the development of tourist destinations. There are numerous formal and informal means for government at all levels to assist in minimising the costs of production for tourism developers. Indeed, the offer of government assistance for development is often used to encourage private investment in a particular region or tourist project. For instance, through the provision of cheap land, tax breaks or government backed low-interest loans. For example, in India several states have created tourism development corporations for the purpose of encouraging tourism development and investment. The Tourism Corporation of Gujarat, for example, developed a tourism plan which included several tax concessions for investors, such as exemption from luxury tax, sales tax, electricity duty, turnover tax and entertainment tax, and long-term loans from state institutions. This, in part, has helped to address the negative image of India overseas as a tourist destination and limitations on foreign direct investment for tourism prior to the government's economic liberalisation measures in the 1990s (Chaudhary 1996).

Stimulation

Similar to the entrepreneurial role is the action that government can take to stimulate tourism development. According to Mill and Morrison (1985) governments can stimulate tourism in three ways. First, financial incentives such as low-interest loans or a depreciation allowance on tourist accommodation, although 'their introduction often reflected both the scarcity of domestic investment funds and widespread ambition to undertake economic development programmes' (Bodlender and Davies 1985, in Pearce 1992 : 11). For example, the creation of incentives to encourage foreign investment in the tourism sector has been closely tied to the creation of new tourism development bodies at the state level in India. Concessions at the state level have also been matched by central government fiscal incentives for tourism projects, including income tax exemptions on 50% of the profits from foreign exchange earnings, exemption on the remaining 50% if the amount is reinvested in new tourism projects, and exemption on import duty on imports for hotel projects. In an effort to use tourism as a tool for regional development, the Indian federal government has explicitly sought to encourage regional tourism development by providing interest subsidies on term loans from eligible financial institutions for hotels in cities other than main centres such as Mumbai (Bombay), Delhi, Calcutta and Chennai (Madras), with higher rates of subsidy available for hotel development in designated tourist areas and heritage hotels. The provision of financial incentives for tourism by the Indian central government in the 1990s is indicative of not only increased attention by government to tourism's potential for generating employment and foreign exchange, but also the wider deregulation of the Indian economy to provide for competition and foreign investment. For example, in the accommodation sector the federal government now allows foreign management and up to 51% foreign ownership of hotels (Hall and Page 1999b).

A second aspect of government stimulation of tourism is through sponsoring research for the general benefit of the tourism industry rather than for specific individual organisations and associations. In the case of Australia, for example, the federal government established a non-statutory intergovernmental agency, the Bureau of Tourism Research (BTR) in late 1987. The BTR was created in accordance with the recommendations of the Australian Government Inquiry into Tourism (1987), to provide government and the private sector with the statistical and analytical support necessary for effectively planned and balanced tourism development. The BTR was a response to the perceived need for a coordinated approach to tourism research and the desire to overcome gaps and deficiencies in the provision of data and, in particular, delays in providing statistical information on overseas visitor arrivals (Hall 1998b). The BTR is jointly funded by the Federal and State/Territory governments and also derives revenue from the sale of data and through its consultancy services. 'The BTR's mission is to provide independent, accurate, timely and strategically relevant statistics and analyses to the tourism industry, government and the community at large in order to enhance the contribution of tourism to the wellbeing of the Australian community' (Department of Tourism 1993b : 50).

The third dimension of the stimulation role is that of marketing and promotion, generally aimed at generating tourism demand, although it can also take the form of investment promotion aimed at encouraging capital investment in tourism attractions and facilities. However, such is the size of the role that government plays in promotion that it is usually recognised as a separate function.

Tourism promotion

> . . . marketing of inbound tourism in large measure has the market failure and public good characteristics that indicate private sector under-provision and justify public sector support via government funding of marketing activity (Access Economics 1997 : 29).

One of the main activities of government is the promotion of tourism through tourism marketing campaigns (Ascher 1984). Tourist commissions and agencies have the task of identifying potential target markets, the best methods of attracting them and, once they want to buy the tourist product, where to direct them. Furthermore, as well as encouraging visits by foreign travellers, tourism promotion agencies will sometimes attempt to retain as many domestic tourists as possible through the conduct of domestic marketing campaigns in order to ensure the minimum of 'leakage' from outside of the national, state or regional tourism system.

Given calls for smaller government in Western society in recent years, there have been increasing demands from government and economic rationalists for greater industry self-sufficiency by industry in tourism marketing and promotion (Jeffries 1989). The political implications of such an approach for the tourism industry are substantial. As Hughes (1984 : 14) noted, 'The advocates of a free enterprise economy would look to consumer freedom of choice and not to governments to promote firms; the consumer ought to be sovereign in decisions relating to the allocation of the nation's resources.' Such an approach means that lobbyists in the tourism industry may be better shifting their focus on the necessity of government intervention to issues of externalities, public goods, and merit wants rather than employment and the balance of payments (Hall 1994). 'Such criteria for government intervention have a sounder economic base and are more consistent with a free-enterprise philosophy than employment and balance of payments effects' (Hughes 1984 : 18). However, the conduct of government involvement in tourism promotion is as much a legacy of effective political lobbying as it is the conduct of economic rationalism, if not more so (Craik 1990, 1991a, 1991b). Nevertheless, as Pearce (1992 : 8) has recognised, 'general destination promotion tends to benefit all sectors of the tourist industry in the place concerned; it becomes a "public good" . . . The question of "freeloaders" thus arises, for they too will benefit along with those who may have contributed directly to the promotional campaign.'

However, the freeloader or freerider problem can be regarded as rational business behaviour in the absence of some form of government intervention in tourism promotion. As Access Economics (1997 : 29) observed: 'There will be a strong incentive for individual producers of tourism/travel services to minimalise their contribution to cooperative marketing, or even not to contribute at all, and other private sector producers have no power to coerce such producers and the beneficiaries of tourism activity, anyway.'

Given the supply-side fragmentation of tourism and the substantial degree of market failure that exists with respect to generic destination promotion, governments may need to determine the most appropriate form of government intervention in order to fulfil their tourism planning and policy goals. In the Australian context, Access Economics (1997) reviewed a number of different forms of intervention including:

- forcing businesses to pay a funding levy
- 'user pays'/cooperative funding systems
- levies on foreign exchange earnings
- making government funding conditional on industry funding;
- levies on tourism investment
- funding from a passenger movement charge
- a bed tax
- funding out of consolidated revenue
- funding out of a possible Goods and Services Tax (GST) [similar to VAT] that emerges from tax reform measures.

After examining the different potential forms of government intervention, Access Economics concluded that the most appropriate form of government intervention is the appropriation of funds from consolidated revenue funds through budget processes. Several reasons for this conclusion were put forward for this conclusion:

- the inability to capture the benefits of generic marketing activity is severe in the light of the fragmented nature of the tourism industry
- levies, user pays charges and business tax arrangements, including bed taxes, will institutionalise the 'freerider' or 'freeloader' problem
- the benefits of successful generic promotion as a travel destination are dispersed across the community.

One of the more unusual features of tourism promotion by government tourism organisations is that they have only limited control over the product they are marketing, with very few governments actually owning the goods, facilities and services that make up the tourism product (Pearce 1992). This lack of control is perhaps testimony to the power of the public good argument used by industry to justify continued maintenance of government funding for destination promotion. However, it may also indicate the political power of the tourism lobby, such as industry organisations (Craik 1990; Hall and Jenkins 1995) to influence government tourism policies.

Social tourism

Social tourism can be defined as 'the relationships and phenomena in the field of tourism resulting from participation in travel by economically weak or otherwise disadvantaged elements of society' (Hunzinger quoted in Murphy 1985 : 23). Social tourism involves the extension of the benefits of holidays to economically marginal groups, such as the unemployed, single-parent families, pensioners and the handicapped. The International Bureau of Social Tourism defines social tourism as meaning, 'the totality of relations and phenomena deriving from the participation in tourism of those social groups with modest incomes – participation which is made possible or facilitated by measures of a well defined social character' (Haulot 1981 : 208).

According to Murphy (1985 : 24) 'Social tourism has become a recognized component and legitimate objective for modern tourism. By extending the physical and psychological benefits of rest and travel to less fortunate people it can be looked upon as a form of preventative medicine.' Haulot (1981 : 212) further extended this perspective by noting that: 'Social tourism . . . finds justification in that its individual and collective objectives are consistent with the view that all measures taken by modern society should ensure more justice, more dignity and improved enjoyment of life for all citizens.' However, the desire of conservative elements in society to reduce the extent of government intervention in economic and private life and focus on individual as opposed to public interest has meant a substantial decline in support for social tourism around the world in recent years.

Government as public interest protector

The final role that government plays in tourism is that of interest protector. Although not necessarily tourism specific, such a role will have major implications for the development of tourism policy. Indeed, public tourism planning, particularly from the community and sustainable approaches in which equity is a major consideration, serves as an arbiter between competing interests. The defence of local and minority interests has traditionally occupied much government activity, particularly as government has had the role of balancing various interest and values in order to meet national or regional public interests, rather than narrow, sectional, private interests, such as that of a specific industry like tourism. This does not, of course, ignore the fact that various tourism interests are represented within the structure of government. 'Statutory authorities and a myriad of state agencies were established to protect sectional groups, to represent key interests in the policy process, and to protect the social order via welfare provisions to many sections of business and society in general' (Davis et al., 1993 : 26). Nevertheless, tourism policy needs to be considered as being potentially subsumed beneath a broader range of government economic, social, welfare and environmental policies. Ideally, policy decisions will reflect a desire to meet the interests of the relevant level of government, e.g. national, provincial/state, or local, rather than the sectionally defined interests of components of the tourism industry (Hall 1994).

The issue of government as protector of the common or public interest lies at the heart of questions surrounding the role of government in tourism planning. It also causes us to question the democratic nature of planning and policy making – the extent to which planning and policy decisions are open to public scrutiny and debate and therefore provide for such decisions to be seen as legitimate in the public sphere. As Saul (1995 : 115–116) states, 'Democracy is simply about the nature of legitimacy and whether the repository of that legitimacy – the citizens – are able to exercise the power its possession imposes upon them. We are having great difficulty today exercising the power of legitimacy. It has . . . shifted away into other hands.'

One of the great ironies of the growth of the enterprise culture of place marketing which extols the virtues of competition and choice (Corner and Harvey 1991; Kotler et al. 1993), is the manner in which debate over representation and redevelopment of place is denied. Throughout much of the western world, in order to ensure that urban leisure and tourism development projects are carried out, 'local authorities have had planning and development powers removed and handed to an unelected institution. Effectively, an appointed agency is, in each case, replacing the powers of local government in order to carry out a market-led regeneration of each inner city' (Goodwin 1993 : 161). Harvey recognised that 'the new entrepreneurialism has, as its centrepiece, the notion of a "public–private partnership" in which a traditional local boosterism is integrated with the use of local government powers to try [to] attract external sources of funding, new direct investments, or new employment sources' (1989a : 7). However, the partnership does not include all members of a community, those who do not have enough money, are not of the right lifestyle, or simply do not have sufficient power, are ignored. For example, in referring to Derwentside in the United Kingdom, Sadler (1993 : 190) argued

> The kind of policy which had been adopted – and which was proving increasingly ineffective even in terms of its own stated objectives – therefore rested not so much on a basis of rational choice, but rather was a simple reflection of the narrow political and intellectual scope for alternatives. This restricted area did not come about purely or simply by chance, but had been deliberately encouraged and fostered.

As Harvey (1993 : 8) asked, 'The question immediately arises as to why people accede to the construction of their places by such a process.' In many cases they do not. Communities may resist such change. However, while victories in short-term battles may save the physical fabric of inner-city communities, this will not usually win the war. The social fabric will usually change through gentrification and touristification of many areas leaving only heritage façades. Furthermore, the very 'rules of the game' by which planning and development decisions are made will often favour business over community interest groups (Hall and Jenkins 1995). Indeed, Harvey also notes that resistance has not checked the overall process of place competition. A mixture of coercion and co-optation centred around maintenance of real estate values, assumptions regarding employment and investment generation, and an assumption that growth is automatically good, has led to the creation of local growth coalitions, in which

> Coercion arises either through interplace competition for capital investment and employment (accede to the capitalist's demands or go out of business; create a 'good business climate' or lose jobs) or more simply, through the direct political repression and oppression of dissident voices (from cutting off media access to the more violent tactics of the construction mafias in many of the world's cities, (Harvey 1993 : 9).

Such changes in government's role as interest protector has major implications for tourism and sustainability. As Blowers (1997 : 36) noted, 'In the UK the long period of privatisation, deregulation, cuts in public expenditure and attacks on local government have resulted in a "democratic deficit" – a dispersal of power to unelected quangos and business interests – and have led to unsustainable developments.' A critique also reflected in the comments of Haughton and Hunter (1994 : 272):

> The unregulated market approach, being relatively amoral, can allow individuals to be immoral. The ethical dimension is important since the market does not provide a sufficient basis for the resolution of the profound moral issues which face us every day; it can play a part in avoiding distorted decision making by individuals and organizations, but alone it cannot reconcile all of the environmental problems facing society.

If government is meant to occupy the role of general interest protector and, more particularly, if public tourism planning is meant to protect the interests of the wider community rather than just short-term sectoral tourism interests, then increasing attention also needs to be given to the manner in which the institutional arrangements of government involvement in tourism are organised and the instruments by which government intervenes to achieve tourism planning and policy goals.

The organisation of government involvement in tourism

As has already been noted several times in this book, the tendency to privatise and commercialise functions that were once performed by government, which has been almost universal in western nations since the late 1970s, has substantially affected the nature of many national governments' involvement in the tourism industry (Hall and Jenkins 1995). According to Davis et al. (1993 : 24) three principal economic reasons for this trend can be identified: 'governments are interested in reducing the dependency of public enterprises on public budgets, in reducing public debt by selling state assets, and in raising technical efficiencies by commercialisation'. However, the economic reasons are themselves shrouded in political rationales that relate to broader philosophical perspectives regarding the question of what are the appropriate roles for the state and the individual within society. Ideology therefore has practical effect in the design of government institutions and their tasks.

As readers would be aware, there are many different organisational structures for government involvement in tourism in the countries around the world. The organisational structures used by governments develop over time in relation to a number of factors, including political philosophies as to the appropriate role of the state, national traditions of public administration, the nature of the political system, and values and interests in the bureaucratic process. New government departments may be established as part of the growth in the activity and influence of government, particularly as new demands and interests, such as environmental concerns, reach a prominent position on the political agenda. As Mercer (1979 : 107) noted:

> The setting up of entirely new government departments, advisory bodies or sections within the existing administration is a well established strategy on the part of governments for demonstrating loudly and clearly that 'something positive is being done' with respect to a given problem. Moreover, because public service bureaucracies are inherently conservative in terms of their approach to problem delineation and favoured mode of functioning . . . administrative restructuring, together with the associated legislation, is almost always a significant indicator of public pressure for action and change.

Tourism has come to occupy a number of different positions in government administrative structures in different parts of the world. Tables 6.1 and 6.2 illustrate the institutional arrangements for government involvement in tourism in New Zealand. In general terms, the institutional arrangements for tourism in New Zealand are similar to other national jurisdictions in that there is a small core group of primary agencies directly responsible for tourism

Table 6.1 Institutional arrangements for government involvement for tourism in New Zealand

Agency	Principal roles*	Enabling legislation	Responsible minister	Principal tourism-related functions
Primary agencies				
Office of Sport and Tourism Ministry of Internal Affairs	Policy Operations	None, but administers several Acts	Sport and Tourism	Advice to government on tourism and sport policy development; represents government's tourism and sport interests internationally and monitors overseas tourism to assess their relevance to New Zealand. Manages Croesus owned land for which the Minister of Tourism is responsible.
New Zealand Tourism Board (crown agency)	Marketing Policy	New Zealand Tourism Board Act 1991	Tourism	Ensures that New Zealand is marketed as a visitor destined to maximise long-term benefits to New Zealand; develop implements and promotes strategies for tourism; and adapt government and industry on the development, promotion implementation of those strategies.
Department of Conservation	Policy Operations Regulation	Conservation Act 1987	Conservation	Management of land in the conservation estate to achieve conservation objectives; gives effect to the principles of Treaty of Waitangi; advocates conservation; education; provision of visitor services and visitor centres; maintain historic and cultural heritage; and liaises with stakehold.

Table 6.1 (cont'd)

Agency	Principal roles*	Enabling legislation	Responsible minister	Principal tourism-related functions
Secondary agencies *Conservation*				
Ministry for the Environment	Policy Regulation	Environment Act 1986	Environment	Advises Government on all aspects of environmental administration; assists in the promotion of sustainable management; administers the Resource Management Act.
New Zealand Conservation Authority	Policy	Conservation Act 1987	Conservation	Advises Government on DOC policy and activities; apply conservation management strategies and plans and National Park Management Plans.
Conservation Boards	Policy	Conservation Act 1987	Conservation	Advise NZCA and regional conservators on policy and concessions.
New Zealand Historic Places Trust	Regulation Operations Policy	Historic Places Act 1993	Conservation	Protects and manages historic and cultural heritage through advocacy, policy advice and direct management.
Fish and Game New Zealand	Regulation Operations Policy	Conservation Act 1987	Conservation	Coordinates the management, enhancement and maintenance of sports fish and game, through policy, advocacy and a management.
Employment, Business, Trade and Economic Development				
Ministry of Maori Development – Te Puni Kokiri	Policy	Ministry of Maori Development Act 1991	Maori Affairs	Mainly provides analysis and policy advice to increase Maori achievement within the tourism sector, and monitor other agencies' delivery of outcomes for Maori.

Organisation	Function	Legislation	Portfolio	Role
Community Development Group, Department of Internal Affairs	Operations Policy	–	Employment	Advises and informs community groups and organisations.
Community Employment Group, Department of Labour	Operations Policy	–	Agriculture	Promotes rural tourism.
Ministry of Agriculture	Policy	–	Agriculture	Promoting rural diversification, including farm tourism.
Ministry of Foreign Affairs and Trade (FA&T)	Policy	–	FA&T	Fosters international links involving tourism, including international expositions, inputs into tourism policy decisions affecting broader diplomatic considerations, e.g. Antarctic tourism policy.
Business Development Group – Ministry of Commerce	Policy	–	Business Development	Provides assistance to businesses, plus programmes and initiatives to promote and sustain international competitiveness of NZ businesses, especially small to medium-sized business.
Business Development Boards	Policy Operations	Business Development Boards Act 1991	Commerce	Stimulates development of small to medium-sized business with information and financial assistance.
Public Health and Public Safety Sector				
Public Health Group Ministry of Health	Policy Operations	Health Act 1956	Health	Manages and regulates activities including those which affect public health.

Table 6.1   (cont'd)

Agency	Principal roles*	Enabling legislation	Responsible minister	Principal tourism-related functions
Occupational Safety and Health Service – Dept of Labour	Regulation Policy	Occupational Safety and Health Act 1992	Labour	The prevention of harm to employees at work and visitors to workplaces.
New Zealand Police	Operations Regulation	–	Police	Protection of the public from criminal activity, traffic service compliance and search and rescue coordination.
Transport and Transport Safety Sector				
Ministry of Transport	Policy	Transport Act 1962	Transport	Provides advice and information relating to the promotion safe, sustainable transport at reasonable cost; sets government framework for the transport sector; is the lead department government policy on external aviation links.
Transit New Zealand (Crown agency)	Operations Policy Information	Transit New Zealand Act 1989	Transport	Controls and manages state highways; includes guideline roads in national parks and conservation reserves; also controls signage.
Civil Aviation Authority (Crown agency)	Policy regulation	Civil Aviation Act 1990	Transoprt	Controls and monitors safety and security in civil aviation includes provision of safety and security information, and policy advice to government.

Agency	Function	Act	Portfolio	Description
Land Transport Safety Authority (Crown agency)	Operations Regulation Policy	Land Transport Act 1993; Transport Services Licensing Act 1989	Transport	Promotes land transport safety; includes monitoring safety standards, education programmes, licence and regulation of passenger services industry.
Maritime Safety Authority (Crown agency)	Regulation	Maritime Transport Act 1994; Marine Pollution Act 1974	Transport	Promotes and monitors standards for safe shipping and the protection of the marine environment.
Border Security				
New Zealand Customs Service	Regulation	Customs and Excise Act 1996	Customs	Ensures smooth passage of people and products in and out New Zealand, controls prohibited or restricted products; as an agent for New Zealand Immigration Service at boom control points, such as airports.
New Zealand Immigration Service – Dept. of Labour	Operations Policy		Immigration	Processes visa applications for people wanting to stay far longer than three months in New Zealand.
Ministry of Agriculture	Policy Operations	Biosecurity Act 1993	Agriculture	Manages risks associated with introduction of unwanted organisms, including inspection of aircraft in compliance with New Zealand Customs.
Recreation Activities				
Ministry of Fisheries	Policy Regulation	Fisheries Act 1996	Fisheries	Manages New Zealand's fisheries, including recreational fishing.
Hillary Commission	Policy Operations	Sport, Fitness and Leisure Act 1987	Sport	Promotes sport, recreation and excellence in high-performance sport. Major initiatives include development of Events with NZTB to promote events tourism.

Table 6.1   (cont'd)

Agency	Principal roles*	Enabling legislation	Responsible minister	Principal tourism-related functions
Information and Research				
Department of Statistics	Information	Statistics Act 1975	Statistics	Gathers statistical information about New Zealand tourism including international arrivals and departures, and accommodation statistics. Looking at establishing a Tourism Satellite Account.
Foundation for Research, Science and Technology (Crown agency)	Information	Foundation for Research, Science and Technology Act 1990	Research, Science and Technology	Allocates money from the Public Good Science Fund for research, including tourism research.
General				
Department of Internal Affairs	Policy Regulation	Local Government Act 1974	Local Government	Administers the Local Government Act 1974, which empowers local government to provide various services including infrastructure development. Also administers Casino Control Act 1990.

Roles:

Infrastructure	Infrastructure development and provision
Information	Information provision and research
Marketing	Marketing and promotion
Operations	Direct land/asset management and/or service provision
Policy	Policy development and analysis, including sector development
Regulation	Managing compliance with legislation

Source: After Office of the Parliamentary Commissioner for the Environment (1997).

Table 6.2   Tourism responsibilities of local government agencies in New Zealand

Agency	Role	Primary acts	Functions
Territorial local authorities	Operations Policy Infrastructure Regulation Information Marketing	Local Government Act 1974 Resource Management Act 1991	Integrated management of the effects of the use, development and protection of land and associated natural and physical resources of the district. Also involved in economic development, local government owned attractions, e.g. art galleries and museums, and the management of visitor information services.
Regional councils	Operations Policy Infrastructure Regulation Information	Local Government Act 1974 Resource Management Act 1991	Integrated management of natural and physical resources.
Regional tourism organisations	Marketing Information Policy		Marketing and promotion of areas within New Zealand, international marketing usually undertaken in conjunction with the NZTB; provide information to operators and to visitors. Funding base is usually from local authorities although some RTOs also have a membership base as well.

Source: After Office of the Parliamentary Commissioner for the Environment (1997).

and a large number of secondary agencies which have part direct involvement. Not listed, but still significant, are those departments and agencies which indirectly affect tourism through their policies and the legislation which they are responsible for. For example, Departments of Finance and Treasury affect the overall economic environment within which tourism occurs through their setting of exchange and interest rates and by their policies on such matters as foreign investment.

The New Zealand example also illustrates the great problem which surrounds coordination of tourism policy and planning for tourism in that there is a plethora of government stakeholders in policy development in terms of different departments and agencies, responsible ministers, and legislative bases for action. In order for more than the simplest policy settings to be achievable in this policy environment it becomes apparent that agencies will need to develop a series of positive inter-organisational relationships in which common goals can be agreed upon and in which information flow is maximised for coordination to occur. Such a situation is extremely difficult. Indeed, it may partially explain why effective tourism policy development has been so difficult in many national jurisdictions (Hall and Jenkins 1995). Instead, in many western nations the policy function of tourism at the national government level has been reduced at the expense of a narrower promotion function. For example, in countries as geographically dispersed as Australia, Austria, Canada, New Zealand and the United Kingdom, the policy function has come to be reduced in recent years often with a split of government departments into separate agencies responsible for promotion and policy respectively. Such an institutional split has raised interesting issues in terms of encouraging sustainable tourism. If promotion and policy are separated how can promotion be seen to be set within sustainable tourism goals? In the short term increasing government funds into promotion at the expense of other functions may be welcomed by industry. However, it may also imply a lack of attention to other aspects of the roles of government in tourism including broader planning and policy functions which look beyond the short-term goal of attracting more tourists.

Given the complex situation which surrounds government involvement in tourism, issues of inter-organisation relationships are therefore an extremely significant component of the tourism planning and policy system. Some of these issues will be dealt with in more detail in the next chapter. However, inter-organisational relations occur not just horizontally, *within* the same level of government, but also vertically, *between* the different levels of government. The previous chapter noted how international and supranational policy actors influenced tourism planning and policy at the national, regional and local level. However, the relationship is clearly two way. Member countries of the international institutions will also be attempting to influence the policy directions of those organisations in an attempt to meet national policy goals. For example, countries such as Australia, Canada, New Zealand and the United States have been trying to encourage the development of increasingly freer trade in the Asia-Pacific region, including trade in services and foreign investment, through APEC by using diplomatic methods to influence APEC agreements. Similarly, the various countries of the EU can be readily seen to be attempting to influence EU policy decisions and settings in order to meet their own national interests.

However, as the scope of international relations has increased in light of the expansion of global interdependence so the role of sub-national government, e.g. provincial, state and regional governments, has also increased in the international sphere. The emergence of international policy areas such as sustainable development, human rights, environmental pollution, migration, international trade flows and tourism in recent years has meant that, unlike traditional diplomatic/strategic/security concerns, these 'new' policy areas are intermestic in nature, that is, they are 'simultaneously, profoundly and inseparably both domestic and international' in character (Manning 1977 : 309). The actions of sub-national actors in the international sphere, also described as paradiplomacy (Soldatos 1993) and constituent diplomacy (Kincaid 1990), is readily apparent in the tourism field, particularly in federal systems where states and provinces compete with each other not only for tourists but also for investment. For example, in Australia nearly all the states and territories have offshore offices from which they try and attract tourists, a situation which has led to confusion in the marketplace at times (Australian Government Committee of Inquiry Into Tourism 1987), while states and territories have also opposed any efforts to coordinate activities by which investment might be attracted for fear of losing out on investment to other states. 'The Northern Territory Government does not see a significant role or need for the co-ordination of foreign tourist development between the States, including the Northern Territory, by the Commonwealth Government' (Northern Territory Government submission in Senate Standing Committee on Environment, Recreation and the Arts 1992 : 248). Similarly, the Canadian provinces compete aggressively in their marketing in the United States, while the American states promote themselves separately in Canada.

The interdependence of local, national and international communities at a level 'that is far greater than any previously experienced' (Rosenau 1990 : 17), has led to a situation in which leaders of subnational governments have become 'acutely aware of the influence which international actors . . . can have on the economic well-being of their constituencies' (Fry 1986 : 301). The success of their leaders in attracting investment, trade and tourism can contribute both to economic development and employment generation and to increasing their chances for re-election. Nevertheless, it is important to note that the international activities of sub-national governments are not simply the result of proactive policy settings. Provincial/state government subsidies are now subject to scrutiny under free trade regimes because of the possibility that they could be considered trade distortions. Therefore, provincial/state governments may seek defensive positions with respect to their policy choices. In addition, environmental and social policies at the state/provincial level may also come under international scrutiny, particular with respect to trans-border and regional policy issues.

The area of transnational relations, 'direct interactions between agencies (government subunits) of different governments where those agencies act relatively autonomously from central government control' (Keohane and Nye 1976 : 4) is therefore becoming of increasing importance in tourism policy and planning, particularly as regions seek to attract increasing amounts of international visitors in a complex and competitive market. Two types of transgovernment relations may be distinguished: first, where the sub-national government is a primary actor whereby it engages directly in international relations, e.g. through direct international promotion. Second, where the sub-national government is a mediating actor and seeks to affect international relations by attempting to influence the central government in its policy deliberations and actions for the purpose of promoting 'general policies that are beneficial to local conditions in such areas as trade and foreign investment' (Hocking 1986 : 484), e.g. trade policy and targeted international tourism promotion. Further, it should be noted that increasingly it is not just provincial/state governments which are playing such an international role, but also cities (e.g. see Cohn and Smith 1995). For example, in the case of tourism, cities are increasingly lobbying to host international events, such as the Olympics and International Expositions, and also competing to be able to attract international investment for tourism infrastructure, such as conference and exhibition centres and sports stadia.

The growing importance of sub-governments in international tourism has significant implications not only for international relations but also for the domestic relations between central and regional governments. The increasing activity of regional and municipal activity in tourism promotion and planning may create substantial tensions between different levels of government and further increase the difficulties that exist in coordinating government activities. As Airey (1983) recognised, different state levels will tend to have different sets of objectives to achieve via tourism development. Similarly, Williams and Shaw (1988b : 230) observed that the study of tourism 'policy formation is made more complex because the aims of the local state may diverge from those of the central state'. For example, in the Australian situation, the Federal Government has not taken an active role in direct national tourism planning in a statutory setting because of the constitutional and political difficulties that it would face and instead has focused on the development of national tourism strategies in which the national government assumes more of a coordination role (e.g. Department of Tourism 1992; Office of National Tourism 1997a, b). Tourism-related land use planning initiatives have occurred at the state level where responsibilities for statutory planning is more clearly defined (e.g. Tourism South Australia 1990, 1991). At times this has meant substantial conflicts between federal and state policy in a number of areas, such as resort and tourism infrastructure development in World Heritage areas. Nevertheless, the Federal Government still assumes a significant role in the tourism planning process at all levels of government through the provision of tourism research, marketing and promotion services, direct funding for local tourism planning and visitor management programmes in such areas as ecotourism and rural tourism (Jenkins 1997; Hall 1998).

Similar conflicts between central and state/provincial government have occurred in Canada and the United States. In the case of Canada, improved coordination between the provinces and Tourism Canada came about through greater emphasis on joint promotion exercises and greater private sector involvement. In the United States the direct tourism promotion and policy role of the Federal Government is extremely weak in comparison with the states. Where the Federal Government does play a significant role in tourism is in relation to the large expanses of federal land tied up in national parks, national monuments, and Forest Service and Bureau of Land Management lands. However, local, state and national governments often come into conflict over land use practices on federal lands as different stakeholders seek to influence various policy levels.

One of the outcomes of the desire to reduce the role of government in Western society has been a devolution of responsibilities from central government to state/provincial and/or local government; in some cases, a withdrawal by central government from the policy area and/or sector has resulted in the vacuum being filled by regional or local government and/or the private sector. For example, many transport systems have been privatised while heritage sites once managed by a national authority have become the responsibility of local government or community groups.

The changing role of government has also led to greater attention to the instruments or means by which government is able to achieve its planning and policy goals. For example, the Austrian National Tourism Organization (ANTO), or Österreich Werbung, which includes the country's federal and provincial governments, was restructured in 1997 in order to streamline the decision-making process and improve the cost-effectiveness of marketing and promotional programmes, with a resultant drop in administrative and other fixed costs from 57% in 1995 to less than 50% of ANTO's total budget in 1998 (World Tourism Organization 1998g).

In line with the national constitution, Austria's nine provincial governments are responsible for tourism development in their respective provinces, while the Federal Government coordinates tourism policy across the country. One of the major focuses of Austrian tourism policy is the development of small and medium-sized tourism enterprises (SMEs). In addition to the aim of providing a more favourable overall framework for tourism development through the restructuring process, the Austrian Government has been developing instruments, such as the use of subsidies, to support SMEs. These include:

- promotion of participation and risk capital, since the Austrian tourism industry suffers from a high share of foreign capital for investment financing as a result of the low equity capital available
- promotion of consultation and training measures in tourism facility design, in order to help develop a more varied tourism plant
- promotion of cooperation – this is intended to show that the creation of voluntary groups and networks provide synergies which improve marketing efficiency
- implementation of pilot projects in the field of cooperation – this can include multiple distribution channels, destination management schemes, or even joint offers and joint brand development (WTO 1998g).

The emphasis given by the Austrian Government to the role of cooperation in tourism development highlights the role given to public–private partnerships and stakeholder collaboration in tourism planning as opposed to command planning approaches. Nevertheless, there is a wide range of instruments available for planners to achieve their objectives.

Table 6.3 illustrates the range of planning and policy instruments that are available to government to give effect to tourism planning and policy objectives. The various measures range from voluntary instruments through to highly coercive mechanisms such as removal of property rights by compulsion. However, there is no one 'perfect' instrument or measure to solve planning and policy problems. Multiple instruments are often used and even these will result in 'imperfect' solutions. As Selman (1992 : 10) commented with respect to environmental planning, 'this inherent variety [of instruments] is instructive . . . as it confirms that there is no single panacea for the regulation of natural resources, but rather a menu of potential mechanisms which may be selected according to the nature of the issue at stake and their political acceptability'. Nevertheless, there are a number of criteria by which different planning and policy instruments may be evaluated. According to Haughton and Hunter (1994):

- an instrument must be capable of attaining its objective in a reliable and consistent fashion, while being adaptable to changing circumstances over time and sensitive to differences in local conditions (this is the measure of effectiveness)
- an instrument should be judged against costs (this is a measure of efficiency)
- an instrument should be equitable in its impact
- compliance costs need to be weighed
- an instrument must be politically acceptable, easy to operate and as transparent and understandable as possible
- an instrument should be compatible with other policy approaches.

Furthermore, as government withdraws more from direct intervention in the economy, so the role of persuasion, argument and the creation of partnerships with various stakeholder groups becomes all the more important. It is to these processes that the next chapter will now turn.

Conclusions

This chapter has examined a number of issues with respect to tourism planning and policy at the national and sub-national level. It has identified the various roles that government and the state play in tourism, with particular reference to the appropriateness of those roles and the role that public planners may pay with respect to attempting to meet the public interest. The chapter also discussed the organisational aspects of government involvement in tourism. Although there are many institutional means and forms by which government involvement in tourism is expressed, it was argued that at the broad level government involvement has been shifting from a developmental to a promotional role. This has corresponded with a change in the role of the central state and increasing importance of the local state expressed through the

Table 6.3 Tourism planning and policy instruments

Categories	Instruments	Examples
Regulatory instruments	1. Laws	Planning laws can give considerable power to government to encourage particular types of tourism development through, for example, land use zoning which determines desirable and undesirable land uses.
	2. Licences, permits, consents and standards	Regulatory instruments can be used for a wide variety of purposes especially at local government level, e.g. restraining undesirable uses, setting materials standards for tourism developments, or they can be used to set architectural standards for heritage streetscapes or properties.
	3. Tradeable permits	Often used in the United States and, increasingly, in Europe to limit pollution or resource use. However, the instrument requires effective monitoring for it to work.
	4. Quid pro quos	Government may require businesses to do something in exchange for certain rights, e.g. land may be given to a developer below market rate, the development is of a particular type or design or there is a guaranteed period of occupancy or use.
	5. Removal of property rights	In order to achieve planning outcomes, such as the development of tourism infrastructure or the removal of inappropriate land uses, government may remove property rights (freehold or leasehold ownership) either on the market or through compulsory acquisition.
Voluntary instruments	1. Information and education	Expenditure on educating the local public, businesses or tourists to achieve specific goals, e.g. appropriate tourist or industry behaviour.
	2. Volunteer associations and non-governmental organisations	Government support of community tourism organisations is very common in tourism. Support may come from direct grants, tax benefit and/or by provision of office facilities. Examples of this type of development include local or regional tourist organisations, heritage conservation groups, mainstreet groups, tour guide programmes, or the establishment of industry associations and networks, including sectoral networks, e.g. farmstay, bed and breakfast, adventure tour operator and winery associations; and regional tourism operator networks.
	3. Technical assistance	Government can provide technical assistance and information to business with regard to planning and development requirements, including the preparation of environmental and social impact statements.

Table 6.3 (cont'd)

Categories	Instruments	Examples
	4. Argument and persuasion	Government may seek the cooperation of stakeholders by persuading them that certain patterns of behaviour or conduct is appropriate for furthering common interest of stakeholders and/or self interest.
Expenditure	1. Expenditure and contracting	This is a common method for government to achieve policy objectives as the government can spend money directly on specific activities, this may include the development of infrastructure, such as roading, or it may include mainstreet beautification programs. Contracting can be used as a means of supporting existing local businesses or encouraging new ones.
	2. Investment or procurement	Investment may be directed into specific businesses or project, while procurement can be used to help provide businesses with a secure custom for their products.
	3. Public enterprise	When the market fails to provide desired outcomes, governments may create their own businesses, e.g. rural or regional development corporations enterprise boards. If successful, such businesses may then be sold off by private sector.
	4. Public–private partnerships	Government may enter into partnership with the private sector in order to develop certain products, locations or regions. These may take the form of a corporation which has a specific mandate to attract business to a certain area for example.
	5. Monitoring and evaluation	Government may allocate financial resources to monitor rural economical environmental and socio-economic indicators. Such measures may not be valuable to government to evaluate the effectiveness and efficiency of tourism planning and development policies and objectives but can also be a valuable source of information to the private sector as well.
	6. Promotion	Government may spend money on promoting a region to visitors either with or without financial input from the private sector. Such promotional activities may allow individual businesses to reallocate their own budget by reducing expenditures that might have made on promotion.

Financial incentives	1. Pricing	Pricing measures may be used to encourage appropriate behaviour, market segments and/or to stimulate or reduce demand, e.g. use of particular walking trails through variations in camping or permit costs.
	2. Taxes and charges	Governments may use these to encourage appropriate behaviours by becoming individuals and businesses, i.e. pollution charges. Taxes and charges, e.g. passenger or bed taxes, may also be used to help fund infrastructure development, e.g. regional airports, or help fund regional tourism promotion.
	3. Grants and loans	Seeding money may be provided to businesses to encourage product development, business relocation, and/or to encourage the retention of heritage and landscape features. Grants and loans may also be used to provide for business retention in marginal economic areas.
	4. Subsidies and tax incentives	Although subsidies are often regarded as creating inefficiencies in markets they may also be used to encourage certain types of behaviour with respect to social and environmental externalities, e.g. heritage and landscape conservation, that are not taken into account by conventional economics. Subsidies and tax incentives are one of the most common methods to establish or retain tourism businesses, especially in peripheral and rural areas.
	5. Rebates, rewards and surety bonds	Rebates and rewards are a form of financial incentive to encourage individuals and businesses to act in certain ways. Similarly, surety bonds can be used to ensure that businesses act in agreed ways; if they do not then the government will spend the money for the same purpose.
	6. Vouchers	Vouchers are a mechanism usually used to affect consumer behaviour by providing a discount on a specific product or activity, e.g. to shop in a specific centre or street.
Non-intervention	1. Non-intervention (deliberate)	Government deciding not to directly intervene in sectoral or regional development is also a policy instrument, in that public policy is what government decides to do and not do. In some cases the situation may be such that government may decide that policy objectives are being met so their intervention may not add any net value to the rural development process and that resources could be better spent elsewhere.

Source: after Hall (1998); Hall and Jenkins (1998).

activities of sub-national governments (state, provincial and municipal governments). Such a shift also means that increasing attention needs to be given to domestic and, increasingly, international interorganisational relationships in tourism planning and policy. Finally, the chapter discussed some of the instruments by which government achieve their policy goals as part of the tourism planning process. The next chapter further continues the emphasis on relational aspects of tourism planning with a focus on the destination level of tourism.

Questions and further reading

What are the main roles of government in tourism? Discuss the extent to which they are given effect in your country at the national and local level.

What is the most equitable approach to funding tourism promotion?

Identify the manner by which the institutional arrangements for government involvement in tourism in your country are organised in terms of primary and secondary agency responsibility? How does this set of arrangements differ from the New Zealand situation (Table 6.1).

Why have tourism related subnational government actors become more important in international relations?

Evaluate the application of tourism policy instruments (Table 6.3) in your country at either the national or local level against the criteria identified by Haughton and Hunter (1994) (see p. 156).

Hall (1994), Hall and Jenkins (1995) and Elliot (1997) provide accounts of the role of government in tourism at the national level. Accounts of various national approaches to tourism are also to be found in Williams and Shaw (1998b, also see later editions), Richter (1989), Pearce (1992), Hall, Jenkins and Kearsley (1997), and Hall and Page (1997, 1999b).

Chapter 7

Planning destinations: creating cooperative structures

Destinations are the focal point for much tourism research. Metelka (1990 : 46) defines a destination as the 'geographic location to which a person is traveling', with Gunn (1994 : 107) equating the idea of a destination to that of a 'travel market area'. Similarly, Medlik (1993 : 148) defines a tourism destination as

> Countries, regions, towns or other areas visited by tourists. Throughout the year their amenities serve their resident and working populations, but at some or all times of the year they also have temporary users – tourists. How important any geographical unit is as a tourism destination, is determined by three prime factors: attractions, amenities and accessibility, which are sometimes called tourism qualities of the destination.

Nevertheless, defining what actually constitutes a destination is highly problematic (Davidson and Maitland 1997) with the term often being equated with that of a 'resort' (Vukonic 1997) and also being applied at a number of scales. Smith (1995) provides a number of ways in which regionalisation may be identified in tourism research through such measures as cartographic regionalisation, perceptual regionalisation, cognitive mapping, functional regionalisation and destination zone identification. Drawing on the work of Gunn (1979), Smith (1995 : 199) identified a number of criteria that might be applied in the identification of destination zones:

- The region should have a set of cultural, physical and social characteristics that create a sense of regional identity.
- The region should contain an adequate tourism infrastructure to support tourism development. Infrastructure includes utilities, roads, business services, and other social services necessary to support tourism businesses and to cater to tourists' needs.
- The region should be larger than just one community or one attraction.
- The region should contain existing attractions or have the potential to support the development of sufficient attractions to draw tourists.
- The region should be capable of supporting a tourism planning agency and marketing initiatives to guide and encourage future development.
- The region should be accessible to a large population base. Accessibility may be by road, scheduled air passenger service, or cruise ships.

Nevertheless, despite the value of such an approach, precise boundaries will still be difficult to identify (Smith 1995). Moreover, from a public planning perspective it should also be noted that perceptual regions or destination zones may run over different government boundaries, making land use planning and even tourism promotion extremely difficult as it raises the potential for conflicts between different government jurisdictions. In attempting to overcome such difficulties, Davidson and Maitland (1997 : 4) defined destinations in terms of 'a single district, town or city, or a clearly defined and contained rural, coastal or mountain area' which share a number of characteristics:

- a complex and multidimensional tourism product based on a variety of resources, products, services and forms of ownership
- other economic and social activities, which may be complementary to or in conflict with the various aspects of tourism
- a host community
- public authorities and/or an elected council with responsibility for planning and management
- an active private sector.

Davidson and Maitland's approach towards tourism destinations is useful as it highlights the complexity of destinations. Although some tourism marketers and promoters and, perhaps, even planners may sometimes seem to propose otherwise, a destination is not just another 'product' or 'commodity'. Destinations are places in which people live, work and play. If we are serious about making places sustainable then we need to treat them as the complex set of relationships and networks that they are. As Hewison argued, 'the time has come to argue that commerce is *not* culture, whether we define culture as the pursuit of music, literature or the fine arts, or whether we adopt Raymond Williams' definition of culture as "a whole way of life". You cannot get a whole way of life into a Tesco's trolley or a V & A Enterprises shopping bag' (1991 : 175). Similarly, Goodwin (1993 : 149) observed:

> The urban region is thus more than a simple coherence of production and consumption (and even this is never guaranteed). It is a complex collection of individuals and communities, which in certain instances develop particular regional and local cultures, formed by social relations and practices outside of capital's narrow logic. Together these movements and cultures can be important in helping to sustain or to destroy the coherence of a particular place. The 'building' and 'revolutionising' of an urban landscape is thus never just physical and economic: it is also social, cultural and political, and changes in these processes can play a vital role in easing economic transformation and helping to form a new round of coherence . . .
> The promotion of new urban images, of new lifestyles and of new 'city myths', is often a necessary prelude to the establishment of new urban economies. Importantly, however, the formation of these new images themselves is an issue of challenge and contestation, an issue which is often fought through particular political agencies and institutions.

For some, places are now commodities to be produced and consumed. The competitive ethos of the marketplace has become translated into a burgeoning 'place market' (Sadler 1993). 'The primary goal of the place marketer is to construct a new image of the place to replace either vague or negative images previously held by current or potential residents, investors and visitors' (Holcomb 1993 : 133), in order to effectively compete with other places within the constraints of a global economy for a share of mobile international capital (Harvey 1987, 1989a). 'This marketing operation involved the construction or selective tailoring of particular images of place, which enmeshed with the dynamics of the global economy and legitimised particular conceptions of what were "appropriate" state policy responses' (Sadler 1993 : 175). The new rhetoric of 'the local' therefore has to be seen as deeply embedded in processes of global accumulation, in a 'fragmented mosaic of uneven development in which competitive places try to secure a lucrative development niche' (Swyngedouw 1989 : 31).

This chapter discusses tourism planning at the local or destination level. It first discusses the nature of place competition within a global economy before going on to examine the ways in which places manage themselves in terms of growth management strategies and cooperate in order both to compete more effectively and deal with conflict.

Destinations and places

Although destinations have long promoted themselves to potential visitors, there has been a qualitative change in the nature of place promotion since the early 1980s when shifts to reduce the role of the state in a globalising economy, otherwise known as 'Thatcherism' (UK), 'Reaganomics' (USA) and 'Rogernomics' (New Zealand), occurred. Within the tourism, geography and marketing literature, the concepts of 'place marketing' (e.g. Madsen 1992) also sometimes described as 'selling places' (e.g. Burgess 1982; Kearns and Philo 1993), 'geographical marketing' (e.g. Ashworth and Voogd 1988) or 'reimaging strategies' (Roche 1992; Hall 1994), have arisen to describe this new phenomenon. As Ashworth and Voogd (1988 : 65) argue, the process of place marketing reflects a 'paradigm structuring the way the complex functioning of cities is viewed . . . [as] many urban activities operate in some kind of a market . . . in which a planned action implies an explicit and simultaneous consideration of both the supply-side and the demand-side . . . [and] such an approach has implications for . . . the way the cities are managed'. Although the notion of place marketing was initially applied in the urban context (Page 1995), the concept has increasingly come to be used to described place promotion in rural regions as well (Butler et al. 1998).

One of the main reasons for the attention given to place as a focus of academic, government and industry interest is the process of globalisation, whereby geographical transformations are now being brought about through the international restructuring of capitalist economies and the consequent changes to the nature and role of cities and regions as they seek to attract ever more mobile investors (Robins 1991).

It has created new centres and peripheries, and also new territorial hierarchies. It has produced new relational contexts and configurations . . . beyond this, there is the overarching global context: 'regional differentiation becomes increasingly organised at the international rather than national level; sub-national regions increasingly give way to regions of the global economy (Smith 1988 : 150)' (Robins 1991 : 24).

Similarly, Kotler et al. have argued that 'In a borderless economy, [places] will emerge as the new actors on the world scene' (1993 : 346). According to Kotler et al. (1993) we are living in a time of 'place wars' in which places are competing for their economic survival with other places and regions not only in their own country but throughout the world. 'All places are in trouble now, or will be in the near future. The globalization of the world's economy and the accelerating pace of technological changes are two forces that require all places to learn how to compete. Places must learn how to think more like businesses, developing products, markets, and customers' (Kotler et al. 1993 : 346).

The profound changes to the global economic and cultural system – technological diffusion, decreasing cost and increasing speed of transportation, increasing diffusion of information, and declining barriers to trade – which are generally characterised under the heading of 'globalisation', have tremendous implications for tourism planning. As has been indicated in the emphasis placed by this book on systems, relationships and the multi-scale nature of tourism planning and policy, 'These changes express themselves both in the relationship of individual cities to each other and to the system of which they form a part; and also in the internal structure of the city' (P. Hall 1995 : 3). 'Major cities of the world are becoming increasingly linked – by global networks of telecommunications, computers and air transport' (Brotchie et al. 1995 : vi). While cities and places are in increased competition with each other they are correspondingly more linked and entwined with each other's fates than ever before. Nevertheless, there is no formal theory of location for 'high touch' industries such as the arts, tourism, leisure and entertainment sectors,

> but it is clear that they tend to cluster strongly in established major metropolitan cities . . . They may also cluster disproportionately in specialised cities such as university towns . . . and places of unique historic character. They thus have a close symbiotic relationship with the more specialised non-mass segments of the tourist industry, notably business tourism and cultural tourism. Only rarely, and only in the mass tourist sector, can entirely new urban spaces be created for this complex of industries; and this sector is the most vulnerable to globalised third world competition exploiting the potential offered by long-haul jets and lower labour costs (P. Hall 1995 : 7–8).

The notion of rapidly circulating international capital within the global economy is also implicit in the work of Kotler et al. (1993), probably the major place marketing text which is oriented within the mainstream empiricist marketing tradition. According to Kotler et al. (1993 : 18) a central proposition of *Marketing Places: Attracting Investment, Industry, and Tourism to*

Plate 7.1   Darling Harbour redevelopment, Sydney, Australia. The Darling Harbour redevelopment established a major leisure/tourism/retail in the inner city in an effort to renew a rundown dockyard area.

Cities, States, and Nations, was that the 'marketplace shifts and changes occur far faster than a community's capacity to react and respond. Buyers of the goods and services that a place can offer (i.e. business firms, tourist, investors, among others) have a decided advantage over place sellers (i.e. local communities, regions, and other places that seek economic growth).'

Kotler et al. (1993 : 18) refer to the need for places to adopt a process of 'strategic place marketing' for urban and regional revitalisation in order to design a community 'to satisfy the needs of its key constituencies'. Such a process embraces four interrelated core activities:

- designing the right mix of community features and services
- setting attractive incentives for the current and potential buyers and users of its goods and services
- delivering a place's products and services in an efficient, accessible way
- promoting the place's values and image so that the potential users are fully aware of the place's distinctive advantages (1993 : 18).

'Place marketing means designing a place to satisfy the needs of its target markets. It succeeds when citizens and businesses are pleased with their communities, and meet the expectations of visitors and investors' (Kotler et al. 1993 : 99). Various investments can be made to a place to 'improve livability, investibility, and visitability', a process made up of the four components of place:

Plate 7.2 Docklands redevelopment, London, England. The massive redevelopment of London's docklands has led to substantial changes in the economic and social mix of the area.

- place as character
- place as a fixed environment
- place as a service provider
- place as entertainment and recreation (Kotler et al. 1993 : 100).

From all of this the reader may well ask, so how is strategic place marketing any different from the strategic tourism planning process discussed earlier in the book? In many ways they are clearly similar. However, there is one fundamental difference when we look towards public tourism planning that is attempting to develop sustainable forms of tourism development, and that is the notion of seeking to meet a public interest through equitable programmes

Plate 7.3   Crown Casino, Melbourne, Australia. The development of the casino complex was aimed not only at redeveloping the waterfront area but also in promoting a more exciting image of the city.

and policies. In objectifying place as a commodity, as within the empiricist tradition of the majority of marketing, including tourism marketing, the people constituting place have often been placed outside of the place marketers and the developer's frame of reference. As Hudson (1988 : 493–494) recognised:

> [T]he point is that for these people the locality is *not just* a space in which to work for a wage but a place where they were born, went to school, have friends and relations etc.; places where they are socialised human beings rather than just the commodity labour-power and, as a result, places to which they have become deeply attached. These localities are places that have come to have socially endowed and shared meanings for people that touch on all aspects of their lives and that help shape who they are by virtue of where they are.

In commodifying place as a product that can be revitalised, advertised and marketed, places are presented not so much 'as foci of attachment and concern, but as bundles of social and economic opportunity *competing* against one another in the open (and unregulated) *market* for a share of the capital investment cake (whether this be the investment of enterprises, tourists, local consumers or whatever)' (Philo and Kearns 1993 : 18). Harvey (1989c) sees four different competitive elements for cities attempting to restructure themselves:

1 competition within the spatial division of labour
2 competition within the spatial division of consumption
3 competition for command functions
4 competition for redistribution

The 'terrain of thinking' about local economic policies and political forms is therefore being shifted (Duncan and Goodwin 1985a, 1985b, 1988), so that a range of local institutions 'now internalise the idea that the interests of a place are best served by lifting the "dead hand" of regulation and by opening it to the sway of market forces' (Philo and Kearns 1993 : 19).

As discussed in Chapter 3, theories are also policies (Hall and Jenkins 1995). Academic, government and industry arguments as to the role of the local state are intimately related. Institutional arrangements are increasingly based around the notions of privatisation and deregulation, twin processes which supposedly promote the unfettered operation of so-called 'market forces' (Cloke 1992). The infrastructure of urban government is becoming increasingly privatised, along with the ideologies and discourses of regeneration and revitalisation. 'Where public agencies were once seen as an essential part of the solution to any urban crisis, they are now viewed as part of the problem itself' (Goodwin 1993 : 148). However, it is ironic that Kotler et al.'s (1993) discussion of strategic place marketing fails to address the means by which the citizenry can actually participate in the place marketing process to decide how their city or region should be presented to consumers, if at all. Within this context, normative assumptions about equal individual access to power and decision-making pervade much of the marketing literature. Yet, clearly, individuals do not have equal access to power and decision-making. As Hall and Jenkins (1995) argued, business interest groups tend to dominate the tourism policy-making process, while Harvey (1988) highlighted the role of growth coalitions in urban redevelopment (see the discussion in Chapter 6 on the role of government as public interest protector). Similarly, Lowe (1993 : 211) commented on the potential power of the 'regional entrepreneur': 'A person of vision, tenacity and skill (such as a charismatic mayor, a clever city administrator, or wealthy business leader) to put a particular stamp upon the nature and direction of urban entrepreneurialism, perhaps to shape it even, to particular political ends' (Harvey 1989a : 7).

Changing places, changing thinking

The focus on the local, on cities and regions, has led to changes in thinking about how places operate. As Brotchie et al. (1995 : 442) observed, there has been a shift in thinking in urban planning and policy theory from macro-analysis to micro levels of analysis, 'from the notion that cities are strong, collectively organised systems to ideas that cities are composed of many groups and individuals in competition, betraying great diversity but also great adaptability, acting locally but generating organisation and order which is manifest at more global scales through the urban hierarchy'. Such sentiments apply equally as well to rural areas as well. Brotchie et al.'s comment illustrates the need to perceive what is happening at the local level in the context of what is happening at the sub-national, national and international scales. As has been previously noted, the relationships which drive the tourism planning process are horizontally and vertically connected within the different scales of governance.

This means that in focusing on local processes which give rise to the aggregates, we observe new approaches to 'organised complexity' (Batty 1995 : 470). However, it must be noted that, as the field of place marketing indicates, the capacity to think globally, act locally, does not necessarily lead to sustainable conclusions. Nevertheless, realisation of the embedded set of relations between local, regional, national and global processes does have substantial value. For example, in the age of ecology and global environmental issues we increasingly recognise the transborder nature of environmental problems. Indeed, there may be significant shortcomings attached to local land use control, including:

- the absence of a comprehensive planning framework
- the predominance of municipal self-interest and the lack of a mechanism to allocate undesirable but socially necessary land uses to optimal sites
- the inherent inability of local governments to address larger environmental questions
- the essentially negative character of local controls (Delogu 1984).

As Cullingsworth (1997 : 125) observed, 'Local governments are severely limited in their ability to manage urban growth. The issues are essentially regional in character. Restraints in one area may simply result in development pressures moving elsewhere in the region.' In such cases resolution of growth issues then moves to another scale, i.e. state or provincial. In response to such problems, growth management has emerged as a highly important approach not only to urban development but the management of tourist destinations as well (Gill and Williams 1994; Gill 1998).

Growth management includes both the promotion of development and the protection of land against development. 'Growth management is inherently a governmental process which involves many interrelated aspects of land use. The process is essentially coordinative in character since it deals with reconciling competing demands on land and attempting to maximize locational advantages for the public benefit' (Cullingsworth 1997 : 149–150). Several elements of growth management can be identified:

- consistency among government units – ensuring that different agencies share similar policy goals, values and instruments
- concurrency – requiring infrastructure to be provided in advance or concurrent with the new development
- containment of urban growth – the substitution of compact development for urban sprawl
- provision of affordable housing – so as to ensure social equity
- broadening of growth management to embrace economic development – the 'managing to grow' aspect
- protection of natural systems, including land, air and water; and a broadened concern for viability of the regional economy (after DeGrove and Miness 1992).

Gill (1998) has noted that in the case of much tourism resort development, it is only after the resort has established itself as a tourist destination then the challenge of addressing the needs of residents is considered. 'While clearly this post-hoc consideration of residents needs seems inappropriate, economic considerations in developer-driven resort projects seem, at least in the past, to have dictated such an approach' (Gill 1998 : 106). Nevertheless, emerging longer-term visions of resort viability linked to the recognition that good resorts are good communities may, however, lead to more integrated approaches in which residents' needs as well as those of the tourist are considered to be of equal importance (Minger 1991).

Growth management is a systematic impact management strategy which calls for an integrated sharing of ideas between citizens and managers (Stein 1993). Such a process is not easy as it requires the identification and reconciliation of the different values of stakeholders regarding ideal conditions. 'Conflicts over natural resources are rarely exactly what they seem. What appears to be a simple collision of purposes is usually a combination of issues, past history, personalities, and emotions' (Amy 1987 in Millar and Aiken 1995 : 628). As Cullingsworth (1997 : 150) noted,

> Acceptability across the spectrum on interests is the key characteristic of successful growth management policies. Securing of this acceptability is difficult, enormously time consuming, and fraught with political problems. Moreover, it is an ongoing process: the determination of land uses, the timing of development, the coordination of development with the provision of infrastructure all involve continuing debate and planning, the achievement of consensus, and the provision of adequate finance. In short, growth management is a major part of the continuing process of government.

The tourism industry needs to be sensitive to the needs of the local community and must, in the long term, be accepted by it if it is to maintain economic sustainability for extended time horizons. This requires an understanding of the mechanisms by which tourism can become a part of the community rather than something that is imposed on it. Ongoing collaborative planning between stakeholders in tourist destinations is surprisingly rare, given attention to community-based tourism planning in the tourism literature, but is becoming an increasingly important component of strategic tourism planning (Go et al. 1992; Simmons 1994; Jamal and Getz 1995; see also Chapter 4). However, as Gill and Williams (1994) have indicated, some resort communities in North America (e.g. Aspen, Colorado; Lake Tahoe, Nevada; Whistler, British Columbia) are turning to growth management practices as a guide to more integrated approaches (Gill and Williams 1994), with Whistler having developed an extremely comprehensive monitoring system (Gill 1998).

The establishment of a monitoring system is a vital aspect of growth management strategies as not only does it provide details by which progress towards desirable futures can be benchmarked, but it also details a series of indicators that serve to provide a basis for informed community stakeholder debate about such futures. As Williams and Gill (1994 : 184) commented, 'Community involvement in establishing desirable conditions is perhaps the single most important element of growth management.' Table 7.1 provides a number of examples of community management-based indicators of tourism impact that can be used in growth management planning strategies. According to Wight (1998) indicators to reflect desired conditions and use should ideally:

Plate 7.4   Whistler, British Columbia, Canada. This resort development has grown into a permanent, thriving community that has a strong growth management strategy in order to maintain the resident's quality of life.

- be directly observable
- be relatively easy to measure
- reflect understanding that some change is normal, particularly in ecological systems, and be sensitive to changing use conditions
- reflect appropriate scales (spatial and temporal)
- have ecological, not just institutional or administrative boundaries
- encompass relevant structural, functional, and compositional attributes of the ecosystem
- include social, cultural, economic and ecological components
- reflect understanding of indicator function/type (e.g. baseline/reference, stress, impact, management, system diagnostic)
- clearly relate to vision, goals and objectives
- be amenable to management.

The evaluation of destination capacities, which is often a component of growth management, parallels project-based planning which is a common feature of tourist development (Pearce 1989). For example, the Shankland Cox partnership, a British-based planning consultancy, has identified four basic studies which are regarded as essential in the preparation of a comprehensive plan for any tourism development.

1 The tourist market: its origin, form, needs, rate of growth and competition for it.
2 The physical capacity of the area: its ability to absorb the requirements of tourism in terms of its natural attractions, infrastructure and economic resources.

Table 7.1 Examples of community management-based indicators of tourism impact

Community management objective	Indicators of impact
Population stabilisation	Out-migration levels In-migration levels Age/gender structure
Employment change	Direct job creation Indirect job creation Employment levels Job retention levels Job displacement levels Job satisfaction Labour force structure
Income change	Person/household income levels Inflation levels Tax revenue levels Direct economic impact Indirect economic impact
Community viability enhancement	Infrastructure levels Public service levels Housing availability Employee housing availability Resident attitudes
Welfare/social services	Health/social service/education access Services distribution Recreation activity access
Cultural enhancement	Cultural facility access Cultural event frequency Resident attitudes
Conservation improvement	Pollution levels Indicator species Measures of biodiversity Conservation practices Cultural feature damage Environmental maintenance costs
Amenity enhancement	Levels of crowding density Privacy access Visual amenity satisfaction

Source: After Getz (1977); Williams (1993); and Williams and Gill (1994).

3 The socio-economic impact on local communities migration, housing and social infrastructure for the support population.
4 The environmental capacity of the area: the limits imposed upon tourist development to protect the quality of the area in terms of landscape, townscape, tranquillity and culture (Mills 1983 : 132).

Project-based planning probably represents the most immediate face of tourism planning for most members of the general public. However, the efficacy and effectiveness of project planning will depend on the emphasis given to its various elements by developers and the receptiveness of planning authorities to its usefulness as a planning tool. Furthermore, while such planning may be described as comprehensive in terms of the range of dimensions it covers, it cannot be described as 'integrated' in that it does not provide for linkages and relationships with stakeholders in terms of the formulation, development, implementation and evaluation of the tourism planning process. Moreover, it tends to be a 'one-shot' study, which although valuable for establishing baseline data, does not become part of an ongoing assessment and evaluation of tourism's affects on the destination, and the community stakeholders' selection of desired futures.

The involvement of people in the planning and decision-making processes which affect their community is extremely important: such activity is likely to foster 'sustainability', as participants will then be more likely to regard themselves as stakeholders in the implementation of programmes. Nevertheless, governments will also need to use a range of instruments by which growth management policies can be implemented. Table 7.2 presents a selection of growth management tools and techniques, while Table 7.3 illustrates potential direct and indirect tourism growth management strategy options. As readers will notice, the strategies reflect the range of instruments available to government noted in the previous chapter. Again, it must be recognised that there is no universally appropriate strategy available for managing growth in tourism destinations. Instead, strategies, tools and techniques will be selected according to local characteristics, the nature of the planning problem and the acceptability of such instruments. Nevertheless, the above discussion of growth management and the changing thinking surrounding how to manage changing places has highlighted the role of stakeholder relationships and collaboration in tourism planning and it is to these lynchpins of strategic tourism planning that we shall now turn.

Relationships and networks

This book has continually stressed the relational aspects of tourism planning. The metaphor of relational webs and social and economic networks provides a useful descriptive way of capturing a conception of relational social dynamics that exist in tourism planning and, of course, everyday life. Spatial planning systems provide a framework to manage the various connections between networks which co-exist in a locality (Healey 1997). Governance, which is the management of the common affairs of political communities, i.e. the public interest, may serve to sustain or transform relational webs. Increasingly, the role of the public tourism planner is to assist in the development and maintenance of networks, whether it be for reasons of tourism development (Jamal and Getz 1995), management of heritage sites (Hall and McArthur 1998), or maintenance of agency support.

Table 7.2   Growth management tools and techniques

Growth management tools	Growth management techniques
1 *Policy and assessment*	By-law requirements
	Comprehensive plans
	Regional plans
	Fair share low-cost housing
	Information services
	Employment/resident balances
2 *Impact analyses*	Fiscal impact
	Social impact
	Cost/benefit analysis
	Environmental impact
	Carrying capacity analysis
3 *Regulatory systems*	
3.1 Environment controls	Environmentally sensitive areas
	Special planning areas
	Pollution controls
3.2 Development right transfers	Development rates and location
3.3 Restrictive covenants	Concession in landowners
	Initial land title documents
3.4 Zoning uses	Conventional zoning
	Conditional zoning
	Planned unit development
	Special permits (e.g. historic districts)
3.5 Other zoning tools	Minimum floor areas/lot sizes
	Height restrictions
	Population density
	Performance standards
	Geographical constraints
3.6 Quota systems	Development/building permits
	Utility connections
3.7 Short-term tools	Moratoria
	Creative foot-dragging
	Negotiation and permit review
	Off-site levy charges
4 *Capital expenditures*	Land banking
	Development rights purchases
	Capital programming
5 *Revenue systems*	
5.1 Exactions	Land/money dedications
	Capital facility dedication
	Low/moderate income housing allocations
5.2 Tax and fee systems	Urban and rural service areas
	Utility fees
	User rates
	Local improvement areas
	Development districts

Source: Schiffman 1989 in Williams and Gill (1994).

Table 7.3 Potential tourism growth management strategy options

Direct strategies	Indirect strategies

Enforcement
 • increased surveillance (formal, informal)
 • impose fines
 • establish by-laws
	Physical alterations
	 • provide guidelines for:
	   – architectural design
	   – development
	   – landscape design
	   – access to infrastructure
	   – capacity

Zoning
 • separate incompatible:
   – activities
   – land uses
   – tourist groups
   – resident/tourist groups
	Information dispersal
	 • disseminate appropriate behaviour information
	 • advertise alternate locations
	 • distribute low impact activity guidelines
	 • distribute codes of ethics for tourists, residents, tourism operators

Use rationing
 • limit use of:
   – specific facilities/sites
   – access routes
 • provide reservation use only
	Economic incentives
	 • create:
	   – differential user-fee structures
	   – differential utility fees
	   – local improvement areas

Activity restrictions
 • restrict:
   – type of use
   – length of stay
   – timing of activity	

Source: after Williams (1993).

Networking refers to a wide range of cooperative behaviour between otherwise competing organisations and between organisations linked through economic and social relationships and transactions. Current government interest in networking stems from the view that the networked firm appears to be an important component of both successful national economies and of highly performing regional economies (e.g. Sabel 1989; Cooke and Morgan 1993) and may offer considerable potential to assist in cushioning the effects of economic restructuring, particularly in rural and peripheral areas (e.g. OECD 1990; Marsden et al. 1993; Butler et al. 1998).

Networks are a distinct, hybrid mode of coordinating economic activity that are alternatives to organisation by markets or within firms (hierarchical transactions) (Harper 1993). Networks involve firms of all sizes in various combinations; they can be locally or internationally based, can occur at all stages of the value chain, and they range from highly informal relationships through to contractual obligations. Network development has received enormous attention in both academic and government circles in recent years. However, networking is not a new phenomenon and has long been a hallmark of innovative organisations. The innovation literature attests to 'the central importance of external collaboration with users and external sources of technical expertise [and] these empirical studies of innovation demonstrated the importance of formal and informal networks, even if the expression "network" was less frequently used' (Freeman, 1991). Nevertheless, as Freeman goes on to observe, 'there has been a major upsurge of formal and semi-formal flexible networks in the 1980s, including some new types of network'. Networks are defined as arrangements of interorganisation cooperation and collaboration. Such collaboration occurs, for example, 'where firms cooperate in production and marketing, to exchange know-how and market intelligence, to jointly train their employees, to develop research capacities and new markets, to purchase raw materials in bulk, to share equipment and infrastructure, and so on. If the collaborators also compete in input and product markets – as is often the case – networks are said to encompass the cooperative elements of otherwise competitive relationships' (Bureau of Industry Economics (BIE) 1991b : 5). Similarly, in a much cited work, Powell notes, that in networks

> Transactions occur neither through discrete exchanges nor by administrative fiat, but through networks of individuals or institutions engaged in reciprocal, preferential, mutually supportive actions. Networks can be complex: they involve neither the explicit criteria of the market, nor the well-organised routines of the hierarchy. A basic assumption of network relationships is that parties are mutually dependent upon resources controlled by another, and that there are gains to be had by the pooling of resources. In network forms of resource allocation, individual units exist not by themselves, but in relation to other units. These relationships take considerable effort to establish and sustain, thus they constrain both partners' ability to adapt to changing circumstances. As networks evolve, it may become more economically sensible to exercise voice rather than exit. Benefits and burdens come to be shared . . . Complementarity and accommodation are the cornerstones of successful production networks (Powell 1990 : 78).

Network relationships are of great significance for tourism promotion. For example, with respect to Baltic Sea tourism destinations World Tourism Organization Chief of Quality of Tourism Development, Henryk Handszuh, commented, the region's 'tourism image must be strengthened, enhanced and, to the extent possible, coordinated. Coordination here does not mean any formal intervention, but identifying and working towards common objectives by tourism enterprises in the region and by their support bodies in the public and private sectors' (WTO 1998h). Similarly, Buhalis and Cooper (1998 : 338) observed that networking will allow small and medium-sized tourism enterprises (SMTEs) to:

- pool their resources in order to increase their competitiveness
- draw up strategic management and marketing plans
- reduce operating costs
- increase their know-how.

Despite increasing recognition of the significance of networks there is an absence of a common set of factors for describing and explaining the development of networks as the conditions which give rise to network formation are quite diverse. Network arrangements have multiple causes and varied 'historical trajectories' (Powell 1990 : 323):

> ... in some cases, the formation of networks anticipates the need for [network] form of exchange; in other situations, there is a slow pattern of development which ultimately justifies the form; and in still other circumstances, networks are a response to the demand for a mode of exchange that resolves exigencies that other forms are ill-equipped to handle.

Nevertheless, several classifications of network relationships have been developed (Harper 1993). For example, the BIE (1991a, b) developed an institutional categorisation (e.g. firm, government), while Powell (1990) developed a classification scheme which emphasised the reasons why the network came into being. Several different types of inter-organisational linkages can be recognised (after Harper 1993). Table 7.4 illustrates the different types of networks, with examples taken from the field of wine tourism (Hall et al. 1997). One of the most significant aspects of all four types of networks is that not only do they represent flows of corporate information, e.g. research and promotion, but, from a tourism perspective, they may also represent flows of tourists on the ground. In other words, the economic and social characteristics of networks parallel the flow of goods and services including tourists. Communicative relationships therefore affect economic and political relationships.

From the perspective of government, such flows are particularly attractive as they represent a potential enhancement of the multiplier effect of tourist spending, particularly in rural and peripheral areas, thereby enhancing regional economic development processes. Furthermore, from a policy perspective, networking is attractive because it reflects a middle ground that 'seeks a more interactive role with firms, and rejects the two extreme cases of total reliance on the market on one hand, and the proliferation of subsidies and "hand outs" on the other' (Australian Manufacturing Council 1991 : 8). However, network formation may be difficult in areas where there are information gaps about the perceived benefits of such linkages, such as in the wine tourism area (Hall et al. 1997).

Two industry areas which have been the focus of considerable national and regional government attention because of their income-generating capacities and economic development potential are the wine and tourism industries (e.g. Institut für Geographie der Universität Würzburg and Geographische Gesellschaft Würzburg 1984; Comté Régional du Tourisme de Languedoc-Roussillon Prodexport 1994; AusIndustry 1996; Macionis and Cambourne 1997; Hall and Macionis 1998). However, despite a broad awareness by policy makers of the potential linkages that exist between the wine and tourism industries there appears to be only a limited understanding of the nature of wine tourism among industry stakeholders, a situation which may substantially

Table 7.4 Network categorisations – using wine tourism examples

Interorganisational relationship		Example
Dyadic linkage	Formed when two organisations find it mutually beneficial to collaborate in achieving a common goal.	A joint venture between a winery and a tour company to promote winery visitation.
Organisation sets	Interorganisational linkages that refers to the *clusters* of dyadic relations maintained by a *focal* organisation.	A visitor information centre or wine tourism organisation develops individual relationships with wineries so as to provide tourists with information on each winery.
Action sets	A coalition of *interacting* organisations that work together in order to achieve a specific purpose.	A visitor information centre and the wineries in a region come together to produce a regional wine tourism promotional campaign.
Networks	Used here in a narrow formal sense, refers to a group of organisations that share common organisational ties and can be recognised as a *bounded* interorganisational system.	A federation or association of wine tourism organisations, e.g. the Movimento del Turismo del Vino; the European Council of Wine Regions (Assembleia das Regioes Europeias Viticolas (AREV)); and the Dyonisos multimedia network of European wine-producing regions.

Source: after Hall et al. (1997).

limit the ability and, therefore, potential benefits of creating linkages between the two industries (Hall et al. 1997).

In a study of the New Zealand wine industry, Hall and Johnson (1997) reported that approximately 85% of wineries were open for cellar door sales. Indeed, many of the smaller wineries could not survive without them as visitors contribute to both direct sales by purchase at the winery and indirectly by placing themselves on mail order lists and purchasing wine later upon their return home. Yet many wineries do not see themselves as dealing with 'tourists' and/or excursionists and therefore as part of the tourism industry.

Hall and Johnson (1997; see also Hall et al. 1997) in their survey reported a range of approaches by wineries in their relationships towards tourism. For example, in responses to questions about their attitudes towards tourism, three Hawke's Bay wineries, on the East coast of the North Island of New Zealand, commented:

> 'Overseas tourists are not as interested in wineries, wine buying, wines. They have not in general, come to the region because of the wines . . . This could be a pointer for the promotion of the region'.
> 'Do you mean overseas or local visitors?'
> 'Generally tourist don't buy much wine but are time consuming for staff'.

with similar reactions from two Canterbury (South Island) wineries: 'Not at this stage – but more money spent on wine promotion instead of administration would be good', and 'I don't really support tourism – most countries I have travelled to which are heavily tourist orientated were ruined countries'. In a reflection of a widely held attitude among over half of those interviewed, a Martinborough (South Island) winery stated: 'As I don't consider being a tourist operator I am in the business of selling my wine all the rest is carried out by us to welcome people to us'. A statement supported by another local winery:

> Our small business is to grow and make wine for sale to customers, whether they are 'tourists' or not. I am coordinator of group visits for the wineries that are prepared to take groups – 5 or 6 at present date. Many groups are not interested at all in wine and groups often only buy 1–6 bottles between them. None of us, if truthful, consider ourselves to be tourist orientated as we are very small establishments and tourism is an extra expense just at present and time consuming without extra (unpaid!) staff.

Nevertheless, in Marlborough, a region in the South Island of New Zealand which has some of the strongest relationships between the wine and tourism industries with a high proportion of wineries offering cellar door sales, the response was much more positive (Hall and Johnson 1997). Following are two responses which are representative of the comments received from the region:

> 'Here in Marlborough we are fortunate that most wineries and tourism operators work together well'.

'Need to look at generating greater volumes of tourists through Marlborough & attempt to cater all seasons. I believe most tourists are intimidated by the atmosphere of some wineries – need to bring these people into a "comfort zone" – in addition – EDUCATE! – people seek information constantly – need to provide professional quality, varied levels of education – improve their awareness and comfort with the wine industry'.

In an extremely supportive statement about wine tourism in the region, one winery commented, 'Although we do not undertake cellar door sales [and] tastings we still see ourselves as part of the tourism industry. Tourism promotion is important to regional wine industries [and] to all small local vineyards . . . We belong to a wine marketing group (sub group of a wine growers [association]) which produces a winery map, undertakes displays [and] could in future mount food and wine events.' Indeed, several responses, even from those who had otherwise been negative about tourism, recognised the value of relevant cooperative relationships and networks. For an example, a Marlborough winery called for 'relationship marketing with parallel industries – arts, music, food, etc'. Similarly, a Martinborough (North Island) winery called for 'linkage of wineries to events held in area – golf tournaments, cycle tours, flower and garden shows, music and entertainments', with another observing a 'lack of cooperative element within the wineries of the region'. Finally, a Central Otago (South Island) winery, noted that New Zealand wineries were 'just babies at wine tourism compared with Australia – need local and central government financial assistance to get further down track'.

The range of responses received by Hall and Johnson (1997) is reflective of the partial industrialisation of tourism discussed in Chapter 3 (Leiper 1989; 1990b). Although, as students of tourism, we can recognise that many segments of the economy may benefit from tourism, it is only those organisations with a direct relationship to tourists and/or who actually *perceive* their customers as tourists that become actively involved in fostering tourism development or in marketing. For example, there are many other businesses, such as food suppliers, petrol stations and retailers, sometimes described as 'allied industries', and as the discussion above notes, wineries, which also benefit from tourists but which are do not readily identify themselves as part of the tourism industry (Hall 1998b). Therefore, in most circumstances, unless there is a clear financial motive for wine businesses to create linkages with tourism businesses it will often require an external inducement, such as the establishment by government at no or minimal cost to individual businesses, to create new network structures which link the wine and tourism sector.

In several parts of the world such organisations have been established with government or external assistance. For example, network development is an important component of European wine tourism initiatives. Many of the European wine trails and routes are being developed with the assistance of the Europäische Weinstrassen (European Council of Wine Routes), incorporated within the European Council of Wine Regions (Assembleia das Regioes Europeias Viticolas (AREV)) which was created within the framework of the Dyonisos multimedia network of European wine producing regions. The network was established in 1992 with European Community support and now encompasses more than 60 European wine regions (Hall and Macionis 1998). According to the Europäische Weinstrassen, winetrails are, 'the best framework for cooperative work between government, private enterprises and associations, the tourism industry, wine and the local council' in encouraging regional development and job creation. In addition, from the perspective of individual producers, 'an opportunity exists for the winegrower to establish advantageous connections and a strategically important means of obtaining trade in high quality produce which encourages the development of direct sales and levels of awareness, and consolidates the image of products as well as creating a loyal consumer market' (translated from Europäische Weinstrassen, n.d., in Hall and Macionis 1998).

Similarly, several Australian state governments have established organisations specifically to facilitate and coordinate the development of wine tourism. In 1993, the Victoria state government established and funded the Victorian Wineries Tourism Council (VWTC), to develop and implement tourism strategies to promote Victoria's wineries and wine regions. In 1996 the South Australian Government developing a state wine tourism strategy and formation of the South Australian Wine Tourism Council (SAWTC) (Hall and Macionis 1998).

The issue of government or external intervention, such as European Union funding, to directly promote networking arrangements raises a number of issues including: if networks are so overwhemingly positive in their effects, why do they not arise spontaneously without government intervention? And, what advantages do public tourism planners and policy makers have in identifying profitable opportunities for increased interorganisational networking that market participants do not have? (Harper 1993). The BIE (1991a, 1991b) identified four potential roles for government in the development of networks:

- disseminating information on the opportunities created by networks
- encouraging cooperation within industries through industry associations
- improving existing networks between the private sector and public sector agencies involved in research and development, education and training
- examining the effects of the existing legislative and regulatory framework on the formation, maintenance and breakup of networks relative to other forms of organisation, such as markets and firms.

In the case of wine tourism, government has directly utilised the first three roles in the creation of specific organisations and/or the provision of funding for research, education, cooperative strategies and mechanisms, and information provision. The BIE (1991a, b) considered information gaps to be a major factor in the impairment of network formation. Indeed, the discussion above indicates substantial negative attitudes towards tourism by wineries, whereas tourism organisations tend to be far more positive towards the wine industry (Hall et al. 1997; Hall and Macionis 1998), a situation which is extremely supportive of Leiper's (1989) concept of tourism's partial industrialisation. However, some negative responses by wineries towards linkages with the tourism industry may not be entirely misplaced: some wineries, by virtue of their market and/or their location, may receive little direct benefit from tourism – for example, if they do not have cellar door sales or, in the case of some major companies, see their direct customers as being wholesale and retail outlets (Hall and Johnson 1997; Hall et al. 1997).

In order to maximise the potential contribution of network development to regional economies it becomes essential that network relationships move from dyadic linkages and organisation sets (such as those which typically exist when the wine tourism organisations are first established) to action sets and formal networks. Indeed, there is already considerable encouragement for such a move given the development of regional wine tourism associations in Europe, North America and Australasia (Hall et al. 1997). Yet, for such networks to be sustained it is important that they be internally driven rather than government maintained. To argue, as do Morris and King (1997), that 'The opportunities abound. It is simply a matter of being sufficiently entrepreneurial to explore the options and work with others to create tourism products that are unique and provide contributing SMEs with a competitive advantage' is inadequate. Wineries, particularly in those areas which are not major tourist destinations, require substantial persuasion and information provision so as not only to illustrate the potential benefits of linkages between wine and tourism but also to dispel myths about what constitutes tourism, particularly the belief that domestic excursionists to the cellar door are not tourists (Macionis 1996; Hall and Johnson 1997). The task for the tourism planner is then to use argument and persuasion in attempting to encourage the development of networks. Not every network will succeed and it should also be recognised that networks, like any organisational structure which is goal driven, will also go through an organisational lifecycle. Moreover, not every business in a given region will want to become part of a network. Nevertheless, great things can still be accomplished through the establishment of such networks that can achieve more by operating in cooperative arrangements than could possibly be achieved by a single business. Finally, network creation and collaborative arrangements can take time to establish and to develop trust between participants, especially if they come from different sectoral or cultural backgrounds (Powell 1990), a situation which is also reflective of the way in which relational approaches to tourism planning may be able to assist in conflict resolution in tourism.

Conflict in destination development

Opposition to the growth of tourism in an area or the establishment of specific tourism developments often arises because access to common resources, e.g. scenic qualities, water, air, public resources (the commons) is coveted by other users with different, often incompatible interests (see Millar and Aiken 1995 for a statement of this problem in terms of coastal zone use in Canada). Opposition is often multifaceted and based on a range of concerns which may range from opposition on macro-level environmental (e.g. habitat destruction, air and water pollution and alterations in scenic values), social (e.g. loss of low-income housing, loss of sense of place, breakdown of communities and lack of employment opportunities to locals) and economic (e.g. failure to purchase locally, localised inflation and increases in rents and government taxes) grounds to micro-level concerns which arise from jealousy and envy (e.g. Hall et al. 1997; Wahab and Pigram 1997; Laws et al. 1998). Moreover, many of these elements are combined with respect to how residents' sense of place is affected by tourism development (Dovey 1989; Craik 1991a). A sense of place arises where people feel a particular attachment or personal relationship to an area in which local knowledge and human contacts are meaningfully maintained. 'People demonstrate their sense of place when they apply their moral or aesthetic discernment to sites and locations' (Tuan 1974 : 235). However, people may only consciously notice the unique qualities of their place when they are away from it or when it is being rapidly altered.

Change is a normal part of the human experience. However, tourism, as with much of modernity, may serve to hasten rates of change above those which are 'comfortable' for many people. New buildings, new economic structures and, perhaps most significantly of all, influxes of new people – the tourists and the people who serve them – can serve to dramatically alter the web of relations that residents have with place, and therefore substantially affect tourism development and planning as well (Pigram and Wahab 1997; Laws et al. 1998). As Millar and Aiken (1995 : 620) commented, 'Conflict is a normal consequence of human interaction in periods of change, the product of a situation where the gain or a new use by one party is felt to involve a sacrifice or changes by others. It can be an opportunity for creative problem solving, but if it is not managed properly conflict can divide a community and throw it into turmoil.' Tourism planners therefore typically have to find accommodation between various stakeholders and interests in tourism development in an attempt to arrive at outcomes which are accepted by stakeholders including the wider community.

Conflict resolution is a process of value change that attempts to manage disputes through negotiation, argument and persuasion by which conflict is eliminated or at least minimised to the extent that a satisfactory degree of progress is made by the interested stakeholders. Substantial attention has been given to issues of conflict resolution in the field of resource and environmental management (e.g. Mitchell 1989); however, relatively little attention to such issues has been forthcoming in tourism, a somewhat surprising situation given the extent to which research on tourism destination development and the social impacts of tourism have highlighted the extent to which dissatisfaction often arises with tourism by residents.

Conflict resolution can take a number of forms, ranging from information exchange to mediation involving a neutral third party, through to binding arbitration in which a decision-making function is mutually given to a third party by the affected stakeholders. In all such situations two primary objectives will be sought. First, an agreed definition of resource use. Second, the creation of a working relationship between the affected parties which will provide for effective implementation of the resource use agreement and ongoing monitoring, evaluation and procedural mechanisms for dealing with new problems that might emerge.

Conflict resolution and mediation is clearly an integral component of sustainable tourism development with the assumption that the various groups and interests involved have doubts about their ability to achieve objectives. For example, Ostrom (1990) noted the following interrelated factors of sustainable development at the community level:

- clearly defined boundaries
- harmony between appropriation and provision rules and local conditions
- participation by all interested parties in changes that may affect them
- accountable monitoring
- graduated sanctions administered by an accountable authority
- low cost and readily accessible mechanisms for conflict resolution
- recognition by governments of the rights to organise
- for those regimes which are part of large systems of governance, appropriate licensing provisions, monitoring, enforcement, conflict resolution and organisational arrangements.

Much conflict resolution, particularly in terms of land-use planning, is based on the interests of the stakeholders engaged in conflicts. Such a process of consultation and bargaining assumes that stakeholders have clearly defined specific interests which are amenable to negotiation. According to Millar and Aiken (1995) the following are the necessary conditions for resolving an interest-based conflict:

- the parties to the conflict identify themselves and are represented
- all parties can agree on the 'facts'
- there is an urgent need for all parties to arrive at an agreement
- the parties want to resolve the matter as soon as possible
- all parties are willing to be flexible
- all parties can be certain that the other parties will abide by the agreement once it is defined.

However, such interest-based approaches only work effectively in a limited range of situations; for example, when there are only a limited number of parties to the resolution process. As Powell (1990 : 326) noted with respect to the creation of networks, 'The more homogenous the group, the greater the trust, hence the easier it is to sustain network-like arrangements.' Therefore, the likelihood of interest-based approaches working can be expected to fall as

- the number of stakeholders increases
- the size of social groups increases
- the membership of social groups becomes more unstable
- stakeholders become more geographical dispersed
- the diversity of participants increases.

Similarly, such an approach will work best in relation to a single project, issue or small site, the more complex the conflict becomes the more difficult will be the possibilities for resolving conflicts based on interests. More significantly, an interest-based approach may do little to resolve conflicts and antagonisms that are rooted in deep-seated differences in values, ideologies and philosophies, 'for as long as the initial motives, understandings, and interests remain, so too will the conflict' (Millar and Aiken 1995 : 621) – for example, as often seems to exist between conservation groups and developers in tourism in areas of perceived high environmental value. Conflict management therefore needs to be able to develop structures that can deal with fundamental value differences in terms of issues of

- *Appropriateness* – how appropriate is a certain type of development or use of technology in an area given its wider impacts?
- *Property rights* – what are the respective rights of neighbouring land uses and the rights of individual property owners in relation to wider public rights?
- *Governance* – who sets the rules and regulations under which the parties operate and how are they enforced and changed?

Fundamental value differences are clearly not unique to tourism-related development; however, little effort has been made to transfer the experience of conflict resolution in other areas of resource management and use to the complex set of stakeholder attitudes and relations which usually surround tourism. Legal regulation is not sufficient to resolve value conflict in tourism planning and development. While 'winners' and 'losers' can be determined through legal processes, fundamental value conflict can continue and even made worse as 'losers' come to feel even further alienated from the 'rules of the game' that set the structures within which conflict resolution may occur (Hall and Jenkins 1995). For example, 'the agenda is often the subject of intense debate since some parties will work hard to add or delete issues of special concern' (Susskind and Madigan 1984 : 185). It is necessary, therefore, to seek to resolve or manage conflict at a deeper level than that represented through mere legal solutions. This deeper level is best recognised as that of 'trust'.

Trust

Embedded in the continuation of a mutually satisfying relationship is a dialogue of trust. While trust is a future-oriented concept, it is based on past performance. Ongoing interactions and flows of information over time have built up a bond of confidence that anticipated outcomes can be relied upon to be achieved. This is a significant departure from transaction cost economics, which assumes that the agent within the principal/agent relationship is not to be trusted (Pavlovich 1997). As Millar and Aitken (1995 : 623) recognised, 'it is a general rule of all agreements that the formal particulars are only effective to the extent that the working relationship is based on trust'.

Trust is one of the basic elements of understanding cooperation and conflict among stakeholders in the tourism planning process. Trust is 'confidence in the reliability of a person or system, regarding a given set of outcomes or events', which is based on 'faith in the probity or love of another, or in the correctness of abstract principles' (Giddens 1990 : 34). It is the glue which holds communities and societies together. Trust creates the potential for voluntary collective action through fostering the assurance necessary for individuals to commit towards a common goal (Coleman 1990).

Trust is a 'collective attribute' based on the relationships between people within a larger social system rather than just the individual recipients. Trust is therefore a set of social expectations, including broad social rules of fair, right, and taken-for-granted assumptions over common understandings that are shared by everyone involved in economic and social exchange. Coleman (1990) acknowledges that the relationship between two actors may well be conditional on the placement of trust on other related actors. The withdrawal of trust by one actor potentially has a domino effect on the system of interactions. Significantly, Coleman likens this to a grid effect with highly sensitive configurations predisposed to breaking down at a single weak point. For networks then, the performance and position of the weakest element is important to the functioning of the total network (Pavlovich 1997).

Where trust is absent, cooperative or voluntary collective action is impossible, particularly in 'commons' situations which rely on the 'curbing of opportunistic impulses toward individual exploitation' (Millar 1996 : 207). Trust therefore provides for a sufficient number of reciprocal and cooperative actions to occur such that there will be a greater return to all stakeholders than would be forthcoming through individual exploitation (Brann and Foddy 1987). Trust requires a sufficiently common set of values between stakeholders in order to operate. Therefore, attention in much conflict resolution and management in tourism development needs to be given to the social and political context within which development occurs and value conflict arises. To place the observations Millar and Aitken (1995 : 623–624) within a tourist context:

> In conflict situations, the social component is critical. The main purpose of [tourism] is to produce and ultimately sell a product, but in conflict situations we must be more concerned with how the local society and resource base are organized to accept such production . . . communities exist within a web of kinship, physical interdependency, and social obligation, and in this context, [tourism] cannot be separated from the social issues of property and morality.

For example, Millar and Aitken (1995) have identified that in many communities faced with new patterns of resource development and use there is a two-part morality of neighbourliness in which, while there is a recognition that everyone has the right to make a living, there is also a belief that everyone who is affected by developments should have the right to be consulted. Where such consultation does not occur and where sufficient resentment is reached, extra-legal means may be used to oppose new developments, including damage or destruction of property.

In the majority of societies, the turmoil that may be created by such developments has clear limits of political and social acceptability. When these limits are reached then government action and intervention becomes the order of the day, particularly as government usually seeks to minimise conflict and encourage consensus. However, the institutional arrangements of government, particularly at higher levels, may be at odds with conflict resolution at the community level. Not because government necessarily wants to be, indeed new government structures may be established so as to try to promote conflict resolution, but because the inherently bureaucratic nature of government is often at odds with the social characteristics of a community. For example, as Bingham (1986 : 115) recognised

> A general problem, particularly for public agencies and corporations, is that often the individuals with decision-making authority who can speak for the organization are not the same as those with specific technical expertise on the issues. Also, in large organisations, it is often not possible for the policy makers to spend their time to be present personally in all negotiations.

'Operating within the community setting, the ethics of a bureaucracy can lead to mistrust and conflict. In a community, heterogeneity and autonomous decision-making, not conformity, are the hallmarks; custom and tradition, not just law and rational arguments, are the guiding principles' (Millar and Aitken 1995 : 626). For example, in a study of public participation in natural resource management, Sewell and Phillips (1979) found that the managing agency provided pragmatic, agency-oriented objectives while the community had a broader set of objectives for being involved in consultation. Specifically, the objectives from the management agency point of view were to develop programs with broad public acceptance, enhance performance and improve the image of the agency. In contrast, Sewell and Phillips found the objectives from the community's point of view were to influence the design and implementation of policy and reduce the power of bureaucracy and its planners.

While public participation is seen as a standard tourism planning mechanism to deal with controversial issues, it should be noted that simply the hosting of a public meeting – a common consultation strategy – for example, will not by itself make it more likely that conflicts will be resolved. Indeed, they may well lead to even greater conflict between parties and serve to reinforce rather than change positions and come closer to agreement. 'Public meetings may help to identify conflicts, but they cannot resolve or manage them. While it is true they allow everyone to have his or her say, the root causes . . . are often neglected. In the end, the government is often left with the task of sorting out what it considers to be the relevant facts' (Millar and Aiken 1995 : 627). The problem has often been a focus on the technique – the public meeting – rather than the process and what the hoped-for outcome of the process actually is. Too often, processes have been interest based rather than values based. However, if long-term agreement and common ground between stakeholders is sought then attention must be given to the values which are involved in the conflict. Public meetings, as with some other forms of public participation, may help in the identification of conflicts and opinions but they do not of themselves manage or resolve them (Hall and McArthur 1998). Smith (1992), for example, recommended that decision-making processes be structured around four principles:

- real and regular consultation – which seeks to be inclusive of all stakeholders and which begins early in any decision-making process
- development of a common information base
- action plans which also involve multiple stakeholders – while more costly in terms of time and often money, savings can be gained in the longer term as parties to any agreement reduce the cost of regulation. Action plans should also seek to encourage ongoing dialogue in order to encourage further cooperation and anticipate difficulties in implementation and/or possible future potential conflict
- the use of a variety of effective mechanisms including mediation and zoning.

If the equity component of sustainability is to be treated seriously, then it therefore becomes vital that tourism planning, and public participation as a component of tourism planning, addresses values and people's perception of the 'truth' rather than just be geared to short-term interest management which deals with the 'facts' as seen by the makers of the rules of the tourism planning game.

This does not mean that community-based tourism planning will automatically lead to either sustainable tourism development or even a reduction in the amount of conflict surrounding tourism development. Instead, a local focus allows for the dynamics of the planning process to be altered as stakeholders face their interdependencies at a place-specific level. However, we should not romanticise the local, as so often seems to be the case in discussions of tourism planning. As Millar and Aiken (1995 : 629) recognised,

> Communities are not the embodiment of innocence; on the contrary, they are complex and self-serving entities, as much driven by grievances, prejudices, inequalities, and struggles for power as they are united by kinship, reciprocity, and interdependence. Decision-making at the local level can be extraordinarily vicious, personal, and not always bound by legal constraints.

Nevertheless, a community-based approach does provide the possibility that the necessity to consult over the use of shared resources and the needs of neighbours opens the way of conflict resolution. Perhaps more significantly, with a reduction in the extent of formal government procedures, a community-based process of management and conflict resolution provides an informality in personal relationships between stakeholders by which trust is able to develop.

Conclusions

This chapter has reviewed some of the contemporary processes within which places find themselves being turned into destinations via the process of place marketing. The chapter has also highlighted the set of interrelationships which exist within destinations which the tourism planner seeks to understand and manipulate in order to achieve certain goals and outcomes. (I realise that some readers may be upset by the use of the word 'manipulation', but that is what we try to do in social settings in order to achieve our objectives, even if these be something like more sustainable planning outcomes.) Network arrangements and conflict resolution are two spheres in which the tourism planner is extremely active in working with relationships with planning stakeholders. In this setting, 'spatial and environmental planning, understood relationally, becomes a practice of building a relational capacity which can address collective concerns about spatial co-existence, spatial organisation and the qualities of place' (Healey 1997 : 69). Tourism planners are therefore more often than not in these more entrepreneurial times involved in 'link-making' work between stakeholders, establishing relationships through the social glue of trust.

Relational resources can be regarded as a form of social capital. Collaborative or relational planning approaches focus attention on the relational webs and networks in which we live our lives. 'The challenge is to make sense of a multiplicity of claims for attention arising from the different relational webs which each actual and potential participant brings to the public arena' (Healey 1997 : 67). Creating and maintaining dialogue therefore becomes a critical role of the tourism planner. The planner will typically be involved in direction setting, which refers to the articulation by stakeholders of the values and interests that guide their individual pursuits in order to appreciate a common sense of purpose and direction, and the establishment of equitable ground rules for participation and negotiation between interests. 'Procedural issues can include deciding whether to allow the use of alternate representatives, selecting meeting sites, scheduling meetings, handling confidential information, using outside experts, deciding how to handle relations with the media, and determining whether agreements will be put in writing and, if so, in what form' (Bingham 1986 : 106).

The revitalisation and planning of place requires more than just the development of product and image. The re-creation of a sense of place is a process which involves the formulation of planning and design strategies based on conceptual models of the cities and regions which are, in turn, founded on notions of civic life and the public realm and the idea of planning as debate and argument (Bianchini and Schwengel 1991). Unfortunately, such models have only limited visibility within the place-marketing and tourism realms, as tourism and place planning is often poorly conceptualised with respect to participatory procedures, while the institutional arrangements for many of the public–private partnerships for urban redevelopment actually exclude community participation in decision-making procedures.

Policy visions, whether they be for places or for industries, typically fail to be developed in the light of oppositional or critical viewpoints. Place visions tend to be developed through the activities of industry experts rather than the broad populace, perhaps because the wider public's vision for a place may not be the same as some segments of business. Community involvement is undertaken through opinion polls, surveys or SWOT analyses rather than through participatory measures (e.g. Hall et al. 1997; Hall and McArthur 1998). Nevertheless, cities and regions 'will be re-imagined in democratic forms only by creating the conditions for the emergence of a genuinely public, political discourse about their future, which should go beyond the conformist platitudes of the "visions" formulated by the new breed of civic boosters and municipal marketers' (Bianchini and Schwengel 1991 : 234).

To enable this to occur it is vital that tourism planners become actively engaged in the places that they seek to plan. Tourism planning is therefore a combination of formal and informal theory (common sense). For example, in conflict management nothing is more valuable and productive than meeting face to face (Amy 1987). Nevertheless, we also have to be able to imagine different possibilities and futures. As Morgan (1986 : 331) commented, 'The images or metaphors through which we read organizational situations help us describe the way organizations are, and offer clear ideas over the way they could be.' 'Our different languages and discourses provide vocabularies of metaphors and reference points. Our understandings are shaped by and filtered through our thoughtworlds, our cultural systems of meaning' (Healey 1997 : 65). In this we have to understand and appreciate other people's values and perspectives as well as our own, and the way in which they change over time.

Tourism planning is imperfect. 'Local-level development is an uncomfortable and often painful process, requiring that new community-based decision-making structures be defined and experimented with' (Millar and Aitken 1995 : 640). Nevertheless, the very diversity of values and interests which make the tourism planner's life difficult at times is also a great strength, as the existence of a diversity of social groups and their values can also offer sources of resilience, resistance and innovation in changing times. Amin and Thrift (1995a and b) and Healey (1997), for example, write of the concept of institutional capacity in reference to the overall quality of the collection of relational networks in a place. One of the planner's tasks may be, therefore, to find ways of enhancing that capacity, and it is to this task that the penultimate chapter will turn.

Questions and further reading

How can place marketing approaches more effectivley incorporate community perception and ownership of place?

What are the key elements of growth management and how can they be applied to tourism?

Using the different categories of networks identified in Table 7.4 identify different tourism network relationships in your destination.

To what extent can conflict resolution be regarded as a process of value change?

What are the necessary conditions for resolving conflict?

How can the equity component of sustainable development best be addressed?

Although it has a particular British orientation, Davidson and Maitland (1997) provides an excellent introduction to issues of destination management and planning. Issues of destination planning are also dealt with in various case studies in Hall and Lew (1998). Kotler et al. (1993) provides an uncritical approach to place marketing. Contrast this book with the more critical and reflexive approach of Kearns and Philo (1993). For a useful introduction to network relationships in business see the highly influential paper by Powell (1990) as well as the literature on collaboration discussed in Chapter Four. The role of relational planning in enhancing network relationships and social capital is well discussed by Healey (1997).

Chapter 8

Designing sustainability

> Loved buildings are the ones that work well, that suit the people in them, and that show their age and history. All it takes is keeping most everything that works, most everything that is enjoyed, much of what doesn't get in the way, and helping the rest evolve. That goes better if the place is neither owned nor maintained by remote antagonists, because they distance the building from its users. What makes a building learn is its physical connection to the people within . . . an adapted state is not an end state. A successful building has to be periodically challenged and refreshed, or it will turn into a beautiful corpse (Brand 1997 : 209).

As several chapters in the book have already noted, many people think of tourism planning in terms of land use. The book has argued that while land use is a major role, the theories, thinking and assumptions behind such planning traditions require much more analysis if we are to envisage sustainable place futures which involve tourism. In order to conceptualise and imagine sustainable futures we have advocated a systems-based approach to tourism planning which emphasises the relational nature of planning and, perhaps, provides a more accurate mental representation of the way in which human–environment interaction actually works. Sustainability is, after all, basically an ecological concept. 'Seeing nature whole, understanding interrelationships and connections between human and non-human life, must, therefore, begin with the places where most people live' (Hough 1995 : 25). This chapter briefly looks at some of the implications of such an approach with respect to design issues in tourism and the way an improved understanding of material change may also lead us to develop more sustainable places.

An ecological approach

The previous chapters have moved down the different levels of tourism planning and policy analysis from the international through to the local. This chapter looks at site-level operations and the interconnections between the site and its urban and regional context. Although tourism facilities and 'resorts do not belong to the category in which much of contemporary debate on architecture is centred' (Beng 1995 : 6), recognition of such relationships are, of course, not new. The field of urban ecology has long stressed such relationships. An environmental view is an essential component of the economic, engineering, political and design processes that shape cities, with the problems facing the larger regional context of the countryside often having their roots in cities; 'solutions must, therefore, also be sought there' (Hough 1995 : 6).

According to Hough (1995 : 20), 'The nature of design is one of initiating purposeful and beneficial change, with ecology and people as its indispensable foundation.' The principles of design which he advocates are reflective of the systems and relational approaches advocated through this book (see also Alexander et al. 1977, 1987; Alexander 1979). Indeed, one only has to reflect on the relationship between ecology and economics in terms of its original Greek root – *oikos* – 'the management of the household so as to increase its value to all members of the household over the long run' (Daly and Cobb 1989 : 138), something which is often forgotten in contemporary development practices. Perhaps we should also note that *domus* meant 'house' in an expanded sense which included the people within the walls, not just the physical structure.

To Hough (1995) three principles underlie good site design:

- *Process* – 'The tendency to view phenomena as static events, frozen in time, is a root cause of the aesthetic dilemmas that we face. When nature is seen as a continuum, the argument of what is beautiful or what is less so in the landscape becomes, if not meaningless, then of a very different order of meaning' (Hough 1995 : 18–19).
- *Diversity* – in ecological terms diversity implies health. In the urban setting, 'Diversity makes social as well as biological sense . . . since the requirements of an infinitely diverse urban society implies choice' (Hough 1995 : 23).
- *Connectedness* – as the systems approach stresses everything is ultimately connected to everything else (Commoner 1971). To understand a local place, therefore, requires an understanding of its larger context, including not only the economic, social and political context but also the environmental context such as 'the watershed and bio-region in which it lies' (Hough 1995 : 24).

Therefore, given these ecological principles, 'One of the fundamental tasks of reshaping the city is to focus on the human experience of one's home places; to recognize the existence and the latent potential of natural, social and cultural environments to enrich urban places' (Hough 1995 : 26). As we noted in the previous chapter with respect to the concept of 'sense of place', over time communities develop a complex web of perceptions and attitudes as to what is appropriate and compatible with 'their' space which may be substantially affected by tourism development. This human ecology is intimately connected with people's relationship with their environment and changes which may occur. Therefore, such linkages and relationships need to be made visible in the tourism planning process in order to minimise negative impacts.

> Much of our daily existence is spent in surroundings designed to conceal the processes that sustain life and which contribute, possibly more than any other factor, the acute sensory impoverishment of our living environment . . . visibility is essential in economic and political terms . . . policies should capitalise on the visibility of the environmental consequences of human actions in the process of daily living (Hough 1995 : 30).

The loss of linkage is a significant theme in tourism, whether it be environmental relationships or culture-driven relationships such as notions of

authenticity. According to Beng (1995 : 6), 'The production of tourist architecture distorts both time and place. There is a tendency to homogeneity
behind the false fronts.' The loss of historically rooted places, including the
attempt to depoliticise them, 'decontextualising them and sucking out of
them all political controversy – so as to sell . . . places . . . to outsiders who
might otherwise feel alienated or encounter encouragements to political defi-
ance' (Philo and Kearns 1993 : 24), appears commonplace in tourism. Heritage
centres and historical anniversaries typically serve to flatten and suppress
contested views of history (Hall and McArthur 1996). However, the presentation of one-dimensional views of the past to the tourist and the community is
also encountered at the destination and resort level. In her excellent study of
tourism, history and ethnicity in Monterey, Norkunas (1993) argues that the
rich and complex ethnic history of Monterey is almost completely absent in
the 'official' historic tours and the residences available for public viewing.
In Monterey, as in many other parts of the world, heritage is presented in
the form of the houses of the aristocracy or elite. 'This synopsis of the past
into a digestible touristic presentation eliminates any discussion of conflict; it
concentrates instead on a sense of resolution. Opposed events and ideologies
are collapsed into statements about the forward movement and rightness of
history' (Norkunas 1993 : 36). Narratives of labour, class, and ethnicity are
typically replaced by romance and nostalgia. Overt conflict, whether between
ethnic groups, classes or, more particularly, in terms of industrial and labour
disputes, are either ignored or glossed over in 'official' tourist histories. The
overt conflict of the past has been reinterpreted by local elites to create a
new history in which heritage takes a linear, conflict-free form. In the case of
Monterey, the past is reinterpreted through the physical transformation of the
canneries. 'Reinterpreting the past has allowed the city to effectively erase
from the record the industrial era and the working-class culture it engendered.
Commentary on the industrial era remains only in the form of touristic interpretations of the literature of John Steinbeck' (Norkunas 1993 : 50–51).

The homogenisation of 'public' life and space, sometimes referred to as
disneyfication, is a major criticism of tourism and contemporary cultural processes. Indeed, to paraphrase Holcomb (1993), at first glance it might be
assumed that place marketing, with its enthusiastic embrace of place, its appeal
to the supposedly unique attractions of particular locations, and its passionate
text, is anything but homogenising.

> Yet ultimately, the deconstructed discourses of the packed newly post-industrial
> cities replicate the same images, amenities, and potentials and contain the same
> silences with respect to poverty, race and blight. The pastiche of upscale places is
> contextless: presumably intentionally so, since the fashionable fern bars are often in
> not-yet-completely gentrified neighbourhoods. The time of places marketed is present
> and future. The only past that matters is the packaged past of the heritage industry
> (Holcomb 1993 : 141).

Diversity and the recognition of linkages are not being acknowledged, let
alone maintained. In this context contemporary postmodern architecture and

design appear 'less as an "architecture of the people", and more as just another mutation in the "architecture of power", with power no longer being so nakedly expressed in city form as in the days of massive skyscrapers "pricking" the skies but being cunningly disguised amidst the homeliness of cultural, historical and (above all) local remembrances' (Philo and Kearns 1993 : 23). Indeed, Mitchell (1993 : 30) comments, 'A range of observers of architecture are now suggesting that the field may be bankrupt, the profession itself impotent, and the methods inapplicable to contemporary design tasks. It is further suggested that collectively they are incapable of producing pleasant livable, and human environments, except perhaps occasionally and then only by chance.' Hough (1995), among others (e.g. Selman 1992; Buckingham-Hatfield and Evans 1996; Blowers 1997; Brand 1997; Evans 1997), argues that as ecology is now an indispensable basis for environmental planning in the regional setting, so an understanding of the natural processes becomes central to design and planning practice in urban areas and other sites. In this context,

> The conventions and rules of aesthetic values have validity only when placed in context with underlying bio-physical determinants . . . We seek a design language whose inspiration derives from making the most of available opportunities; one that re-establishes the concept of multi-functional, productive and working landscapes that integrate ecology, people and economy (Hough 1995 : 31).

What might such a design language look like? One strong possibility is in the idea of adaptive architecture. Brand (1997), expanding on the work of Duffy (1990), argues that buildings should not be conceived of as unchanging architecture, rather they should be seen as several layers of longevity of different built components. Brand identifies six layers of change which, in turn, we can locate within the local, regional, national and international contexts discussed earlier in this book. The six S's of layered change in a building are

- *Site* – refers to the geographical setting and the legally defined property boundaries. Site can be an extremely long-lasting influence on urban form in particular as witnessed in the extent to which the street pattern for the cores of many present-day cities in Europe and the Middle East have been in existence for many hundred of years and in some cases thousands of years.
- *Structure* – refers to the foundation and load-bearing elements of buildings, which may also last hundreds of years.
- *Skin* – this is the exterior surface of the building which changes according to fashion, technologies and maintenance needs, often measured in tens of years.
- *Services* – refers to such things as the wiring, plumbing, air conditioning, heating, ventilation, elevators and such like. These are often replaced within seven to 15 years.
- *Space* – this is the interior layout and refers to such things as the location of walls and doors. Rates of change here may vary from approximately three years in commercial buildings to 30 years in residential properties.
- *Stuff* – refers to furniture and personal belongings that may be relatively mobile.

The layering of change helps defines how a building and places relate to people:

Organizational levels of responsibility match the pace levels. The building interacts with individuals at the level of stuff; with the tenant organization (or family) at the Space plan level; with the landlord via the Services (and slower levels) which must be maintained; with the public via the Skin and entry; and with the whole community through city or county decisions about the footprint and volume of the structure and restrictions on the Site. The community does not tell you where to put your desk or your bed; you do not tell the community where your building will go on the Site (unless you're way out in the country) (Brand 1997 : 17).

Most interaction is within the same level of pace of change. 'The dynamics of the system will be dominated by the slow components, with the rapid components simply following along' (O'Neil et al. 1986 : 98). Nevertheless, interaction and influence is a two-way process. Indeed, it is at times of major change in a system that the quick processes appear most to influence the slow. However, as Brand (1997 : 18) records, 'Slow is healthy. Much of the wholesome evolution of cities can be explained by the steadfast persistence of Site.' The pattern of ownership of land and property is extremely important for the way in which places change. Small lots allow for ongoing fine-grain change as opposed to the sudden wholesale change that can occur with large parcels of land. The more owners the more gradual and adaptive will be the change.

> Small lots will support resilience because they allow many people to attend directly to their needs by designing, building and maintaining their own environment. By ensuring that property remains in many hands, small lots bring important results: many people make many different decisions, thereby ensuring variety in the resulting environment. And many property owners slow down the rate of change by making large-scale real estate transactions difficult (Moudon 1986 : 188).

Such an observation has many significant implications for the way in which tourism development is managed, particularly in urban areas. Appropriate tourism development may well mean relatively gradual small-scale change with the inclusion of large numbers of stakeholders as opposed to large-scale developments with limited numbers of 'owners' of the project. While the large-scale project may well be a grand gesture which politicians and boosters support by virtue that they are seen to be 'doing something', the more unspectacular gradual change is likely to be more sustainable. For example, in the case of Vancouver in British Columbia, Canada, the gradual redevelopment of Granville Island as a mixed use area which maintained associations with traditional waterfront businesses, e.g. chandlers, boat repairs and moorings, as well as providing for new uses such as a hotel, markets, bookshops and theatres, has proven to be a far more sustainable development than the large-scale development of other parts of the former dock area through the hosting of the 1986 Expo. Over a decade later, many parts of the former Expo site were still undeveloped.

According to Brand (1997) good urban design is respect for what came before. 'Age plus adaptivity is what makes a building come to be loved. The building learns from its occupants, and they learn from it' (Brand 1997 : 23). Similarly, Jacobs (1993 : 245) recognised that 'Old ideas can sometimes use

Plate 8.1 Granville Island, Vancouver, British Columbia, Canada. This redevelopment has worked because it has focused on retaining a diverse economic, social and cultural base and in developing through a series of incremental steps.

Plate 8.2 Cement works, Granville Island. The retention of industrial use adds to the attractiveness of the development as it is a 'living' community.

Plate 8.3   Post Expo derelict land, Vancouver. This parcel of prime waterfront land less than 100 m from Granville Island lay derelict post Expo 1986 for almost a decade.

new buildings. New ideas must come from old buildings.' From this position the preservation movement has been one of the great design revolutions which has had substantial implications for tourism, particularly with respect to conveying place identity. Vernacular buildings evolve 'a search for pattern in folk material yields regions, where a search for pattern in popular material yields periods' (Glassie 1968 : 33). 'Preservationists have a philosophy of time and responsibility that includes the future' (Brand 1997 : 90). In this sense, the preservation movement is creating a form of inter-generational equity through the maintenance and adaptive re-use of buildings and structures from one generation to another, while also contributing to substantial economic and energy savings. For example, 'even extensive rehabilitation (services, windows, roof) typically costs 3 to 16 per cent less than demolishing and replacing an old building' (Rypkema 1992 : 27), while preservation can also help conserve the 'embodied energy' of buildings and reducing the solid-waste burden of demolition (Rathje and Murphy 1992). However, with respect to preservation and recycling of old buildings cultural and aesthetic arguments only go so far; economic issues tend to remain at the forefront of site preservation. In many places the greatest impact of tourism is through the effect that tourism development can have on real estate values, although such effects are generally little discussed in terms of their impacts on sustainability. According to Brand (1997 : 87):

> Nearly everything about real estate estranges buildings from their users and interrupts any form of sustained continuity. A triumph of abstraction, real estate operates distant from the daily life of building use, distant from the real. The 'real' in

'real estate' derives from *re-al* – 'royal' – rather than *res* – 'thing' which is the root
of 'reality'. Realty is in many ways the opposite of reality.
    All that is sold melts into cash. Real estate turns buildings into money, into
fungible units devoid of history and therefore of learning (Brand 1997 : 87).

Rapid changes in real estate value are extremely dangerous to the lives of
buildings and places. Substantial increases or decreases in value can dramatically affect land use development strategies as well as municipal charges placed
on residents and owners. Tourism development is often used by cities in
conjunction with private sector partners to try to improve real estate values.
However, such developments may have ripple effects across the social and
economic fabric of the city: for example, through the hosting of mega-events
such as the Olympics or through the construction of flagship developments
and retail/leisure/tourism complexes often associated with waterfronts, the
development of stadia and/or the convention and exhibition centres (Smyth
1994; Page 1995). Moreover, the overall long-term impacts of large-scale
tourism developments on a destination are often ignored in the planning
process despite the role that such events and facilities clearly play in urban
redevelopment strategies. If there are no lasting benefits and no identifiable
economic opportunity costs from urban redevelopment programmes, then
we are left with the proposition of Bourdieu (1984): 'the most successful
ideological effects are those with which have no words' (quoted in Harvey
1989b : 78). The function of a flagship development is then 'reduced to
inducing social stability, assuming the generated experience is sustainable for
enough people over a long period and is targeted towards those who are
potentially the harbingers of disruption what is the purpose of marketing the
city?' (Smyth 1994 : 7) (See Table 8.1 on lessons of flagship developments.)
As Hughes (1993 : 162) argued with respect to the Olympics, tourism

> can only be a component of an overall strategy for urban regeneration rather than
> a major force in its own right. Tourism associated with the Olympics, given its
> short-term nature, provides even less direct opportunity for urban regeneration.
> The hopes of regeneration lie largely in the belief that inward investment in
> other industries and increased long-term tourist flows will result. The prospect
> is based on improvements to the environment and infrastructure and a generally
> enhanced image or awareness of an area. The case for this has, however, not yet
> been demonstrated.

    Property-led urban regeneration has had some success in terms of localised
economic regeneration, 'but it has not provided a solution to the problem of
urban regeneration, even during the property boom of the mid- and late-
1980s' (Smyth 1994 : 12). Urban regeneration must be therefore seen as a
long-term activity in which diversity and relationships are enhanced not minimised. As Worpole (1991 : 145) observed:

> A town centre in which it is no longer possible to buy a pint of milk, a tin of paint,
> a fishing rod, a ball of wool, a bicycle tyre, or get a pair of shoes mended – and
> there are many such towns in Britain – will be in serious trouble in the future,

Table 8.1   Lessons of flagship developments

- flagship developments require an overt marketing strategy;
- flagship developments require management of the policy formulation, implementation and evaluation process;
- the strategy and management may be project, area and/or city-based;
- marketing concerns the creation and bringing together of supply and demand factors in an implicit exchange in the urban context;
- success is not contingent upon public versus private finance or initiation;
- design and planning should arise from the social relations of residents, business and organisations in the affected areas and those envisaged for the area;
- economic benefits do not trickle down to the disadvantaged;
- all organisations must take responsibility for the impact of their development on others in order to make the market work, as well as for moral reasons;
- political legitimacy and economic necessity will increasingly demand the participation of the local residents and other interests in the policy and development process in order to help maintain social stability, create a 'saleable' urban 'product' and create new development markets within the urban economy;
- participation may produce benefits for all parties, yet it will be a politicised process, the balance of the benefits being the object of confict and the outworking of transforming city lives and economies;
- participation is essential to the transformation of the urban economy and of relations within it and is a key management issue; and
- management must identify techniques and means to facilitate and accelerate the policy and the development process, rather than closing down the process. The management approach must be one of serving not controlling.

Source: Adapted from Smyth (1994 : 259–60).

when mobile companies and populations start relocating again and look for self-reliant towns and cities that exhibit an economic and cultural dynamic and its associated quality of life.

A diverse base not only protects the local population from the extremes of recession and external decision-making, but also attracts and helps retain inward investment (Worpole 1991). As Jane Jacobs (1965) argued with respect to the role of diversity within an urban system (an equally valid point holds with tourism systems):

> So long as we are content to believe that city diversity represents accident and chaos, of course its erratic generation appears to represent a mystery. However, the conditions that generate city diversity are quite easy to discover by observing places in which diversity flourishes and studying the economic reasons why it can flourish in these places. Although the results are intricate and the ingredients producing them may vary enormously, this complexity is based on tangible economic relationships which, in principle, are much simpler that the intricate urban mixtures they make possible (Jacobs 1965 : 162).

However, diversity also implies adopting policies of inclusiveness and equity in planning strategies. Yet the results can be extremely beneficial, as Harvey

(1989b : 14) noted, 'If everyone, from punks and rap artists to the "yuppies" and the haute bourgeoise can participate in the production of social space, then all can at least feel some sense of belonging to that place.' Although, according to Smyth (1994 : 242) 'planners tend to fear diversity and their ability to control it. Postmodernism is ostensibly trying to create diversity, yet this frequently results in efforts to create a "sense of place", a local identity, which squeezes out the most disadvantaged in terms of labour market opportunities and geographically through planning and development decisions'.

Indeed, Hughes (1993 : 162) went on to note that the hosting of a mega-event, such as the Olympics, may even disturb 'the "normal" development of tourism and other activity', with the possibility that they be 'a distraction from the pursuit of a more fundamental development strategy that will ensure long-term sustainable growth'. In these situations higher-use value of existing buildings, facilities and structures should be encouraged in order to reflect and serve long-term value, with tourism obviously being a major mechanism to provide for this. According to Brand (1997 : 80), 'The degree of institutionalization of real estate value over use value is odious enough as an invasion of privacy, but it also prevents buildings from exercising their unique talent for getting better with time.' Similarly, Jacobs has commented,

> Time makes the high building costs of one generation the bargains of a following generation. Time pays off original capital costs, and this depreciation can be reflected in the yields required from a building. Time makes certain structures obsolete for some enterprises, and they become available to others. Time can make the space efficiencies of one generation the space luxuries of another generation. One century's building commonplace is another century's useful aberration (Jacobs 1993 : 247).

Nevertheless, the ideas of preservation – space-planning, scale, mutability, adaptivity, materials, functional tradition and originality – may also be applied to new construction and development. 'Hindsight is *better* than foresight. That's why evolutionary forms such as vernacular building types always work better than visionary designs such as geodesic domes. They grow from experience rather than from somebody's forehead' (Brand 1997 : 188). Attention to the vernacular also highlights the role that process plays in design.

'An organic process of growth and repair must create a gradual sequence of changes, and these changes must be distributed evenly across every level of scale' (Alexander et al. 1975 : 68), while, according to Hough (1995 : 19), 'Design and maintenance, based on the concept of process, become an integrated and continuing management function, rather than separate and distinct activities, guiding the development of the human-made landscape over time.' Indeed, in terms of creating options for future use, one of the tenets of sustainability, Lynch (1972) writes of 'future preservation': 'Our most important responsibility to the future is not to coerce it but to attend to it. Collectively, [such actions] might be called "future preservation", just as an analogous activity carried out in the present is called historical preservation' (Lynch 1972 : 115). In tourism, notions akin to that of future preservation are generally found in the area of ecotourism, rather than in mainstream large-scale tourism

Plate 8.4 Adaptive use of vernacular design for a hotel complex, near Lillehammer, Norway. Use of traditional design principles, such as earth roofs, is energy efficent, environmentally friendly and fits into the region's natural and cultural landscape.

development. For example, Matthews (1998) argued that tourism developments in high latitude regions 'can only be truly sustainable, that is, supportable where there is a framework based on the (relatively simple) parameters of

- researching local historical models for design elements;
- utilisation of appropriate materials;
- the selection of either (or both) of the basic design tenets of integrated or camou-flaged design; and
- design by local partnership with consultants and advisors who have either no, or reduced voting rights.'

Stadia, festival marketplaces and convention centres are often constructed with the likelihood of relatively short-term periods of use in the order of 15–30 years, before they are replaced. Such patterns of development have little in common with the comments of one of the founders of the preservation movement: 'When we build, let us think that we build forever. Let it not be for present delight, nor for present use alone; let it be such work as our descendants will thank us for' (Ruskin 1989 : 186). For Lynch, future preservation not only implies longer-term thinking in construction but also that such buildings are favoured because of the way in which they contribute to a sense of place and a city's 'wholeness'. 'Longevity and evanescence gain savor in each other's presence . . . We prefer a world that can be modified progressively, against a background of valued remains, a world in which one can leave a personal mark alongside the marks of history' (Lynch 1972 : 38–39). However, longevity has no chance without serious Structure: 'A building's foundation and frame should be capable of living 300 years. That's beyond the economic lifetime of any of the players. But construction for longlife is what invites the long-term tampering it takes for a building to reach an adapted state' (Alexander in Brand 1997 : 194), which is also often described as representing something which is 'authentic' of that place. Yet this does not mean that a building is frozen in time. Indeed, Hewison's (1987) scathing attack on Britain's heritage industry was not because he considered some things were not worth preserving but because the focus on heritage appeared to exclude the potential for new possibilities and innovations that would continue the life of the heritage in question in response to the world around it. As Beng (1995 : 218) observed with respect to the design of resort developments in Southeast Asia,

> historicism can be avoided if the design has been based on the generational prin-
> ciples of the past rather than on acknowledged forms and symbols. The continued
> regeneration of traditional forms or literal, kitsch variants of past models, no
> matter how sensually or carefully crafted, can only at its best, result in the stagna-
> tion of the operational idea of tradition. At its worse, it debases both itself and the
> past model.

'To change is to lose identity; yet to change is to be alive . . . buildings partially resolve the paradox by offering the hierarchy of pace – you can fiddle with the Stuff and Space plan all you want while the Structure and Site remain solid and reliable' (Brand 1997 : 167). In seeking to extend the lifespan of tourism developments can there be any planning principles which can support some of the design principles discussed above? The answer is a definite yes and seeks to place some of the principles already discussed with respect to regional and local planning at the site level. One of the clearest planning principles is that of consultation. Brand (1997), for example, notes that in addition to failing to understand the faster areas of change in a building and the urban environment, many architects are image- and fad-driven and often fail to consult with the users. This failure to interrelate is also recorded by Moreno (1989) who noted the lack of post-occupancy evaluation by architects of the people who occupied their buildings.

At the level of policy greater attention can be given by planners to the conflict between use value and market value. As Brand (1997 : 73) observed, 'Every building leads three contradictory lives – as habitat, as property, and as component of the surrounding community.'

> A building is the interface between two human organizations – the intense group
> within and the larger, slower, more powerful community outside. The building's
> Site, Structure, Skin, and the connection to its Services are all shaped by the
> community at large . . . What you see on the street is the product of the unending
> conflict between the organizations inside and outside – buildings pretending to fit
> in or defying fitting in (Brand 1997 : 73).

Planning legislation and regulation through land use controls are extremely significant in determining the life of buildings. However, overzealous control-oriented planning also has the potential 'to defeat every imaginable future problem, that any possibility of life, spontaneity, or flexible response to unanticipated events is eliminated' (Garreau 1991 : 453). While providing broad frameworks, planning needs to be both responsive to stakeholder needs and flexible enough to allow places to evolve and change to meet the local needs. As Krier (1984 in Brand 1997 : 79) noted, 'Functional zoning is not an innocent instrument; it has been the most effective means in destroying the infinitely complex social and physical fabric of pre-industrial urban communities, of urban democracy and culture.' In design, as in planning, 'at each level of scale, it is those actually using the space who understand best how it can be made/altered to have the character of being conducive to the work, and this group should be given sole control over that space' (Alexander in Brand 1997 : 173). Environmental planners and architects such as Brand (1997), Colenutt (1997) and Hough (1995) practise what Brand describes as 'subsumption architecture', meaning that a bottom-up decision-making process is used for design and planning. Such an approach is reflective of much of the community-based approach in tourism planning and the desire for greater equity for stakeholders in sustainable tourism strategies.

Conclusions

Sustainability stimulates thinking about durability. While many natural tourist attractions are relatively durable, many human-made attractions are not, while the infrastructure which surrounds much of the tourism industry also has a relatively short lifespan. Responsibility and adaptivity are keys to the survival of buildings (Alexander et al. 1987) because of the ways in which they are responsive to the immediate users and the wider community. They are allowed to evolve. 'You cannot predict or control adaptivity. All you can do is make room for it – room at the bottom. Let the mistakes happen small and disposable . . . Adaptivity is a fine grained process. If you let it flourish, you get a wild ride, but you also get sustainability for the long term. You'll never be overspecified at the wrong scale' (Brand 1997 : 174). However, evolution is generally built of series of small changes by which adaption is made to the environment. 'Authenticity can perhaps be viewed as the attainment of an integrated, unstrained totality derived from . . . meaningful dialectical relationships between . . . different contexts' (Beng 1995 : 218). Rapid, large-scale adaptations may work in the short term but in the long term they are the least easy to change as environmental conditions again change. 'Instant-gratification, universal-standard buildings *are* corrupting. What is called for is the slow moral plastic of the "many ways" diverging, exploring, insidiously improving. Instead of discounting time, we can embrace and exploit time's depth. Evolutionary design is healthier than visionary design' (Brand 1997 : 221). In a similar fashion, Hough (1995) writes of the principle of least effort as a guiding element in urban design:

> The greatest or the most significant results that spring from an undertaking usually come from the least amount of effort and energy expended rather than the most. It involves the idea that from minimum resources and energy, maximum environmental, economic and social benefits are available. It also involves the idea of doing things small, since it suggests that making small mistakes is infinitely preferable

Plate 8.5 Where is this place? This hotel in Crete could be almost anywhere in the world given its design.

to making very large ones. Over time small mistakes can be adapted to social and environmental conditions; large ones may last indefinitely (Hough 1995 : 21).

In thinking about sustainable design, one can consider Brand's (1997 : 49) statement that 'the product of careful continuity is love'. Unfortunately, many tourist developments are not loved. In part this has been a failure of architects, politicians and planners to place such developments in a relevant local context. However, it also reflects the failure to appreciate the role of process and adaptive change. Such developments are also not sustainable.

Questions and further reading

What are the three principles which underlie good site design? How might they be applied to tourism?

What are the six S's of layered change in a building? Examine how they might be applied to a tourism development of your choice?

How do rates of change and patterns of ownership affect the sustainability of tourism developments?

In what way is the use of old buildings for heritage tourism purposes a form of intergenerational equity?

For further discussion of the value of sustainable adaptive approaches to places and sites see Alexander et al. (1977, 1987), Hough (1995) and Brand (1997) (Brand's book was also developed in conjunction with a TV series of the same name which is well worth viewing which is likely to be available through architecture libraries). Smyth (1994) provides an extremely good account of the problems encountered with flagship redevelopments.

Chapter 9

Conclusions and reflections: thinking sustainable planning

Sustainability is an 'overarching societal value' or collection of values (Evans 1997) which we increasingly find being enacted in legislation, regulations, institutional arrangements and planning processes at different scales around the globe. 'Sustainability' is also an 'ecological word' (Meier 1995 : 454). 'Global thinking must become a framework for local action, since the two are inextricably linked' (Hough 1995 : 286). Any approach to sustainable tourism planning needs to be based on sound ecological principles. This means not just an appreciation of the physical environment but also a deeper understanding of the economic, social, political and physical systems of which tourism is a part.

One of the key principles of systems thinking is that of the principle of requisite variety (Ashby 1956): in order to control or plan systems, towards some explicit goal, there must be as much variety in the controller as there is in the system itself. Such a situation lays a clear challenge to the student of tourism. What capacities do we possess to be able to understand the system we are interacting with and trying to direct along certain paths? This book has argued that our capacities are increased by an improved understanding of the process nature of planning and our role within it. Planning is not rational. It is highly political. The goal of sustainability is not a given. It is a contested concept that as students of tourism we need to be arguing for. The field of planning therefore represents an ongoing effort to interrelate conceptions of the qualities of places with notions of the social processes of 'shaping' and 'representing' places through the articulation, development and implementation of policies (see Healey 1997).

Tourism planning must also be theory rich in order to be effective in the long term so that it can adapt to its own environment. A focus on techniques at the expense of understanding different theories on the way in which planning operates, their assumptions and intended contributions, denies students a deeper understanding of planning problems. Moreover, it limits their own capacity to adapt. As Morgan (1986 : 336) argued,

> Many practical people believe that theory gets in the way of practice and that, by and large, theorizing is a waste of time. But there is a great fallacy in this way of thinking. For in recognizing how taken-for-granted images or metaphors shape understanding and action, we are recognizing the role of theory. Our images or

205

metaphors *are* theories or conceptual frameworks. Practice is never theory-free, for it is always guided by an image of what we are trying to do. The real issue is whether or not we are aware of the theory guiding our action.

Tourism planning, within the policy analysis tradition which this book takes, is a style of governance which involves long-term and strategic outlooks at the direction of public activity, and the attempt to interrelate different spheres of such activity. Planning is relational. Tourism planning may also serve to challenge forms of governance if stakeholder interests and values are not being met. Indeed, one of the biggest challenges facing tourism planners is the relevance of their work in terms of who benefits. As has been noted throughout, one of the tenets of sustainability is the idea of equity. However, the means by which such equity may be achieved in the context of tourism has been little discussed in the tourism literature.

Process and change are also major themes in tourism planning (see also Laws et al. 1998). Innovative planning is especially prevalent in rapidly changing social systems. It is even more difficult to succeed in establishing effective organizational linkages among institutions engaged in innovative planning, although clearly where a massive effort for change is intended, as in the case of sustainable development, this is a necessary condition for the successful transformation of the system. 'The strategic problem is to identify the critical points for system transformation and to activate innovative planning at these points. But if a system is already undergoing rapid change, the importance of this strategic problem decreases sharply; for the system generates change automatically' (Friedmann 1973 : 365). Tourism planners therefore need to be able to understand the direction of those changes and attempt to influence and adapt to them accordingly. However, planning is not perfect, things do go wrong. Peter Hall (1992) outlined several reasons why planning goes wrong:

- knowledge about the planning environment may change rapidly
- there are complex interrelationships between different levels of the planning system, and between different elements of the planning system
- values change over time
- there are often difficulties in reconciling values
- planning is political in character
- trade-offs are made between the interests of different generations.

Planning 'measures vary greatly in their effectiveness and ease of implementation, and attempted action over . . . issues will often be frustrated by lack of last-resort powers. Suffice for the moment to say that part of the skill of planning lies in the imaginative combination of legal remedies, negotiation, mediation and persuasion' (Selman 1992 : 11). Tourism planning is also increasingly collaborative in nature unlike the old-fashioned command and control model (Selin 1998). Such a shift has dramatic implications not only in the development of theories and models of planning but also for the individuals involved as well. How well are planners able to adapt to roles of mediator and convenor which require different interpersonal skills? How well do you think that you would be able to take on the role of a convenor, 'lacking any formal authority but having the intent to form a collaboration', and using your 'credibility, influence, knowledge of the problem domain, knowledge of stakeholder interrelationships, and personal charisma to persuade stakeholders to participate'? (Wood and Gray 1991 : 153).

A general theory of collaborative planning must be able to articulate the role of the collaborative planner in establishing, legitimising and guiding the collaborative alliance. However, 'no firm conclusions have yet been drawn as to how the convener uses various forms of authority to identify and persuade stakeholders to participate, which differences can be observed when conveners are responsive to stakeholder initiatives or are proactive in implementing their own ideas, or which specific roles conveners might play in helping organize the problem domain' (Wood and Gray 1991 : 149). Nevertheless, some significant factors may be identified (Gray 1989; Wood and Gray 1991); the convenor/planner must:

- have the ability to identify stakeholders and then induce them to participate, often this power may be based on formal planning authority, although such powers only have a limited range of application in forming partnerships
- have legitimacy among stakeholders
- be perceived by stakeholders as having a fair and even-handed approach to the planning problem
- appreciate the value of collaboration and possess the necessary interpersonal and communication skills which help establish the collaborative process and facilitate interaction between stakeholders
- be responsive to the needs of stakeholders
- be trusted.

In tourism planning there has often been far too much concentration on the techniques of planning without a look at the processes which are occurring. Nevertheless, despite the potential contribution of tourism planning towards more sustainable forms of tourism and the creation of sustainable place, planning 'should not claim the instant ability to solve complex problems'.

> It should not even necessarily claim unique expertise. It should certainly not claim to know what is good for people. Rather, it should be exploratory and instructive. It should aim to help communities think clearly and logically about resolving their problems, and in particular some of the more subtle underlying issues that concern such matters as equity and growth. It should try to examine alternative courses of action and trace through, as far as possible, the consequences of each of these for different groups of people in different places. It should not seek to avoid the difficult questions of who exercises political power on behalf of whom, and by what legitimacy. It should make recommendations, but it should not seek to impose prescriptions. It should claim modestly that planners may perhaps be more capable than the average person to conduct this kind of analysis, but not they are uniquely expert. In other words, it should aim to provide a resource for democratic and informed decision-making. This is all planning can legitimately do, and all it can pretend to do. Properly understood, this is the real message of the systems revolution in planning and its aftermath' (P. Hall 1992 : 249–250).

Reflections

This book has emphasised the relational and, ideally, collaborative nature of tourism planning. In focusing on the interplay of substance and process it has made a departure from much of the existing focus of tourism planning on techniques, control and land use to attempt to provide a more integrative approach to the complexity of tourism planning problems. This book has also stressed the role of argument and persuasion in the planning process. Tourism planning is not value free. Neither is the tourism planner. Instead, tourism planning should be recognised as being value laden. However, this should be seen as a positive as it provides the planner with the relational resources with which to appropriately adapt and change in the global environment. Nevertheless, the argumentative turn in planning (Fischer and Forester 1993), the desire to 'speak truth to power' (Wildavsky 1979) will at times prove difficult. As Reade (1997 : 71) comments

> In every society there is a dominant ideology. There must be, for without this ideological support, the ruling class could not rule. What every ruling class does, however, is to persuade the population that the ideology that legitimates is rule is no ideology at all, but a set of factual statements about the objective nature of the world. It is *the others*, they tell us (i.e. those without power, and who want it) who peddle ideology. They themselves, our rulers tell us, are pragmatists and realists, their policies and actions reflect nothing but what, given the facts of the situation, common sense dictates, and in fact no reasonable human beings could do more than they are doing.

Yet, as public tourism planners we should be engaged in the notion of the public interest and the challenge of sharing spaces. The idea of community is more than just the people who live in an area, it conveys an image of an integrated place world (*gemeinschaft*). The idea of a place-based community is both illusion and fact (Healey 1997). Nevertheless, such illusions are extremely important as we are often as willing to take a stand for something which is an ideal – such as community, democracy or sustainability – knowing that although what we end up with is always imperfect, it is still worth fighting for. Table 9.1 outlines some characteristics of a sustainable community. They are characteristics which could probably not wholly apply to any community on the planet for an extended period of time but they are still important.

This book began with a personal observation and so it will finish with one. This book has emphasised the complex, relational world in which we live. It has also noted the multiple layers of analysis within planning systems from the international to the site level. Clearly, within all of this, the next level, that of the individual actor in the tourism planning and policy-making process, is important throughout.

In my master's thesis I quoted a wonderfully inspirational geographer by the name of Gilbert White as a kind of research credo: 'Speaking only as one individual, I feel strongly that I should not go into research unless it promises results that would advance the aims of the people affected and unless I am

Table 9.1 The four characteristics of a sustainable community

Economic security
A more sustainable community includes a variety of businesses, industries, and institutions which are environmentally sound (in all aspects), financially viable, provide training, education, and other forms of assistance to adjust to future needs, provide jobs and spend money within a community, and enable employees to have a voice in decisions which affect them. A more sustainable community also is one in which residents' money remains in the community.

Ecological integrity
A more sustainable community is in harmony with natural systems by reducing and converting waste into non-harmful and beneficial purposes, and by utilizing the natural ability of environmental resources for human needs without undermining their ability to function over time.

Quality of life
A more sustainable community recognizes and supports people's evolving sense of well-being which includes a sense of belonging, a sense of place, a sense of self-worth, a sense of safety, a sense of connection with nature, and provision of goods and services which meet their needs, both as they define them and as can be accommodated within the ecological integrity of natural systems.

Empowerment and responsibility
A more sustainable community enables people to feel empowered and to take responsibility based on a shared vision, equal opportunity, ability to access expertise and knowledge for their own needs, and a capacity to affect positively the outcome of decisions which affect them.

Source: After *Wingspread Journal* (1997)

prepared to take all practicable steps to help translate the results into action' (White 1972 : 102). Some 15 years on from using that quote, I find myself sitting at my desk at 2 am on a cool Dunedin morning writing the final sentences to this book and asking myself if I still believe that credo. On reflection I can say I do. But the optimism of a younger me has been somewhat battered by the experiences of politics and life.

Establishing and maintaining collaborative and stakeholder relationships can be extremely difficult. There are clearly some people we find it difficult to get on with, whether it be personality, ego, attitudes, value differences or sheer bloody-mindedness. Yet as a collaborative planner one still has to try and do so, but I fully admit that this process is not easy and I would not pretend otherwise. Similarly, somewhat obviously by now, you would realise the extent to which I believe that argument and persuasion play such an important part in tourism planning and policy. This book is part of those arguments. However, there is also the more public role that one can play in communicating ideas. In my private and professional life, working with political parties and conservation groups, appearing in court cases and speaking in public meetings have all been part of the process of argument and the attempt to influence policy decisions, even though at times I have also wanted to avoid such arguments because of the effect that they can have on one's private life. But, as in all arguments, you win some and you lose some. Indeed, perhaps the hardest thing to accept is one's sometime inability to communicate ideas effectively and win policy and planning arguments. Yet, that is the nature of tourism planning and policy. It deals with the richness and variety of human values and existence, it is therefore gloriously imperfect, and must be accepted as such, much to the chagrin of some economic rationalists and those who would prefer things in black and white rather than shades of grey. Nevertheless, I still believe that tourism planning and public planning in particular has a vital role to play.

The last chapter noted the wonderful concept of adaptive architecture. Perhaps this book is an example of adaptive academia. It is an attempt to understand the complexity of tourism planning and, from that, to also try to see how tourism and places can be made more sustainable. This book is also part of a process, a staging post on a route to hopefully deeper understanding and better communicated observations on the nature and direction of tourism planning. I don't think that systems thinking alone will guarantee people become more environmentally and socially aware in their actions and therefore more likely to support sustainable tourism strategies. People still have to make conscious decisions about their actions and endeavours. I am not sure if I believe anymore that one act can change the world, though I do think that we can still all influence it. Nevertheless, ideas are powerful things which reverberate throughout the web of relations within which we exist. The idea of sustainability is a very powerful notion that clearly provides the possibility of a more positive future. It is to be hoped that this book will make one small contribution towards that goal.

Questions and further reading

Lew and Hall (1998) outline five 'lessons' of sustainable tourism (see p. 39). To what extent are these lessons supported or not by the discussions and observations in this book?

Why must tourism planning be theory rich?

Does planning have to achieve 100 per cent of its objectives in order to be regarded as successful?

What personal attributes do you think are required for a planner to more effectively advance more sustainable tourism outcomes?

How effectively do you feel that you can 'Speak Truth to Power' (Wildavsky 1979)?

The role of argument in planning and policy is also taken up by Wildavsky (1979), Majone (1989), Fischer and Forester (1993), and Healey (1997). In the tourism context it was taken up by Hall (1994) and Hall and Jenkins (1995).

Bibliography

Access Economics (1997) *The Economic Significance of Travel & Tourism & Is There a Case for Government Funding for Generic Tourism Marketing*, prepared by Access Economics, Tourism Council Australia, Property Council of Australia and Tourism Task Force, Canberra.

Ackoff, R.L. (1974) *Redesigning the Future*, Wiley, New York.

Airey, D. (1983) 'European government approaches to tourism', *Tourism Management*, 4: 234–44.

Alexander, C. (1979) *Timeless Way of Building*, Oxford University Press, New York.

Alexander, C., Ishikawa, S., Silverstein, M., Jacobson, M., Fiksdahl-King, I. and Angel, S. (1977) *A Pattern Language*, Oxford Unviersity Press, New York.

Alexander, C., Silverstein, A., Ishikawa, S. and Abrams, D. (1975) *The Oregon Experiment*, Oxford University Press, New York.

Alexander, C., Neis, H., Anninou, A. and King, I. (1987) *A New Theory of Urban Design*, Oxford University Press, New York.

Allison, G. (1971) *The Essence of Decision*, Little & Brown, Boston.

Amin, A. and Thrift, N. (1995a) 'Globalisation, institutional "thickness" and the local ecomony', in P. Healey, S.J. Cameron, S. Davoudi, S. Graham and A. Madani Pour (eds), *Managing Cities: The New Urban Context*, John Wiley, Chichester.

Amin, A. and Thrift, N. (1995b) *Globalisation, Institutions and Regional Development*, Oxford University Press, Oxford.

Amy, D.J. (1987) *The Politics of Environmental Mediation*, Columbia University Press, New York.

Anderson, L.T. (1995) *Guidelines for Preparing Urban Plans*, Planners Press, Chicago.

Archer, B.H. (1982) 'The value of multipliers and their policy implications', *Tourism Management*, 3 : 236–41.

Arnstein, S. (1969) 'A ladder of citizen participation', *Journal of American Institute of Planners*, 35 : 216–24.

Ascher, B. (1984) 'Obstacles to international travel and tourism', *Journal of Travel Research*, 22 : 2–16.

Ashby, W.R. (1956) *Introduction to Cybernetics*, Methuen, London.

Ashby, W.R. (1966) *Design for a Brain: the Origin of Adaptive Behaviour*, Chapman and Hall, London.

Ashworth, G.J. and Tunbridge, J.E. (1990) *The Tourist Historic City*, Belhaven, London.

Ashworth, G.J. and Voogd, H. (1988) 'Marketing the city: concepts, processes and Dutch applications', *Town Planning Review*, 59(1): 65–80.

AusIndustry (1996) *Network News: AusIndustry Business Networks Program*, December, no.6: 8.

Australian Government Committee of Inquiry Into Tourism (1987) *Report of the Australian Government Committee of Inquiry Into Tourism*, Vol. 1, Australian Government Publishing Service, Canberra.

Australian Heritage Commission (1983) *Manual*, Australian Heritage Commission, Canberra.

Australian Manufacturing Council (1991) *Networking Seminar Program: A Report on a Nationwide Series of Seminars*, Australian Manufacturing Council, Melbourne.

Barbier, E.B. (1987) 'The concept of sustainable economic development', *Environmental Conservation*, 14(2): 101–10.

Barnes, I. and Barnes, P. (1993) 'Tourism policy in the European Community', in W. Pompl and P. Lavery (eds), *Tourism in Europe: Structures and Developments*, CAB International, Wallingford, 36–54.

Barrett, S. and Fudge, C. (1981) *Policy and Action*, Methuen, London.

Bates, G. (1983) *Environmental Law in Australia*, Butterworths, Sydney.

Batty, M. (1995) 'Cities and complexity: implications for modeling sustainability', in J. Brotchie, M. Batty, E. Blakely, P. Hall, and P. Newton (eds), *Cities in Competition: Productive and Sustainable Cities for the 21st Century*, Longman Australia, South Melbourne, 469–86.

Bayliss, D. and Walker, G. (1996) 'Environmental monitoring and planning for sustainability', in S. Buckingham-Hatfield and B. Evans (eds), *Environmental Planning and Sustainability*, John Wiley & Sons, Chichester, 87–103.

Beng, T.H. (1995) *Tropical Resorts*, Page One Publishing, Singapore.

Bianchini, F. and Schwengel, H. (1991) 'Re-imagining the city', in J. Corner and S. Harvey (eds), *Enterprise and Heritage: Crosscurrents of National Culture*, Routledge, London, 212–34.

Bingham, G. (1986) *Resolving Environmental Disputes: A Decade of Experience*, Conservation Foundation, Washington DC.

Blank, U. (1989) *The Community Tourism Industry Imperative: The Necessity, The Opportunities, Its Potential*, Venture Publishing, State College, PA.

Blowers, A. (1997) 'Environmental planning for sustainable development: the international context', in A. Blowers and B. Evans (eds), *Town Planning Into the 21st Century*, Routledge, London and New York, 34–53.

Bohm, D. (1980) *Wholeness and the Implicate Order*, Routledge and Kegan Paul, London.

Botterill, T.D. (1991) 'A new social movement: tourism concern, the first two years', *Leisure Studies*, 10(3): 203–17.

Bramwell, B. and Lane, B. (1993) 'Sustainable tourism: an evolving global approach', *Journal of Sustainable Tourism*, 1(1): 6–16.

Bramwell, B., Henry, I., Jackson, G. and van der Straaten, J. (1996) 'A framework for understanding sustainable tourism management', in B. Bramwell, I. Henry, G. Jackson, A.G. Prat, G. Richards and J. van der Straaten (eds), *Sustainable Tourism Management: Principles and Practice*, Tilburg University Press, Tilburg, 23–71.

Bramwell, B. and Sharman, A. (1999) 'Collaboration in local tourism policymaking', *Annals of Tourism Research*, 26(2): 392–415.

Brand, S. (1997) *How Buildings Learn: What Happens After They're Built*, Phoenix Illustrated, London.

Brann, P. and Foddy, M. (1987) 'Trust and the consumption of a deteriorating common resource', *Journal of Conflict Resolution*, 31: 615–30.

Britton, S.G. (1989) 'Tourism, capital, and places: a contribution to the geography of tourism', a paper prepared for the New Zealand Geographic Society Conference, 20–24 August, University of Otago, Dunedin.

Britton, S.G. (1991) 'Tourism, capital and place: towards a critical geography of tourism', *Environment and Planning D: Society and Space*, 9(4): 451–78.

Brookfield, H. (1988) 'Sustainable development and the environment', *Journal of Development Studies*, 25(1): 126–35.

Brotchie, J., Batty, M., Blakely, E., Hall, P. and Newton, P. (eds) (1995) *Cities in Competition: Productive and Sustainable Cities for the 21st Century*, Longman Australia, South Melbourne.

Buckingham-Hatfield, S. and Evans, B. (eds) (1996) *Environmental Planning and Sustainability*, Wiley, Chichester.

Buhalis, D. and Cooper, C. (1998) 'Competition or co-operation? small and medium-sized tourism enterprises at the destination', in E. Laws, B. Faulkner and G. Moscardo (eds), *Embracing and Managing Change in Tourism: International Case Studies*, Routledge, London, 324–46.

Bramwell, B. and Sharman, A. (1999) 'Collaboration in local tourism policy making', *Annals of Tourism Research*, 26(2): 312–28.

Bull, A. (1994) *The Economics of Travel and Tourism*, 2nd edn, Longman Australia, South Melbourne.

Bureau of Industry Economics (BIE) (1991a) *Networks: A Third Form of Organisation*, Discussion Paper 14, Bureau of Industry Economics, Canberra.

Bureau of Industry Economics (BIE) (1991b) 'Networks: A third form of organisation', *Bulletin of Industry Economics*, 10: 5–9.

Burgess, J. (1982) 'Selling places: environmental images for the executive', *Regional Studies*, 16: 1–17.

Burns, J.P.A. and Mules, T.L. (1986) 'A framework for the analysis of major special events', in J.P.A. Burns, J.H. Hatch, T.L. Mules (eds), *The Adelaide Grand Prix: The Impact of a Special Event*, The Centre for South Australian Economic Studies, Adelaide, 5–38.

Burns, T. and Stalker, G.M. (1961) *The Management of Innovation*, Tavistock, London.

Butler, R.W. (1980) 'The concept of a tourist area cycle of evolution, implications for management of resources', *Canadian Geographer*, 24(1): 5–12.

Butler, R.W. (1990) 'Alternative tourism: pious hope or trojan horse', *Journal of Travel Research*, 28(3): 40–45.

Butler, R.W. (1991) 'Tourism, environment, and sustainable development', *Environmental Conservation*, 18(3): 201–9.

Butler, R.W. (1992) 'Alternative tourism: the thin end of the wedge', in V. Smith and W. Eadington (eds), *Tourism Alternatives: Potentials and Problems in the Development of Tourism*, University of Pennsylvania Press, Philadelphia, 31–46.

Butler, R.W. (1998) 'Sustainable tourism – looking backwards in order to progress', in C.M. Hall and A. Lew (eds), *Sustainable Tourism Development: Geographical Perspectives*, Addison Wesley Longman, Harlow, 25–34.

Butler, R.W., Hall, C.M. and Jenkins, J. (eds) (1998) *Tourism and Recreation in Rural Areas*, John Wiley, Chichester.

Burns, P. (1999) 'Paradoxes in planning: tourism elitism or brutalism?' *Annals of Tourism Research*, 26(2): 329–48.

Byars, L.L. (1984) *Strategic Management: Planning and Implementation*, Harper & Row, New York.

Campbell, S. and Fainstein, S.S. (1996) 'The structure and debates of planning theory', in S. Campbell and S.S. Fainstein (eds), *Readings in Planning Theory*, Blackwell Publishers, Oxford, 1–18.

Capra, F. (1997) *The Web of Life: A New Synthesis of Mind and Matter*, Flamingo, London.

Carpenter, S.L. and Kennedy, W.J.D. (1988) *Managing Public Disputes: A Practical Guide to Handling Conflict and Reaching Agreements*, Jossey-Bass, San Francisco.

Cauley, D.N. (1993) 'Evaluation: does it make a difference?', *Evaluation Journal of Australasia*, 5(2): 3–15.

Chadwick, G. (1971) *A Systems View of Planning*. Pergamon Press, Oxford.

Chaffee, E.E. (1985) 'Three models of strategy', *Academy of Management Review*, 10(1): 89–96.

Chaudhary, M. (1996) 'India's tourism – a paradoxical product', *Tourism Management*, 17(8): 616–19.

Clarke, J. (1997) 'A framework of approaches to sustainable tourism', *Journal of Sustainable Tourism*, 5(3): 224–33.

Cloke, P. (1992) *Policy and Planning in Thatcher's Britain*, Pergamon, Oxford.

Coggins, G.C. and Wilkinson, C.F. (1981) *Federal Public Land and Resources Law*, Foundation Press, New York.

Cohn, T.H. and Smith, P.J. (1995) 'Developing global cities in the Pacific Northwest: the cases of Vancouver and Seattle', in P.K. Kresl and G. Gappert (eds), *North American Cities and the Global Economy: Challenges and Opportunities*, Sage Publications, Thousand Oaks, 251–85.

Coleman, J.S. (1990) *Foundations of Social Theory*, Belknap Press, Cambridge.

Colenutt, B. (1997) 'Can town planning be for people rather than property', in A. Blowers and B. Evans (eds), *Town Planning Into the 21st Century*, Routledge, London and New York, 105–18.

Commoner, B. (1971) *The Closing Circle*, Knopf, New York.

Comté Régional du Tourisme de Languedoc-Roussillon Prodexport (1994) *Route des vins en Languedoc-Roussillon: projet de valorisation du patrimone viticole par le tourisme*, Comté Régional du Tourisme de Languedoc-Roussillon Prodexport, Blaye.

Cooke, K. (1982) 'Guidelines for socially appropriate tourism development in British Columbia', *Journal of Travel Research*, 21(1): 22–28.

Cooke, P. and Morgan, K. (1993) 'The network paradigm: new departures in corporate and regional development', *Environment and Planning D: Society and Space*, 11: 543–64.

Coper, M. (1983) *The Franklin Dam Case*, Butterworths, Sydney.

Corner, J. and Harvey, S. (1991) *Enterprise and Heritage: Crosscurrents of National Culture*, Routledge, London and New York.

Cowell, R. and Owens, S. (1997) 'Sustainability: the new challenge', in A. Blowers and B. Evans (eds), *Town Planning Into the 21st Century*, Routledge, London and New York, 15–31.

Craik, J. (1988) 'The social impacts of tourism', in Canberra, B. Faulkner and M. Fagence (eds), *Frontiers in Australian Tourism: The Search for New Perspectives in Policy Development and Research*, Bureau of Tourism Research, 17–31.

Craik, J. (1990) 'A classic case of clientelism: the Industries Assistance Commission Inquiry into Travel and Tourism', *Culture and Policy*, 2(1): 29–45.

Craik, J. (1991a) *Resorting to Tourism: Cultural Policies for Tourist Development in Australia*, Allen & Unwin, St Leonards.

Craik, J. (1991b) *Government Promotion of Tourism: the Role of the Queensland Tourist and Travel Corporation*, The Centre for Australian Public Sector Management, Griffith University, Brisbane.

Cullingsworth, B. (1997) *Planning in the USA: Policies, Issues and Processes*, Routledge, London and New York.

Cupitt, D. (1987) *The Long Legged Fly: A Theology of Language and Desire*, SCM Press, London.

Daly, H.E. and Cobb, J.B., Jnr (1989) *For the Common Good*, Beacon, Boston.

Damette, F. (1980) 'The regional framework of monopoly exploitation: new problems and trends', in J. Carney, R. Hudson and J.R. Lewis (eds), *Regions in Crisis*, Croom Helm, London.

Davidson, R. and Maitland, R. (1997) *Tourism Destinations*, Hodder and Stoughton, London.

Davis, B.W. (1984) 'How the World Heritage Convention works', *Environmental and Planning Law Journal*, 1: 196–8.

Davis, B.W. (1985) 'Federalism and environmental politics: an Australian overview', *The Environmentalist*, 5: 269–78.

Davis, B.W. (1989a) 'Federal–State tensions in Australian environmental management: the World Heritage issue', *Environmental and Planning Law Journal*, 6(2): 66–78.

Davis, B.W. (1989b) 'Wilderness conservation in Australia: eight governments in search of a policy', *Natural Resources Journal*, 29: 103–13.

Davis, G., Wanna, J., Warhurst, J. and Weller, P. (1993) *Public Policy in Australia*, 2nd edn, Allen and Unwin, St Leonards.

de Kadt, E. (ed.) (1979) *Tourism: Passport to Development?*, Oxford University Press, Oxford.

DeGrove, J.M. and Miness, D.A. (1992) *The New Frontier for Land Policy: Planning and Growth Management in the States*, Lincoln Institute of Land Policy, Cambridge.

Delbecq, A.L. (1974) 'Contextual variables affecting decision-making in program planning', *Journal of the American Institute for Decision Sciences*, 5(4): 726–42.

Delogu, O.E. (1984) 'Local land use control: an idea whose time is passed', *Maine Law Review*, 36: 261–310.

Department of Tourism (Australia) (1992) *Tourism Australia's Passport to Growth A National Tourism Strategy*, Commonwealth Department of Tourism, Canberra.

Department of Tourism (Australia) (1993a) *Rural Tourism, Tourism Discussion Paper No. 1*, Commonwealth Department of Tourism, Canberra.

Department of Tourism (Australia) (1993b) *Annual Report 1992–93*, Commonwealth Department of Tourism, Canberra.

De-Shalit, A. (1997) 'Is liberalism environmentally friendly?', in R. Gottlieb (ed.) *The Ecological Community: Environmental Challenges for Philosophy, Politics and Morality*, Routledge, London, 82–103.

Douglas, D. (1992) 'Program evaluation and performance measurement in Queensland', in C. O'Faircheallaigh and B. Ryan (eds), *Program Evaluation and Performance Monitoring: An Australian Perspective*, Macmillan, South Melbourne, 19–34.

Dovey, K. (1989) 'Old scabs/new scars: the hallmark event and the everyday environment', in G.J. Syme, B.J. Shaw, D.M. Fenton, and W.S. Mueller (eds), *The Planning and Evaluation of Hallmark Events*, Avebury, Aldershot, 73–80.

Dowling, R.K. (1993a) 'Tourism planning, people and the environment in Western Australia', *Journal of Travel Research*, 31(4): 52–58.

Dowling, R.K. (1993b) 'Tourist and resident perceptions of the environment–tourist relationship in the Gascoyne region, Western Australia', *Geojournal*, 29(3): 243–51.

Dowling, R.K. (1997) 'Plans for the development of regional ecotourism: theory and practice', in C.M. Hall, J. Jenkins and G. Kearsley (eds), *Tourism Planning and Policy in Australia and New Zealand: Cases, Issues and Practice*, Irwin Publishers, Sydney, 110–26.

Dredge, D. and Moore, S. (1992) 'A methodology for the integration of tourism in town planning', *Journal of Tourism Studies*, 3(1): 8–21.

Dror, Y. (1973) 'The planning process: a facet design', in A. Faludi (ed.), *A Reader in Planning Theory*, Pergamon Press, Oxford, 323–43.

Drost, A. (1996) 'Developing sustainable tourism for World Heritage sites', *Annals of Tourism Research*, 23(2): 479–92.

Duffy, F. (1990) 'Measuring building performance', *Facilities*, May: 17.

Duncan, S.S. and Goodwin, M. (1985a) 'Local economic policies: local regeneration or political mobilisation', *Local Government Studies*, 11(6): 75–96.

Duncan, S.S. and Goodwin, M. (1985b) 'The local state and local economic policy: Why the fuss?', *Policy and Politics*, 13: 27–53.

Duncan, S.S. and Goodwin, M. (1988) *The Local State and Uneven Development*, Polity Press, Cambridge.

Dutton, I. and Hall, C.M. (1989) 'Making tourism sustainable: the policy/practice conundrum', *Proceedings of the Environment Institute of Australia Second National Conference*, Melbourne, 9–11 October.

Dye, T. (1992) *Understanding Public Policy*, 7th edn, Prentice Hall, Englewood Cliffs.

Ecotourism Association of Australia (1993) Membership Brochure, Ecotourism Association of Australia, Brisbane.

Edgell, D.L. (1990) *International Tourism Policy*, Van Nostrand Reinhold, New York.

Edwards, S.N., McLaughlin, W.J., and Ham, S.H. (1998) *Comparative Study of Ecotourism Policy in the Americas, Volume III USA and Canada*, Department of Resource Recreation and Tourism College of Forestry, Wildlife and Range Resources University of Idaho/Inter-Sectoral Unit for Tourism Organization of American States, Moscow.

Eidsvik, H.K. (1980) 'National parks and other protected areas: some reflections on the past and prescriptions for the future', *Environmental Conservation*, 7(3): 185–90.

Ekins, P. (1993) 'Making development sustainable', in W. Sachs (ed.), *Global Ecology: A New Arena of Conflict*, Fernwood Publications, Halifax, 91–103.

Elkington, J. and Hailes, J. (1992) *Holidays That Don't Cost the Earth*, Victor Gollancz, London.

Elliot, J. (1997) *Tourism: Politics and Public Sector Management*, Routledge, London.

European Commission (1995) *Green Paper on Tourism*, DGXXIII European Commission, Brussels.

European Commission (1996) *The European Union's Policies for Regional Development and Cohesion*, DGXVI, European Commission, Brussels.

European Union (1993) *Resolution of the Council and the Representatives of the Governments of the Member States, Meeting Within the Council of 1 February 1993 on a Community Programme of Policy and Action in Relation to the Environment and Sustainable Development – A European Community Programme of Policy and Action in Relation to the Environment and Sustainable Development*, Official Journal NO. C 138, 17/05/1993 P. 0001–0004, EUR-Lex: Document no. 493Y0517(01).

European Union (1998) *Special Report No 3/96 on Tourist Policy and the Promotion of Tourism, Together with the Commission's Replies*, Official Journal NO. C 017, 16/01/1997 P. 0001–0023, EUR-Lex: Document 397Y0116(01), Court of Auditors, Luxembourg (http://europa.eu.int/eur-lex/en/lif/dat/en_397Y0116_01.html (accessed 27 August 1998)).

Evans, B. (1997) 'From town planning to environmental planning', in A. Blowers and B. Evans (eds), *Town Planning Into the 21st Century*, Routledge, London and New York, 1–14.

Fagence, M. (1979) *The Political Nature of Community Decision-making*, Planning Research Paper no.1, Department of Regional and Town Planning, University of Queensland, St Lucia.

Fischer, F. and Forester, J. (1993) *The Argumentative Turn in Policy Analysis and Planning*, UCL Press, London.

Freeman, C. (1991) 'Networks of innovators: a synthesis of research issues', *Research Policy*, 20: 499–514.

Friedmann, J. (1959) 'Introduction', *International Social Science Journal*, 11(3): 327–34.

Friedmann, J. (1973) 'A conceptual model for the analysis of planning behaviour', in A. Faludi (ed.), *A Reader in Planning Theory*, Pergamon Press, Oxford, 344–70.

Fry, E.H. (1986) 'The economic competitiveness of the western states and provinces: the international dimension', *American Review of Canadian Studies*, 16(3): 301.

Gallie, W.B. (1955–56) 'Essentially contested concepts', *Proceedings of the Aristotelian Society*, 56: 167–98.

Garratt, B. (1987) *The Learning Organisation*, Fontana, London.

Garreau, J. (1991) *Edge City*, Doubleday, New York.

Gergen, K.J. (1991) *The Saturated Self: Dilemmas of Identity in Contemporary Life*, Basic Books, New York.

Getz, D. (1977) 'The impact of host communities: a research approach', in B.S. Duffield (ed.), *Tourism: A Tool for Regional Development*, Tourism and Recreation Research Unit, University of Edinburgh, Edinburgh, 9.1–9.3.

Getz, D. (1982) 'A rationale and methodology for assessing capacity to absorb tourism', *Ontario Geography*, 19: 92–101.

Getz, D. (1986) 'Models in tourism planning towards integration of theory and practice', *Tourism Management*, 7(1): 21–32.

Getz, D. (1987) *Tourism Planning and Research: Traditions, Models and Futures*, paper presented at The Australian Travel Research Workshop, Bunbury, Western Australia, 5–6 November.

Getz, D. (1994) 'Resident's attitudes towards tourism: A longitudinal study in Spey Valley, Scotland', *Tourism Management*, 15(4): 247–58.

Giddens, A. (1984) *The Constitution of Society*, Polity Press, Cambridge.

Giddens, A. (1990) *The Consequences of Modernity*, Standford University Press, Standford.

Gill, A. (1998) 'Local and resort development', in R. Butler, C.M. Hall and J. Jenkins (eds), *Tourism and Recreation in Rural Areas*, Wiley, Chichester, 97–111.

Gill, A. and Williams, P.W. (1994) 'Managing growth in mountain tourism communities', *Tourism Management*, 15(3): 212–20.

Glassie, H. (1968) *Pattern in the Material Folk Culture of the Eastern United States*, University of Pennsylvania, Philadelphia.

Gluck, F.W., Kaufman, S.P. and Walleck, A.S. (1980) 'Strategic management for competitive advantage', *Harvard Business Review*, July–August, 154–61.

Go, F., Milne, D. and Whittles, L. (1992) 'Communities as destinations: a marketing taxonomy for the effective implementation of the tourism action plan', *Journal of Travel Research*, Spring: 31–37.

Goodwin, M. (1993) 'The city as commodity: the contested spaces of urban development', in G. Kearns and C. Philo (eds), *Selling Places: The City as Cultural Capital, Past and Present*, Pergamon Press, Oxford, 145–62.

Gray, B. (1985) 'Conditions facilitating interorganizational collaboration', *Human Relations*, 38(10): 911–36.

Gray, B. (1989) *Collaborating: Finding Common Ground for Multiparty Problems*, Jossey-Bass, San Francisco.

Greenberg, G.D., Miller, J.A., Mohr, L.B. and Vladeck, B.C. (1977) 'Developing public policy theory – perspectives from empirical research', *American Political Science Review*, 71(4): 1532–43.

Gunn, C.A. (1977) 'Industry pragmatism vs tourism planning', *Leisure Sciences*, 1(1): 85–94.

Gunn, C.A. (1979) *Tourism Planning*, Crane Russak, New York.

Gunn, C.A. (1988) *Tourism Planning*, 2nd edn, Taylor & Francis, New York.

Gunn, C.A. (1994) *Tourism Planning*, 3rd edn, Taylor & Francis, Washington.

Haggett, P. (1965) 'Scale components in geographical problems', in R.J. Chorley and P. Haggett (eds), *Frontiers in Geographical Teaching*, Methuen, London, 164–85.

Hales, D.F. (1984) 'The World Heritage Convention: status and directions', in J.A. McNeely and K.R. Miller (eds), *National Parks, Conservation and Development: The Role of Protected Areas in Sustaining Society*, Proceedings of the World Congress on National Parks, Bali, Indonesia, 11–12 October 1982, Smithsonian Institution Press, Washington, 744–50.

Hall, C.M. (1992) *Wasteland to World Heritage: Conserving Australia's Wilderness*, Melbourne University Press, Carlton.

Hall, C.M. (1994) *Tourism and Politics: Policy, Power and Place*, John Wiley, Chichester.

Hall, C.M. (1998a) 'Historical antecedents of sustainable development and ecotourism: new labels on old bottles?', in C.M. Hall and A. Lew (eds), *Sustainable Tourism Development: Geographical Perspectives*, Addison Wesley Longman, Harlow, 13–24.

Hall, C.M. (1998b) *Tourism: Development, Dimensions and Issues*, 3rd edn, Addison Wesley Longman, South Melbourne.

Hall, C.M. and Butler, D. (1995) 'In search of common ground: Reflections on sustainability, complexity and process in the tourism system', *Journal of Sustainable Tourism*, 3(2): 99–105.

Hall, C.M., Cambourne, B., Macionis, N. and Johnson, G. (1997) 'Wine tourism and network development in Australia and New Zealand: Review, establishment and prospects', *International Journal of Wine Marketing*, 9(2/3) : 5–31.

Hall, C.M. and Jenkins, J.M. (1995) *Tourism and Public Policy*, Routledge, London.

Hall, C.M. and Jenkins, J.M. (1998) 'The policy dimensions of rural tourism and recreation', in R. Butler, C.M. Hall and J. Jenkins (eds), *Tourism and Recreation in Rural Areas*, Wiley, Chichester, 16–42.

Hall, C.M., Jenkins, J.M. and Kearsley, G. (eds) (1997) *Tourism Planning and Policy in Australia and New Zealand, Cases, Issues and Practice*, Irwin, Sydney.

Hall, C.M. and Johnson, G. (1997) 'Wine tourism in New Zealand: Larger bottles or better relationships?', in J. Higham (ed.), *Trails, Tourism and Regional Development Conference Proceedings*, Centre for Tourism, University of Otago, Dunedin.

Hall, C.M. and Lew, A. (eds) (1998) *Sustainable Tourism: A Geographical Perspective*, Addison Wesley Longman, Harlow.

Hall, C.M. and Macionis, N. (1998) 'Wine tourism in Australia and New Zealand', in R.W. Butler, C.M. Hall and J. Jenkins (eds), *Tourism and Recreation in Rural Areas*, John Wiley and Sons, Chichester, 267–98.

Hall, C.M. and McArthur, S. (eds) (1993) *Heritage Management in New Zealand and Australia: Interpretation, Marketing and Visitor Management*, Oxford University Press, Auckland.

Hall, C.M. and McArthur, S. (1996) 'Strategic planning: integrating people and places through participation', in C.M. Hall and S. McArthur (eds), *Heritage Man-*

agement in Australia and New Zealand: The Human Dimension, Oxford University Press, Melbourne, 22–36.

Hall, C.M. and McArthur, S. (1998) *Integrated Heritage Management*, Stationery Office, London.

Hall, C.M. and Page, S. (eds) (1997) *Tourism in the Pacific*, International Thompson Business Publishing, London.

Hall, C.M. and Page, S. (1999a) *The Geography of Tourism and Recreation*, Routledge, London.

Hall, C.M. and Page, S. (1999b) 'Developing tourism in South Asia: India, Pakistan and Bangladesh – SAARC and beyond', in C.M. Hall and S. Page (eds), *Tourism in South and Southeast Asia: Critical Perspectives*, Butterworth-Heinemann, Oxford.

Hall, D.R. (1991) 'Eastern Europe and the Soviet Union: overcoming tourism constraints', in D.R. Hall (ed.), *Tourism and Economic Development in Eastern Europe and the Soviet Union*, Belhaven Press, London, 49–78.

Hall, P. (1982) *Urban and Regional Planning*, 2nd edn, Penguin, Harmondsworth.

Hall, P. (1992) *Urban and Regional Planning*, 3rd edn, Routledge, London and New York.

Hall, P. (1995) 'Towards a general urban theory', in J. Brotchie, M. Batty, E. Blakely, P. Hall and P. Newton (eds), *Cities in Competition: Productive and Sustainable Cities for the 21st Century*, Longman Australia, South Melbourne, 3–35.

Ham, C. and Hill, M.J. (1984) *The Policy Process in the Modern Capitalist State*, Simon and Shuster, New York.

Ham, C. and Hill, M.J. (1994) *The Policy Process in the Modern Capitalist State*, 2nd edn, Prentice Hall, New York.

Hardin, G. (1968) 'The tragedy of the commons', *Science*, 162: 1243–48.

Harper, D.A. (1993) *An Analysis of Interfirm Networks*, NZ Institute of Economic Research, Wellington.

Harrison, D. (ed.) (1992) *Tourism and the Less Developed Countries*, Belhaven, London.

Harvey, D. (1969) *Explanation in Geography*, Edward Arnold, London.

Harvey, D. (1987) 'Flexible accumulation through urbanisation', *Antipode*, 19: 260–86.

Harvey, D. (1988) 'Voodoo cities', *New Statesman and Society*, 30 September, 33–35.

Harvey, D. (1989a) 'From managerialism to entrepreneurialism: the transformation in urban governance in late capitalism', *Geografiska Annaler*, 71B: 3–17.

Harvey, D. (1989b) *The Condition of Postmodernity: An Enquiry into the Origins of Cultural Change*, Basil Blackwell, Oxford.

Harvey, D. (1989c) *The Urban Experience*, Blackwell, Oxford.

Harvey, D. (1993) 'From space to place and back again: reflections on the condition of postmodernity', in J. Bird, B. Curtis, T. Putnam, G. Robertson and L. Tickner (eds), *Mapping the Futures: Local Cultures, Global Change*, Routledge, London and New York, 3–29.

Harvey, D.W. (1995) 'A geographer's guide to dialectical thinking', in A.D. Clift, P.R. Gould, A.G. Hoare and N.J. Thrift (eds), *Diffusing Geography: Essays for Peter Haggett*, The Institute of British Geographers Special Production Series 31, Blackwell, Oxford, 3–21.

Haughton, G. and Hunter, C. (1994) *Sustainable Cities*, Regional Policy and Development Series 7, Jessica Kingsley Publishers, London.

Haulot, A. (1981) 'Social tourism: current dimensions and future developments', *Tourism Management*, 2: 207–12.

Haywood, K.M. (1988) 'Responsible and responsive tourism planning in the community', *Tourism Management*, 9(2): 105–18.

Healey, P. (1992a) 'Planning through debate: the communicative turn in planning theory', *Town Planning Review*, no.632: 143–62.

Healey, P. (1992b) 'A planner's day: knowledge and action in communicative perspective', *Journal of the American Planning Association*, 58(1): 9–20.

Healey, P. (1993) 'The communicative work of development plans', *Environment and Planning B: Planning and Design*, 20: 183–94.

Healey, P. (1996) 'The communicative turn in planning theory and its implication for spatial-strategy making', *Environment and Planning B: Planning and Design*, 23: 217–34.

Healey, P. (1997) *Collaborative Planning: Shaping Places in Fragmented Societies*, Macmillan Press, Basingstoke.

Heath, E. and Wall, G. (1992) *Marketing Tourism Destinations: A Strategic Planning Approach*, John Wiley & Sons, New York.

Heclo, H. (1974) *Modern Social Politics in Britain and Sweden*, Yale University Press, New Haven.

Heeley, J. (1981) 'Planning for tourism in Britain', *Town Planning Review*, 52: 61–79.

Hewison, R. (1987) *The Heritage Industry: Britain in a Climate of Decline*, Methuen, London.

Hewison, R. (1991) 'Commerce and culture', in J. Corner and S. Harvey (eds), *Enterprise and Heritage: Crosscurrents of National Culture*, Routledge, London and New York, 162–77.

Hewison, R. (1991) 'Commerce and culture', in J. Corner and S. Harvey (eds), *Enterprise and Heritage: Crosscurrents of National Culture*, Routledge, London, 162–77.

Hill, G. and Rosier, J. (1989) 'Seabird ecology and resort development on Heron Island', *Journal of Environmental Management*, 27: 107–14.

HMSO (1994) *Sustainable Development: The UK Strategy*, Cm2426, HMSO, London.

Hocking, B. (1986) 'Regional governments and international affairs: foreign policy problems or deviant behaviour?', *International Journal*, 41: 484.

Hogwood, B. and Gunn, L. (1984) *Policy Analysis for the Real World*, Oxford University Press, Oxford.

Holcomb, B. (1993) 'Revisioning place: de- and re-constructing the image of the industrial city', in G. Kearns and C. Philo (eds), *Selling Places: The City as Cultural Capital, Past and Present*, Pergamon Press, Oxford, 133–43.

Hollick, M. (1993) *An Introduction to Project Evaluation*, Longman Cheshire, South Melbourne.

Hollinshead, K. (1992) ' "White" gaze, "red" people – shadow visions: the disidentification of "Indians" in cultural tourism', *Leisure Studies*, 11: 43–64.

Hough, M. (1995) *Cities and Natural Process*, Routledge, London and New York.

Hudson, R. (1988) 'Uneven development in capitalist societies: changing spatial divisions of labour, forms of spatial organisation of production and service provision, and their impacts upon localities', *Transactions of the Institute of British Geographers*, 13(NS): 484–96.

Hughes, H.L. (1984) 'Government support for tourism in the U.K.: a different perspective', *Tourism Management*, 5(1): 13–19.

Hughes, H.L. (1993) 'Olympic tourism and urban regeneration', *Festival Management and Event Tourism*, 1: 157–62.

Hula, R.C. (1988) 'Using markets to implement public policy', in R.C. Hula (ed.), *Market-based Public Policy*, St Martin's Press, New York.

Hunter, C. and Green, H. (1995) *Tourism and the Environment: A Sustainable Relationship?*, Routledge, London.

ICOMOS (1993) *Cultural Tourism. Tourism at World Heritage Cultural Sites: The Site Manager's Hand Book*, The ICOMOS International Specialized Committee on Cultural Tourism, Sri Lanka National Committee of ICOMOS, Colombo.

Innes, J. (1995) 'Planning theory's emergent paradigm: communicative action and interactive practice', *Journal of Planning Education and Research*, 58: 440–53.

Inskeep, E. (1987) 'Environmental planning for tourism', *Annals of Tourism Research*, 14: 118–35.

Inskeep, E. (1991) *Tourism Planning: An Integrated and Sustainable Development Approach*, Van Nostrand Reinhold, New York.

Institut für Geographie der Universitat Würzburg and Geographische Gesellschaft Würzburg (1984) *Die Verflechtung von Fremdenverkehr und Weinbau in Mainfranken* [The link between tourism and wine growing in Mainfranken]. Institut für Geographie, Universitat Würzburg, Würzburg.

International Union for Conservation of Nature and Natural Resources (IUCN) (1980) *World Conservation Strategy*, with the advice, cooperation and financial assistance of the United Nations Environment Education (UNEP) and the World Wildlife Fund (WWF) and in collaboration with the Food and Agricultural Organization of the United Nations (FAO) and the United Nations Educational, Scientific and Cultural Organization (UNESCO), IUCN, Morges.

International Union of Official Travel Organizations (IUOTO) (1974) 'The role of the state in tourism', *Annals of Tourism Research*, 1(3): 66–72.

Jacobs, J. (1965) *The Death and Life of Great American Cities: the Failure of Town Planning*, Penguin, Harmondsworth.

Jacobs, J. (1993) *The Death and Life of Great American Cities*, Random House, New York.

Jacobs, M. (1991) *The Green Economy*, Pluto Press, London.

Jamal, T.B. and Getz, D. (1995) 'Collaboration theory and community tourism planning', *Annals of Tourism Reseach*, 22: 186–204.

Jeffries, D. (1989) 'Selling Britain – a case for privatisation?', *Travel and Tourism Analyst*, no.1: 69–81.

Jenkins, C. and Henry, B. (1982) 'Government involvement in tourism in developing countries', *Annals of Tourism Research*, 9(4): 499–521.

Jenkins, J. (1993) 'Tourism policy in rural New South Wales – policy and research priorities', *Geojournal*, 29(3): 281–90.

Jenkins, J. (1997) 'The role of the Commonwealth Government in rural tourism and regional development in Australia', in C.M. Hall, J. Jenkins and G. Kearsley (eds), *Tourism Planning and Policy in Australia and New Zealand: Cases, Issues and Practice*, Irwin Publishers, Sydney, 181–91.

Jenkins, J., Hall, C.M. and Troughton, M. (1998) 'The restructuring of rural economies: rural tourism and recreation as a government response', in R. Butler, C.M. Hall and J. Jenkins (eds), *Tourism and Recreation in Rural Areas*, Wiley, Chichester, 43–68.

Jenkins, W.I. (1978) *Policy Anaysis: A Political and Organizational Perspective*, St Martin's Press, New York.

Johnston, R.J. (1991) *Geography and Geographers: Anglo-American Human Geography since 1945*, 4th edn, Edward Arnold, London.

Kast, E. and Rosenzweig, J.E. (1973) *Contingency Views of Organization and Management*, Science Research Associates, Chicago.

Kearney, E.P. (1992) 'Redrawing the political map of tourism: the European view', *Tourism Management*, March, 34–36.

Kearns, G. and Philo, C. (1993) 'Preface', in G. Kearns and C. Philo (eds), *Selling Places: The City as Cultural Capital, Past and Present*, Pergamon Press, Oxford, ix–x.

Keohane, R.O. and Nye, J.S., Jnr (1976) 'Introduction: the complex politics of Canadian–American interdependence', in A.B. Fox, A.O. Hero Jnr and J.S. Nye Jnr (eds), *Canada and the United States: Transnational and Transgovernmental Relations*, Columbia University Press, New York, 4.

Kincaid, J. (1990) 'Constituent diplomacy in federal politics and the nation state: conflict and co-operation', in H.J. Michelmann and P. Soldatos (eds), *Federalism and International Relations: The Role of Subnational Units*, Oxford University Press, New York, 54–75.

Kirby, V.G. (1993) 'Landscape, heritage and identity: stories from the West Coast', in C.M. Hall and S. McArthur (eds), *Heritage Management in New Zealand and Australia: Visitor Management, Interpretation and Marketing*, Oxford University Press, Auckland, 119–29.

Knox, P. and Agnew, J. (1989) *The Geography of the World Economy*, Edward Arnold, London.

Kotler, P., Haider, D.H. and Rein, I. (1993) *Marketing Places: Attracting Investment, Industry, and Tourism to Cities, States, and Nations*, The Free Press, New York.

Krier, L. (1984) 'Houses, palaces, cities', *A.D. Profile 54*, Architectural Design, London.

Krippendorf, J. (1987) *The Holiday Makers: Understanding the Impact of Leisure and Travel*, Heinemann Professional Publishing, Oxford.

Kroll, M. (1969) 'Policy and administration', in F.J. Lyden, G.A. Shipman and M. Kroll (eds), *Policies, Decisions and Organisations*, Appleton-Century-Crofts, New York.

Lang, R. (1986) 'Achieving integration in resource planning', in R. Lang (ed.), *Integrated Approaches to Resource Planning and Management*, University of Calgary Press, Calgary, 27–50.

Laws, E., Faulkner, B. and Moscardo, G. (eds) (1998) *Embracing and Managing Change in Tourism: International Case Studies*, Routledge, London.

Le Pelley, B. and Laws, E. (1998) 'A stakeholder-benefits aapproach to tourism management in a historic city centre: The Canterbury City Centre Initiative', in E. Laws, B. Faulkner and G. Moscardo (eds), *Embracing and Managing Change in Tourism: International Case Studies*, Routledge, London, 70–94.

LEADER II (1995a) *Welcome to the Rural Europe Site*, LEADER II Background Note, Rural Europe.

LEADER II (1995b) *Marketing Quality Rural Tourism*, LEADER technical dossier, LEADER II Library, Rural Europe.

LEADER II (1995c) *LEADER II, Development of Disadvantaged Rural Areas of the European Union*, LEADER II Community Measures, Rural Europe.

Leiper, N. (1989) *Tourism and Tourism Systems*, Occasional Paper No.1, Department of Management Systems, Massey University, Palmerston North.

Leiper, N. (1990a) *Tourism Systems An Interdisciplinary Perspective*, Occasional Papers No.2, Department of Management Systems, Business Studies Faculty, Massey University, Palmerston.

Leiper, N. (1990b) 'Partial industrialization of tourism systems', *Annals of Tourism Research*, 17: 600–5.

Leiper, N. (1993) 'Industrial entrophy in tourism systems', *Annals of Tourism Research*, 20(1): 221–26.

Levins, R. and Lewontin, R. (1985) *The Dialectical Biologist*, Harvard University Press, Cambridge.

Lew, A. and Hall, C.M. (1998) 'The geography of sustainable tourism: lessons and prospects', in C.M. Hall and A. Lew (eds), *Sustainable Tourism: A Geographical Perspective*, Addison Wesley Longman, Harlow, 199–203.

Lickorish, L.J., Jefferson, A., Bodlender, J. and Jenkins, C.L. (1991) *Developing Tourism Destinations: Policies and Perspectives*, Longman, Harlow.

Lindberg, K. and McKercher, B. (1997) 'Ecotourism: a critical overview', *Pacific Tourism Review*, 1: 65–79.

Lindblom, C.E. (1980) *The Policy-Making Process*, 2nd edn, Prentice Hall, Englewood Cliffs.

Lowe, M. (1993) 'Local hero! An examination of the role of the regional entrepreneur in the regeneration of Britain's regions', in G. Kearns and C. Philo (eds), *Selling Places: The City as Cultural Capital, Past and Present*, Pergamon Press, Oxford, 211–30.

Lyden, F.J., Shipman, G.A. and Kroll, M. (eds) (1969) *Policies, Decisions and Organisations*, Appleton-Century-Crofts, New York.

Lynch, K. (1972) *What Time Is This Place?*, MIT Press, Cambridge.

Lyster, S. (1985) *International Wildlife Law: An Analysis of International Treaties Concerned with the Conservation of Wildlife*, Grotius Publications, Cambridge.

Macbeth, J. (1997) 'Planning in action: a report and reflections on sustainable tourism in the ex-Shire of Omeo', in C.M. Hall, J. Jenkins and G. Kearsley (eds) *Tourism Planning and Policy in Australia and New Zealand: Cases, Issues and Practice*, Irwin Publishers, Sydney, 145–53.

Macionis, N. (1996) 'Wine tourism in Australia', in *Proceedings of Tourism Down Under II: A Tourism Research Conference*, Centre for Tourism, University of Otago, Dunedin, 264–68.

Macionis, N. and Cambourne, B. (1997) 'Wine and tourism: building sustainable partnerships', *Tourism and Hospitality Update*, September: 26–28.

Madsen, H. (1992) 'Place-marketing in Liverpool: a review', *International Journal of Urban and Regional Research*, 16(4): 633–40.

Majone, G. (1980a) 'The uses of policy analysis', in B.H. Raven (ed.), *Policy Studies Annual Review*, Sage, Beverley Hills, Vol. 4: 161–80.

Majone, G. (1980b) 'An anatomy of pitfalls', in G. Majone and E.S. Quade (eds), *Pitfalls of Analysis*, International Institute for Applied Systems Analysis/John Wiley and Sons, Chichester, 7–22.

Majone, G. (1989) *Evidence, Argument and Persuasion in the Policy Process*, Yale University Press, New Haven.

Manning, B. (1977) 'The Congress, the executive and intermestic affairs: three proposals', *Foreign Affairs*, 55: 309–25.

Marsden, T., Lowe, P. and Whatmore, S. (eds) (1993) *Rural Restructuring: Global Processes and their Response*, David Fulton Publishers, London.

Mason, P. and Mowforth, M. (1996) 'Codes of conduct in tourism', *Progress in Tourism and Hospitality Research*, 2(2): 151–67.

Mathieson, A. and Wall, G. (1982) *Tourism: Economic, Physical and Social Impacts*, Longman, Harlow.

Matthews, L.D. (1998) 'Tourism developments in sensitive environments. The design of architectural/infrastructural elements, processes and solutions', Paper presented at Harnessing the High Latitudes Conference, University of Surrey, Guildford, June.

McArthur, S. and Hall, C.M. (1993) 'Strategic planning for visitor heritage management: integrating people and places through participation', in C.M. Hall and S. McArthur (eds), *Heritage Management in New Zealand and Australia: Interpretation, Marketing and Visitor Management*, Oxford University Press, Auckland.

McConnell, S. (1981) *Theories for Planning*, Heinemann, London.

McCool, S.F. (1994) 'Planning for sustainable nature dependent tourism development: the limits of acceptable change system', *Tourism Recreation Research*, 19(2): 51–55.

McIntosh, R.W. and Goeldner, C.R. (1986) *Tourism: Principles, Practices, Philosophies*, 5th edn, John Wiley & Sons, New York.

McKercher, B. (1993a) 'Some fundamental truths about tourism: understanding tourism's social and environmental impacts', *Journal of Sustainable Tourism*, 1(1): 6–16.

McKercher, B. (1993b) 'The unrecognized threat to tourism: can tourism survive sustainability', *Tourism Management*, 14(2): 131–36.

McKercher, B. (1997) 'Benefits and costs of tourism in Victoria's Alpine National Park: comparing attitudes of tour operators, management staff and public interest group leaders', in C.M. Hall, J. Jenkins and G. Kearsley (eds), *Tourism Planning and Policy in Australia and New Zealand: Cases, Issues and Practice*, Irwin Publishers, Sydney, 99–110.

McLoughlin, J.B. (1969) *Urban and Regional Planning: A Systems Approach*, Faber and Faber, London.

McMichael, D.F. and Gare, N.C. (1984) 'Keynote address: the Australian realm', in J.A. McNeely and K.R. Miller (eds), *National Parks, Conservation and Development: The Role of Protected Areas in Sustaining Society*, Proceedings of the World Congress on National Parks, Bali, Indonesia, 11–12 October 1982, Smithsonian Institution Press, Washington, 258–66.

McNeely, J.A. and Miller, K.R. (1983) 'IUCN, National Parks, and protected areas: priorities for action', *Environmental Conservation*, 10(1): 13–21.

McNeely, J.A. (1984) 'The World Heritage Convention: protecting natural and cultural wonders of global importance – a slide presentation', in J.A. McNeely and K.R. Miller (eds), *National Parks, Conservation and Development: The Role of Protected Areas in Sustaining Society*, Proceedings of the World Congress on National Parks, Bali, Indonesia, 11–12 October 1982, Smithsonian Institution Press, Washington, 735–36.

Medlik, S. (1993) *Dictionary of Travel, Tourism and Hospitality*, 2nd edn, Butterworth Heinemann, Oxford.

Meier, R.L. (1995) 'Sustainable urban ecosystems: working models and computer simulations for basic education', in J. Brotchie, M. Batty, E. Blakely, P. Hall and P. Newton (eds), *Cities in Competition: Productive and Sustainable Cities for the 21st Century*, Longman Australia, South Melbourne, 455–68.

Mellor, A. (1991) 'Enterprise and heritage in the dock', in J. Corner and S. Harvey (eds), *Enterprise and Heritage: Crosscurrents of National Culture*, Routledge, London and New York, 93–115.

Mercer, D. (1979) 'Victoria's Land Conservation Council and the alpine region', *Australian Geographical Studies*, 17(1): 107–30.

Mercer, D. (1995) *'A Question of Balance' Natural Resources Conflict Issues in Australia*, 2nd edn, The Federation Press, Sydney.

Metelka, C.J. (1990) *The Dictionary of Hospitality, Travel and Tourism*, 3rd edn, Delmar Publishers, Albany.

Mill, R.C. and Morrison, A.M. (1985) *The Tourism System: An Introductory Text*, Prentice-Hall International, Englewood Cliffs.

Millar, C. (1996) 'The Shetland way: morality in a resource regime', *Coastal Management*, 24: 195–216.

Millar, C. and Aiken, D. (1995) 'Conflict resolution in aquaculture: a matter of trust', in A. Boghen (ed.), *Coldwater Aquaculture in Atlantic Canada*, 2nd edn, Canadian Institute for Research on Regional Development, Moncton, 617–45.

Mills, E.D. (1983) *Design for Holidays and Tourism*, Butterworths, London.

Minger, T. (1991) 'The green resort: environmental stewardship and the resort community', in A. Gill and R. Hartmann (eds), *Mountain Resort Development: Proceedings of the Vail Conference*, Centre for Tourism Policy and Research, Simon Fraser University, Burnaby, 66–69.

Mitchell, B. (1989) *Geography and Resource Analysis*, 2nd edn, Longman, Harlow.

Mitchell, C.T. (1993) *Redefining Design*, Van Nostrand Reinhold, New York.

Moore, C.W. (1986) *The Mediation Process: Practical Strategies for Resolving Conflict*, Jossey-Bass, San Francisco.

Moreno, E.R.M. (1989) 'The many uses of postoccupancy evaluation', *Architecture*, April: 119–21.

Morgan, G. (1986) *Images of Organization*, Sage Publications, Newbury Park.

Morris, R. and King, C. (1997) 'Cooperative marketing for small business growth and regional economic development: A case study in wine tourism entrepreneurship', in S.W. Kunkel and M.D. Meeks (eds), *The Engine of Global Economic Development*, Proceedings of the 42nd World Conference International Council for Small Business, San Francisco, June 1997, (http://www.icsb.org/conferences/w97/papers/FullPapers/index.htm).

Moudon, A.V. (1986) *Built for Change*, MIT Press, Cambridge.

Mulford, C.L. and Rogers, D.L. (1982) 'Definitions and models', in D.L. Rogers and D.A. Whetten (eds), *Interorganizational Coordination*, Iowa State University Press, Ames.

Murphy, P.E. (1985) *Tourism: A Community Approach*, Methuen, New York.

Murphy, P.E. (1988) 'Community driven tourism planning', *Tourism Management*, 9(2): 96–104.

Nordlinger, E. (1981) *On the Autonomy of the Democratic State*, Harvard University Press, Cambridge.

Norkunas, M.K. (1993) *The Politics of Memory: Tourism, History, and Ethnicity in Monterey, California*, State University of New York Press, Albany.

O'Faircheallaigh, C. and Ryan, B. (eds) (1992) *Program Evaluation and Performance Monitoring: An Australian Perspective*, Macmillan, South Melbourne.

O'Neil, R.V., DeAngelis, D.L., Wade, J.B. and Allen, T.F.H. (1986) *A Hierarchical Concept of Ecosystems*, Princeton University Press, Princeton.

Office of National Tourism (1997a) *Towards a National Tourism Plan: A Discussion Paper*, Office of National Tourism, Canberra.

Office of National Tourism (1997b) *Getting it Right for the Millennium*, report by Jon Hutchison to the Minister for Industry, Science and Tourism, Office of National Tourism, Canberra.

Office of the Parliamentary Commissioner for the Environment (1997) *Management of the Environmental Effects Associated with the Tourism Sector*, Office of the Parliamentary Commissioner for the Environment, Wellington.

Ohmae, K. (1983) *The Mind of the Strategist*, Penguin Books, New York.

Olds, K. (1998) 'The housing impacts of mega-events', *Current Issues in Tourism*, (1).

Ollman, B. (1993) *Dialectical Investigations*, Routledge, London.

Ophuls, W. (1977) *Ecology and the Politics of Scarcity*, W.H. Freeman, San Franciso.

Organisation for Economic Co-operation and Development (OECD) (1974) *Government Policy in the Development of Tourism*, OECD, Paris.

Organisation for Economic Co-operation and Development (OECD) (1990) *Partnerships for Rural Development*, OECD, Paris.

Organisation for Economic Co-operation and Development (OECD) (1991) *Inventory of Measures Perceived as Obstacles to International Tourism in the OECD Area*, OECD, Paris.

Organisation for Economic Co-operation and Development (OECD) (1999) *What is OECD?* http://www.oecd.org/about/general/index.htm (accessed 15 March 1999).

Organization of American States (1997) *Declaration of San José*, XVII Inter-American Travel Congress, San José, Costa Rica. (http://www.oas.org/EN/PROG/TOURISM/decla.htm (accessed 11 January 1999)).

Ostrom, E. (1990) *Governing the Commons: the Evolution of Institutions for Collective Action, The Political Economy of institutions and Decisions*, Cambridge University Press, Cambridge.

Ostrom, E. (1990) *Governing the Commons: The Evolution of Institutions for Collective Action, The Political Economy of institutions and Decisions*, Cambridge University Press, Cambridge.

Page, S. (1995) *Urban Tourism*, Routledge, London.

Pavlovich, K. (1997) unpublished manuscript, University of Waikato, Hamilton.

Pearce, D.G. (1989) *Tourism Development*, 2nd edn, Longman Scientific and Technical, Harlow.

Pearce, D.G. (1992) *Tourism Organisations*, Longman, Harlow.

Pearce, D.G. (1995) *Tourism Today: A Geographical Analysis*, 2nd edn, Longman Scientific and Technical, Harlow.

Pearce, D.W., Barbier, E.B. and Markandya, A. (1988) *Sustainable Development and Cost-Benefit Analysis*, IIED/UCL London Environment Economics Centre, LEEC Paper 88–03.

Pearce, D.W., Markandya, A. and Barbier, E. (1989) *Blueprint for a Green Economy*, Earthscan, Lonon.

Pearce, D.W. and Turner, R.K. (1990) *Economics of Natural Environments and the Environment*, Harvester Wheatsheaf, Hemel Hempstead.

Philo, C. and Kearns, G. (1993) 'Culture, history, capital: a critical introduction to the selling of places', in G. Kearns and C. Philo (eds), *Selling Places: The City as Cultural Capital, Past and Present*, Pergamon Press, Oxford, 1–32.

Pigram, J. and Wahab, S. (1997) 'Sustainable tourism in a changing world', in S. Wahab and J. Pigrim (eds), *Tourism, Development and Growth: The Challenge of Sustainability*, Routledge, London and New York, 17–32.

Pocock, D. (1997) 'Some reflections on World Heritage', *Area*, 29(3): 260–68.

Porritt, J. (1984) *Seeing Green*, Basil Blackwell, Oxford.

Porter, M. (1980) *Competitive Strategy: Techniques for Analyzing Industries and Competitors*, The Free Press, New York.

Powell, W. (1990) 'Neither market nor hierachy: network forms of organization', in B. Straw and L. Cummings (eds), *Research in Organizational Behaviour*, Vol. 12, JAI Press, Greenwich, 295–336.

PPK Planning (1993a) *Victor Harbor Tourism Strategy*, PPK Planning in association with Graham Gaston & Associates and Hannaford Benson Ainslie on behalf of Tourism SA and the District Council of Victor Harbor, Adelaide.

PPK Planning (1993b) *Lower Mid North Region (Clare-Burra) Tourism Strategy*, PPK Planning in association with Hannaford Benson Ainslie on behalf of Tourism SA, the District Councils of Burra Burra, Clare, Riverton and Saddleworth and Auburn, and the Mid North Region Regional Development Board, Adelaide.

Pressman, J.L. and Wildavsky, A.B. (1973) *Implementation*, University of California Press, Berkeley.

Primozic, K., Primozic, E. and Leben, R. (1991) *Strategic Choices: Supremacy, Survival, or Sayonara*, McGraw-Hill, New York.

Rakoff, S.M. and Schaefer, G.F. (1970) 'Politics, policy and political science: theoretical alternatives', *Politics and Society*, 1(1): 51–77.

Rathje, W. and Murphy, C. (1992) *Rubbish!*, HarperCollins, New York.

Reade, E. (1997) 'Planning *in* the future or planning *of* the future', in A. Blowers and B. Evans (eds), *Town Planning into the 21st Century*, Routledge, London, 71–103.

Redclift, M. (1987) *Sustainable Development: Exploring the Contradictions*, Methuen, London.

Redclift, M. and Sage, C. (1994a) 'Introduction', in M. Redclift and C. Sage (eds), *Strategies for Sustainable Development: Local Agendas for the Southern Hemisphere*, Wiley, Chichester, 1–16.

Redclift, M. and Sage, C. (1994b) 'Preface', in M. Redclift and C. Sage (eds), *Strategies for Sustainable Development: Local Agendas for the Southern Hemisphere*, Wiley, Chichester, ix.

Richardson, B. and Richardson, R. (1989) *Business Planning: An Approach to Strategic Management*, Pitman, London.

Richter, L.K. (1989) *The Politics of Tourism in Asia*, University of Hawaii Press, Honolulu.

Ritchie, J.R.B. and Goeldner, C. (1994) *Travel, Tourism, and Hospitality Research: A Handbook for Managers and Researchers*, 2nd edn, John Wiley and Sons, New York.

Roberts, N.C. and King, P.J. (1989) 'The stakeholder audit goes public', *Organizational Dynamics*, 17(3): 63–79.

Robins, K. (1991) 'Tradition and translation: national culture in its global context', in J. Corner and S. Harvey (eds), *Enterprise and Heritage: Crosscurrents of National Culture*, Routledge, London, 21–44.

Roche, M. (1992) 'Mega-events and micro-modernization: on the sociology of the new urban tourism', *British Journal of Sociology*, 43(4): 563–600.

Rosenau, J.N. (1990) *Turbulence in World Politics: A Theory of Change and Continuity*, Princeton University Press, Princeton.

Ross, G. (1991) 'Tourist destination images of the Wet Tropical rainforests of North Queensland', *Australian Psychologist*, 26(3): 153–57.

Ruskin, J. (1989) *The Seven Lamps of Architecture*, Dover, New York.

Ryan, C. and Montgomery, D. (1994) 'The attitudes of Bakewell residents to tourism and issues in community responsive tourism', *Tourism Management*, 15(5): 358–70.

Rypkema, D. (1992) 'Making renovation feasible', *Architectural Record*, January: 27.

Sabel, C. (1989) 'The re-emergence of regional economies', in P. Hirst and J. Zeitlin (eds), *Reversing Industrial Decline?*, Berg, Leamington Spa, 17–70.

Sachs, W. (ed.) (1993) *Global Ecology: A New Arena of Political Conflict*, Fernwood Publications, Halifax.

Sadler, D. (1993) 'Place-marketing, competitive places and the construction of hegemony in Britain in the 1980s', in G. Kearns and C. Philo (eds), *Selling Places: The City as Cultural Capital, Past and Present*, Pergamon Press, Oxford, 175–92.

Sager, T. (1994) *Communicative Planning Theory*, Avebury, Aldershot.

Sagoff, M. (1988) *The Economy of the Earth*, Cambridge University Press, Cambridge.

Saul, J.R. (1995) *The Unconscious Civilization*, Anansi, Concord.

Sautter, E.T. and Leisen, B. (1999) 'Managing stakeholders: a tourism planning model', *Annals of Tourism Research*, 26(2): 312–28.

Schiffman, I. (1989) *Alternative Techniques for Managing Growth*, Institute of Government Studies, University of California at Berkeley, Berkeley.

Schrecker, T. (1991) 'Resisting environmental regulations', in R. Paehlke and D. Torgerson (ed.), *Managing Leviathan*, Belhaven Press, London, 165–99.

Selin, S. (1993) 'Collaborative alliances: new interorganizational forms in tourism', *Journal of Travel and Tourism Marketing*, 2(2/3): 217–27.

Selin, S. (1998) 'The promise and pitfalls of collaborating', *Trends*, 35(1): 9–13.

Selin, S. and Beason, K. (1991) 'Interorganizational relations in tourism', *Annals of Tourism Research*, 18: 639–52.

Selin, S. and Chavez, D. (1994) 'Characteristics of successful tourism partnerships: a multiple case study design', *Journal of Park and Recreation Administration*, 12(2): 51–62.

Selin, S. and Chavez, D. (1995) 'Developing a collaborative model for environmental planning and management', *Environmental Management*, 19(2): 189–96.

Selin, S. and Myers, N. (1995) 'Correlates of partnership effectiveness: the coalition for unified recreation in the Eastern Sierra', *Journal of Park and Recreation Administration*, 13(4): 38–47.

Selin, S. and Myers, N. (1998) 'Tourism marketing alliances: member satisfaction and effectiveness attributes of a regional initiative', *Journal of Travel and Tourism Marketing*, 7(3): 79–94.

Selin, S., Schuett, M. and Carr, D. (1997) 'Has collaborative planning taken root in the National Forests?', *Journal of Forestry*, 95(5): 25–28.

Selman, P. (1992) *Environmental Planning: The Conservation and Development of Biophysical Resources*, Paul Chapman Publishing, London.

Senate Standing Committee on Environment, Recreation and the Arts (1992) *The Australian Environment and Tourism Report*, Senate Standing Committee on Environment, Recreation and the Arts, The Parliament of the Commonwealth of Australia, AGPS, Canberra.

Sewell, W.R.D. and Phillips, S.D. (1979) 'Models for the evaluation of public participation programmes', *Natural Resources Journal*, 19: 180–89.

Sewell, W.R.D. and Phillips, S.D. (1979) 'Models for the evaluation of public participation programmes', *Natural Resources Journal*, 19(2): 338–57.

Shackley, M. (1998) 'Introduction – world cultural heritage sites', in M. Shackley (ed.), *Visitor Management: Case Studies from World Heritage Sites*, Butterworth-Heinemann, Oxford, 1–9.

Simeon, R. (1976) 'Studying public policy', *Canadian Journal of Political Science*, 9(4): 558–80.

Simmons, D. (1994) 'Community participation in tourism planning', *Tourism Management*, 15(2): 98–108.

Slatyer, R.O. (1983) 'The origin and evolution of the World Heritage Convention', *Ambio*, 12(3–4): 138–39.

Slatyer, R.O. (1984) 'The World Heritage Convention: introduction comments', in J.A. McNeely and K.R. Miller (eds), *National Parks, Conservation and Development: The Role of Protected Areas in Sustaining Society*, Proceedings of the World Congress on National Parks, Bali, Indonesia, 11–12 October 1982, Smithsonian Institution Press, Washington, 734.

Smith, L.G. (1992) 'From condescension to conflict resolution: adjusting to the changing role of the public in impact assessment', in *Proceedings of an International Symposium on Hazardous Materials/Waste: Social Aspects of Facility Planning and Management*, Institute for Social Impact Assessment, Toronto, 96–101.

Smith, S.L.J. (1995) *Tourism Analysis: A Handbook*, 2nd edn, Longman, Harlow.

Smith, V. (ed.) (1977) *Hosts and Guests: The Anthropology of Tourism*, University of Pennsylvania Press, Philadelphia.

Smith, V.L. (ed.) (1989a) *Hosts and Guests: The Anthropology of Tourism*, 2nd edn, University of Pennsylvania Press, Pennsylvania.

Smith, V.L. (1989b) 'Preface', in V. Smith (ed.), *Hosts and Guests: The Anthropology of Tourism*, 2nd edn, University of Pennsylvania Press, Philadelphia, ix–xi.

Smith, V.L. and Eadington, W.R. (eds) (1992) *Tourism Alternatives: Potentials and Problems in the Development of Tourism*, 2nd edn, University of Pennsylvania Press, Pennsylvania.

Smyth, H. (1994) *Marketing the City: the Role of Flagship Developments in Urban Regeneration*, E & FN Spon, London.

Soldatos, P. (1993) 'Cascading subnational paradiplomacy in an interdependent and transnational world', in D.M. Brown and E.H. Fry (eds), *States and Provinces in the International Economy*, Institute of Governmental Studies Press, Berkeley.

Sorensen, A.D. (1993) 'Approaches to policy', in A.D. Sorensen and R. Epps (eds), *Prospects and Policies for Rural Australia*, Longman Cheshire, South Melbourne.

Spann, R.N. (1979) *Government Administration in Australia*, George Allen and Unwin, Sydney.

Stein, J.M. (ed.) (1993) *Growth Management: The Planning Challenge of the 1990s*, Sage, Newbury Park.

Stephen, N. (1991) 'The growth of international environmental law', *Environmental and Planning Law Journal*, 8(3): 183–89.

Stoddart, D.R. (1965) 'Geography and the ecological approach: the ecosystem as a geographic principle and method', *Geography*, 49: 369–76.

Stoddart, D.R. (1967) 'Organism and ecosystem as geographical models', in R.J. Chorley and P.J. Haggett (eds), *Models In Geography*, Methuen, London, 511–48.

Stoddart, D.R. (1972) 'Geography and the ecological approach: the ecosystem as a geographic principle and method', in P.W. English and R.C. Mayfield (eds), *Man, Space and Environment: Concepts in Contemporary Human Geography*, Oxford University Press, New York, 156–64.

Susskind, L. and Madigan, D. (1984) 'New approaches to solving disputes in the public sector', *Justice System Journal*, 9(2): 197–203.

Suter, K.D. (1991) 'The UNESCO World Heritage Convention', *Environmental and Planning Law Journal*, 8(1): 4–15.

Swyngedouw, E. (1989) 'The heart of the place: the resurrection of locality in an age of hyperspace', *Geografiska Annaler*, 71B: 31–42.

Tansley, A.G. (1935) 'The use and abuse of vegetational concepts and terms', *Ecology*, 16: 284–307.

Timothy, D.J. (1999) 'Participatory planning: a view of tourism in Indonesia', *Annals of Tourism Research*, 26(2): 371–91.

Tourism South Australia (1990) *Planning for Tourism: A Handbook for South Australia*, Tourism South Australia, Adelaide.

Tourism South Australia (1991) *Making South Australia Special: South Australian Tourism Plan 1991–1993*, Tourism South Australia, Adelaide.

Tuan, Y-F. (1974) 'Space and place: humanistic perspectives', *Progress in Geography*, 6: 211–52.

Ungar, D.G. (1994) *The USDA Forest Service Perspective on Ecosystem Management*, Symposium on Ecosystem Management and Northeastern Area Association of State Foresters Meeting, Burlington, Vermont, July 18.

United Nations Educational, Scientific and Cultural Organization (UNESCO) (1972) *Convention Concerning the Protection of the World Cultural and Natural Heritage, Operational Guidelines for the Implementation of the World Heritage Convention*, UNESCO, Paris, http://www.unesco.org:80//whc/opgutoc.htm (accessed 11 January 1999).

United Nations, Conference on International Travel and Tourism (1963) *Recommendations on International Travel and Tourism*, United Nations, Rome.

Valentine, P. (1992) 'Review. Nature-based tourism', in B. Weiler and C.M. Hall (eds), *Special Interest Tourism*, Belhaven Press, London.

Veal, A.J. (1992) *Research Methods for Leisure and Tourism*, Longman, Harlow.

von Droste, B. (1995) *World Heritage Newsletter*, no.9, December.

Vukonic, B. (1997) 'Selective tourism growth: targeted tourism destinations', in S. Wahab and J. Pigrim (eds), *Tourism, Development and Growth: The Challenge of Sustainability*, Routledge, London, 95–108.

Waddock, S.A. and Bannister, B.D. (1991) 'Correlates of effectiveness and partner satisfaction in social partnerships', *Journal of Organizational Change Management*, 4(2): 74–89.

Wahab, S. and Pigram, J. (eds) (1997) *Tourism, Development and Growth: The Challenge of Sustainability*, Routledge, London and New York.

Wheeller, B. (1993) 'Sustaining the ego', *Journal of Sustainable Tourism*, 1(2): 121–29.

White, G. (1972) 'Geography and public policy', *Professional Geographer*, 24: 101–4.

Wight, P.A. (1993a) 'Sustainable ecotourism: balancing economic, environmental and social goals within an ethical framework', *Journal of Tourism Studies*, 4(2): 54–66.

Wight, P.A. (1993b) 'Ecotourism: ethics or eco-sell?', *Journal of Travel Research*, 29: 40–5.

Wight, P.A. (1998) 'Tools for sustainability analysis in planning and managing tourism and recreation in the destination', in C.M. Hall and A. Lew (eds), *Sustainable Tourism Development: A Geographical Perspective*, Addison Wesley Longman, London, 75–91.

Wildavsky, A. (1987) *Speaking Truth to Power: The Art and Craft of Policy Analysis*, 2nd edn, Transaction, New Brunswick.

Williams, A.M. and Shaw, G. (1988a) 'Tourism and development: introduction', in A.M. Williams and G. Shaw (eds), *Tourism and Economic Development: Western European Experiences*, Belhaven Press, London, 1–11.

Williams, A.M. and Shaw, G. (1988b) 'Tourism policies in a changing economic environment', in A.M. Williams and G. Shaw (eds), *Tourism and Economic Development: Western European Experiences*, Belhaven Press, London, 230–39.

Williams, M.V. (1993) Growth Management in Community Tourism Planning, unpublished research project for the Master of Natural Resource Management, School of Resource and Environmental Management, Simon Fraser University, Burnaby.

Williams, P.W. and Gill, A. (1994) 'Tourism carrying capacity management issues', in W. Theobold (ed.), *Global Tourism: The Next Decade*, Butterworth-Heinemann, Oxford, 174–87.

Williams, R. (1981) *Culture*, Fontana, London.

Williams, R. (1997) *Marxism and Literature*, Oxford University Press, Oxford.

Wilson, A.G.W. (1986) 'System', in R.J. Johnston, D. Gregory and D.M. Smith (eds), *Dictionary of Human Geography*, 2nd edn, Blackwell, Oxford, 476–77.

Wingspread Journal (1997) 'Four characteristics of a sustainable community', *Wingspread Journal* (accessed 17/3/97).

Wood, D.J. and Gray, B. (1991) 'Toward a comprehensive theory of collaboration', *Journal of Applied Behavioral Science*, 27(2): 139–62.

Wood, K. and House, S.L. (1991) *The Good Tourist*, Mandarin, London.

World Commission on Environment and Development (the Brundtland Report) (1987) *Our Common Future*, Oxford University Press, London.

World Heritage Committee (UNESCO, Intergovernmental Committee for the Protection of the World Cultural and Natural Heritage) (1984) *Operational Guidelines for the Implementation of the World Heritage Convention*, WHC/2 Revised, UNESCO, Paris.

World Tourism Organization (1993) *Indicators for the Sustainable Management of Tourism: Report of the International Working Group on Indicators of Sustainable Tourism to the Environment Committee World Tourism Organization*, World Tourism Organization, Madrid.

World Tourism Organization (1996) *Tourism Trends 1995*, World Tourism Organization, Madrid.

World Tourism Organization (1998a) 'Asia warned about too much red tape', *WTO News*, September/October.

World Tourism Organization (1998b) 'Education seminar: unleashing tourism's job potential', *WTO News*, April/March.

World Tourism Organization (1998c) 'Governments' role in tourism', *WTO News*, September/October.

World Tourism Organization (1998d) 'Public private partnerships', *WTO News*, May/June.

World Tourism Organization (1998e) 'Public–private strategy group formed', *WTO News*, May/June.

World Tourism Organization (1998f) 'European Tourism Forum: SG calls for European tourism strategy', *WTO News*, September/October.

World Tourism Organization (1998g) 'Austria streamlines its national tourism organization', *WTO News*, January/February.

World Tourism Organization (1998h) 'Baltic Sea destinations posed for tourism growth', *WTO News*, September/October/November.

World Tourism Organization (1999) http://www.world-tourism.org/.

World Travel and Tourism Council (1990) *Environmental Impact Assessment and Audit Guidelines*, World Travel and Tourism Council, Brussels.

Worpole, K. (1991) 'Trading places: the city workshop', in M. Fisher and U. Owen (eds), *Whose Cities?*, Penguin, Harmondsworth.

Worster, D. (1977) *Nature's Economy: A History of Ecological Ideas*, Cambridge University Press, Cambridge.

Index